‹A HISTORY OF THE INTERNET
AND THE DIGITAL FUTURE›

A HISTORY OF THE INTERNET AND THE DIGITAL FUTURE

Johnny Ryan

REAKTION BOOKS

For Yvonne, Inga, Hanna, Suzanna, Sarah, Tara and, most especially,
for Caroline

PUBLISHED BY REAKTION BOOKS LTD
33 Great Sutton Street
London EC1V 0DX

www.reaktionbooks.co.uk

First published 2010
First published in paperback 2013

Printed and bound in Great Britain by Bell & Bain, Glasgow

British Library Cataloguing in Publication Data

Ryan, Johnny.
   A history of the Internet and the digital future.
   1. Internet. 2. Internet–History. 3. Internet–Social aspects.
   I. Title
   303.4'834–DC22

ISBN 978 1 78023 112 9

Contents

> Preface: The Great Adjustment 7

PHASE I: DISTRIBUTED NETWORK, CENTRIFUGAL IDEAS

<1> A Concept Born in the Shadow of the Nuke 11
<2> The Military Experiment 23
<3> The Essence of the Internet 31
<4> Computers Become Cheap, Fast and Common 45

PHASE II: EXPANSION

<5> The Hoi Polloi Connect 65
<6> Communities Based on Interest, not Proximity 74
<7> From Military Networks to the Global Internet 88
<8> The Web! 105
<9> A Platform for Trade and the Pitfalls of the Dot-com 120

PHASE III: THE EMERGING ENVIRONMENT

<10> Web 2.0 and the Return to the Oral Tradition 137
<11> New Audiences, the Fourth Wall and Extruded Media 151
<12> Two-way Politics 164
<13> Promise and Peril 178

> glossary 198
> references 201
> select bibliography 229
> acknowledgements 234
> index 235

Preface: The Great Adjustment

The Internet, like many readers of this book, is a child of the industrial age. Long before the arrival of digital communications, the steam engine, telegraph pole and coalmine quickened the pace of the world. Industrialized commerce, communications and war spun the globe ever faster and increasingly to a centripetal beat. Control in the industrialized world was put at the centre. The furthest reaches of the globe came under the sway of centres of power: massive urbanization and a flight from the land created monstrous cities in the great nations; maritime empires brought vast swathes of the globe under the sway of imperial capitals. The training of workmen, the precise measurement of a pistol barrel's calibre, the mass assembly of automobiles, all were regimented, standardized in conformity with the centripetal imperative. The industrial revolution created a world of centralization and organized hierarchy. Its defining pattern was a single, central dot to which all strands led. But the emerging digital age is different.

A great adjustment in human affairs is under way. The pattern of political, commercial and cultural life is changing. The defining pattern of the emerging digital age is the absence of the central dot. In its place a mesh of many points is evolving, each linked by webs and networks. This story is about the death of the centre and the development of commercial and political life in a networked system. It is also the story about the coming power of the networked individual as the new vital unit of effective participation and creativity.

At the centre of this change is the Internet, a technology so unusual and so profoundly unlikely to have been created that its existence would be a constant marvel were it not a fact of daily life. No treatise or arch plan steered its development from beginning to end. Nor did its success come from serendipity alone, but from the peculiar ethic that emerged among engineers and early computer lovers in the 1960s and '70s, and through the initiative of empowered users and networked communities. The combination of these elements has put power in the hands of the individual, power to challenge even the state, to compete for markets across the globe, to demand and create new types of media, to subvert a society – or to elect a president.

We have arrived at the point when the Internet has existed for a sufficiently long time for a historical study to reveal key characteristics that will have an impact on business, politics and society in the coming decades. Like all good histories, this book offers insight into the future by understanding the past. The first section of this book (Chapters 1–4) examines the concepts and context from which the Internet emerged. The second section (Chapters 5–9) traces how the technology and culture of networking matured, freeing communities for the first time in human history from the tyranny of geography in the process. This section also describes the emergence of the Web and the folly of the dotcom boom and bust. The final section (Chapters 10–13) shows how the defining characteristics of the Internet are now transforming culture, commerce and politics.

Three characteristics have asserted themselves throughout the Internet's history, and will define the digital age to which we must all adjust: the Internet is a centrifugal force, user-driven and open. Understanding what these characteristics mean and how they emerged is the key to making the great adjustment to the new global commons, a political and media system in flux and the future of competitive creativity.

< 8 >

<PHASE I>
DISTRIBUTED NETWORK, CENTRIFUGAL IDEAS

<1>

A Concept Born in the Shadow of the Nuke

The 1950s were a time of high tension. The US and Soviet Union pre-pared themselves for a nuclear war in which casualties would be counted not in millions but in the hundreds of millions. As the decade began President Truman's strategic advisors recommended that the US embark on a massive rearmament to face off the Communist threat. The logic was simple:

> A more rapid build-up of political, economic, and military strength . . . is the only course . . . The frustration of the Kremlin design requires the free world to develop a successfully function-ing political and economic system and a vigorous political offen sive against the Soviet Union. These, in turn, require an adequate military shield under which they can develop.[1]

The report, NSC-68, also proposed that the US consider pre-emptive nuclear strikes on Soviet targets should a Soviet attack appear immi-nent. The commander of US Strategic Air Command, Curtis LeMay, was apparently an eager supporter of a US first strike.[2] Eisenhower's election in 1952 did little to take the heat out of Cold War rhetoric. He threat-ened the USSR with 'massive retaliation' against any attack, irrespective of whether conventional or nuclear forces had been deployed against the US.[3] From 1961, Robert McNamara, Secretary of Defense under Presidents Kennedy and Johnson, adopted a strategy of 'flexible response' that dropped the massive retaliation rhetoric and made a point of avoiding the targeting of Soviet cities. Even so, technological change kept tensions high. By the mid-1960s the Air Force had upgraded its nuclear missiles to use solid-state propellants that reduced their launch time from eight hours to a matter of minutes. The new

<11>

Minuteman and Polaris missiles were at hair-trigger alert. A nuclear conflagration could begin, literally, in the blink of an eye.

Yet while us missiles were becoming easier to let loose on the enemy, the command and control systems that coordinated them remained every bit as vulnerable as they had ever been. A secret document drafted for President Kennedy in 1963 highlighted the importance of command and control. The report detailed a series of possible nuclear exchange scenarios in which the President would be faced with 'decision points' over the course of approximately 26 hours. One scenario described a 'nation killing' first strike by the Soviet Union that would kill between 30 and 150 million people and destroy 30–70 per cent of us industrial capacity.[4] Though this might sound like an outright defeat, the scenario described in the secret document envisaged that the President would still be required to issue commands to remaining us nuclear forces at three pivotal decision points over the next day.

The first of these decisions, assuming the President survived the first strike, would be made at zero hour (0 H). 0 H marked the time of the first detonation of a Soviet missile on a us target. Kennedy would have to determine the extent of his retaliatory second strike against the Soviets. If he chose to strike military and industrial targets within the Soviet Union, respecting the 'no cities doctrine', us missiles would begin to hit their targets some thirty minutes after his launch order and strategic bombers already on alert would arrive at H + 3 hour. Remaining aircraft would arrive at between H + 7 and H + 17 hours.

Next, the scenario indicated that the President would be sent an offer of ceasefire from Moscow at some time between 0 H and H + 30 minutes. He would have to determine whether to negotiate, maintain his strike or escalate. In the hypothetical scenario the President reacted by expanding us retaliation to include Soviet population centres in addition to the military and industrial targets already under attack by the us second strike. In response, between H + 1 and H + 18 hours, the surviving Soviet leadership opted to launch nuclear strikes on western European capitals and then seek a ceasefire. At this point, European nuclear forces launched nuclear strikes against Soviet targets. At H + 24 the President decided to accept the Soviet ceasefire, subject to a withdrawal of the Soviet land forces that had advanced into western Europe during the 24 hours since the initial Soviet strike. The President also told his Soviet counterpart that any submerged Soviet nuclear missile submarines would remain subject to attack. The scenario concludes at

< 12 >

some point between H + 24 and H + 26 when the Soviets accept, though the US remain poised to launch against Soviet submarines.

In order for the President to make even one of these decisions, a nuclear-proof method of communicating to his nuclear strike forces was a prerequisite. Unfortunately, this did not exist. A separate briefing for Kennedy described the level of damage that the US and USSR would be likely to sustain in the first wave of a nuclear exchange.[5] At the end of each of the scenarios tested both sides would still retain 'substantial residual strategic forces' that could retaliate or recommence the assault. This applied irrespective of whether it had been the US or the Soviet Union that had initiated the nuclear exchange. Thus, despite suffering successive waves of Soviet strikes the United States would have to retain the ability to credibly threaten and use its surviving nuclear arsenal. However, the briefs advised the President, 'the ability to use these residual forces effectively depends on survivable command and control . . .' In short, the Cold War belligerent with the most resilient command and control would have the edge. This had been a concern since the dawn of the nuclear era. In 1950 Truman had been warned of the need to 'defend and maintain the lines of communication and base areas' required to fight a nuclear war.[6] Yet, for the next ten years no one had the faintest idea of how to guarantee command and control communications once the nukes started to fall.

A nuclear detonation in the ionosphere would cripple FM radio communications for hours, and a limited number of nuclear strikes on the ground could knock out AT&T's highly centralized national telephone network. This put the concept of mutually assured destruction (MAD) into question. A key tenet of MAD was that the fear of retaliation would prevent either Cold War party from launching a first strike. This logic failed if a retaliatory strike was impossible because one's communications infrastructure was disrupted by the enemy's first strike.

RAND, a think tank in the United States, was mulling over the problem. A RAND researcher named Paul Baran had become increasingly concerned about the prospect of a nuclear conflagration as a result of his prior experience in radar information processing at Hughes.[7] In his mind improving the communications network across the United States was the key to averting war. The hair-trigger alert introduced by the new solid fuel missiles of the early 1960s meant that decision makers had almost no time to reflect at critical moments of crisis. Baran feared that 'a single accidental[ly] fired weapon could set off an unstoppable

<13>

nuclear war'.[8] In his view command and control was so vulnerable to collateral damage that 'each missile base commander would face the dilemma of either doing nothing in the event of a physical attack or taking action that could lead to an all out irrevocable war'. In short, the military needed a way to stay in contact with its nuclear strike force, even though it would be dispersed across the country as a tactical precaution against enemy attack. The answer that RAND delivered was revolutionary in several respects – not least because it established the guiding principles of the Internet.

Nuclear-proof communications

Baran came up with a solution that suggested radically changing the shape and nature of the national communications network. Conventional networks had command and control points at their centre. Links extended from the centre to the other points of contact in a hub-and-spoke design. In 1960 Baran began to argue that this was untenable in the age of ballistic missiles.[9] The alternative he began to conceive of was a centrifugal distribution of control points: a distributed network that had no vulnerable central point and could rely on redundancy. He was conscious of theories in neurology that described how the brain could use remaining functions effectively even when brain cells had died.[10] An older person unable to recall a word or phrase, for example, would come up with a suitable synonym. Using the neurological model every node in the communications network would be capable of relaying information to any other node without having to refer to a central control point. This model would provide reliable command and control of nuclear forces even if enemy strikes had wiped out large chunks of the network.

In his memorandum of 1962, 'On Distributed Communication Networks', Baran described how his network worked. Messages travelling across the network would not be given a pre-defined route from sender to destination.[11] Instead they would simply have 'to' and 'from' tags and would rely on each node that they landed at on their journey across the network to determine which node they should travel to next to reach their destination in the shortest time. The nodes, by a very simple system that Baran describes in less than a page, would each monitor how long messages had taken to reach them from other nodes on the network,[12] and could relay incoming messages to the quickest node in the direction of the message's destination. By routing the messages like 'hot potatoes', node-to-node, along the quickest routes as chosen by the nodes themselves, the network could route around areas damaged by nuclear attacks.

Rewiring the nation's communications system in this manner was a conundrum. The analogue systems of the early 1960s were limited in the number of connections they could make. The process of relaying, or 'switching', a message from one line to another more than five times significantly degraded signal quality. Yet Baran's distributed network required many relay stations, each capable of communicating with any other by any route along any number of relay stations. His concept was far beyond the existing technology's capabilities. However, the new and almost completely unexplored technology of digital communications could theoretically carry signals almost any distance. This proposal was radical. Baran was suggesting combining two previously isolated technologies: computers and communications. Odd as it might appear to readers in a digital age, these were disciplines so mutually distinct that Baran worried his project could fail for lack of staff capable of working in both areas.[13]

Baran realized that digital messages could be made more efficient if they were chopped up into small 'packets' of information. (Acting independently and unaware of Baran's efforts, Donald Davies, the Superintendent of Computer Science Division of the UK's National Physics Laboratory, had developed his own packet-switched networking theory at about the same time as Baran.) What Baran, and Davies, realized was that packets of data could travel independently of each other from node to node across the distributed network until they reached their destination and were reconstituted as a full message. This meant that different types of transmissions such as voice and data could be mixed, and that different parts of the same message could avoid bottlenecks in the network.

Remarkably, considering the technical leap forward it represented, the US did not keep Baran's concept of distributed communications secret. The logic was that:

we were a hell of a lot better off if the Soviets had a better command and control system. Their command and control system was even worse than ours.[14]

< 15>

Thus, of the twelve memoranda explaining Baran's system, only two, which dealt with cryptography and vulnerabilities, were classified.[15] In 1965 RAND officially recommended to the Air Force that it should proceed with research and development on the project.[16]

Baran's concept had the same centrifugal character that defines the Internet today. At its most basic, what this book calls the 'centrifugal' approach is to flatten established hierarchies and put power and responsibility at the nodal level so that each node is equal. Baran's network focused on what he called 'user-to-user rather than ... centre-to-centre operation'.[17] As a sign of how this would eventually empower Internet users en masse, he noted that the administrative censorship that had occurred in previous military communications systems would not be possible on the new system. What he had produced was a new mechanism for relaying vast quantities of data across a cheap network, while benefiting from nuclear-proof resilience. Whereas analogue communications required a perfect circuit between both end points of a connection, distributed networking routed messages around points of failure until it reached its final destination. This meant that one could use cheaper, more failure-prone equipment at each relay station. Even so, the network would be very reliable.[18] Since one could build large networks that delivered very reliable transmissions with unreliable equipment, the price of communications would tumble. It was nothing short of a miracle. AT&T, the communications monopoly of the day, simply did not believe him.

When the Air Force approached AT&T to test Baran's concept, it 'objected violently'.[19] There was a conceptual gulf between the old analogue paradigms of communication to which AT&T was accustomed and the centrifugal, digital approach that Baran proposed. Baran's centrifugal model was the antithesis of the centralized, hierarchical technology and ethos on which AT&T had been founded. AT&T experts in analogue communications were incredulous at Baran's claims made about digital communications. AT&T, used to analogue communications that relied on consistent line quality that relayed a message as cleanly as possible from point to point, could not accept that cutting messages into packets as Baran proposed would not hinder voice calls. Explaining his idea in a meeting at AT&T headquarters in New York, Baran was interrupted by a senior executive who asked:

< 16 >

Wait a minute, son. Are you trying to tell me that you open the switch before the signal is transmitted all the way across the country?[20]

Yet the theoretical proofs that digital packet switching could work were beginning to gather. In 1961 a young PhD student at MIT named Leonard Kleinrock had begun to investigate how packets of data could flow across networks.[21] In the UK, Donald Davies's packet-switching experiment within his lab at the National Physics Laboratory in 1965 proved that the method worked to connect computer terminals and prompted him to pursue funding for a national data network in the UK. Though Davies was unable to secure sufficient funding to pursue a network project on the scale that would emerge in the US, his laboratory did nonetheless influence his American counterparts. Also in 1965 two researchers called Lawrence Roberts and Tomas Marill connected a computer at MIT's Lincoln Laboratory in Boston with a computer at the System Development Corporation in California.[22]

Despite these developments, AT&T had little interest in digital communications, and was unwilling to accept that Baran's network, which had a projected cost of $60 million in 1964 dollars, could replace the analogue system that cost $2 billion per year.[23] One AT&T official apparently told Baran, 'Damn it, we're not going to set up a competitor to ourselves.'[24] AT&T refused the Air Force's request to test Baran's concept. The only alternative was the Defense Communications Agency (DCA). Baran believed that the DCA 'wasn't up to the task'[25] and regarded this as the kiss of death for the project. 'I felt that they could be almost guaranteed to botch the job since they had no understanding for digital technology . . . Further, they lacked enthusiasm.' Thus in 1966 the plan was quietly shelved, and a revolution was postponed until the right team made the mental leap from centralized analogue systems to centrifugal digital ones.

Innovation incubator: RAND

The breadth of Baran's ideas and the freedom that he had to explore them had much to do with the organization in which he worked. RAND was a wholly new kind of research establishment, one born of the military's realization during the Second World War that foundational science research could win wars. Indeed it is perhaps in the Second World

<17>

War rather than in the Cold War that the seeds of the Internet were sown. Even before America's entry into the War, President Roosevelt had come to the view that air power was the alternative to a large army and that technology, by corollary, was the alternative to manpower. In Roosevelt's mind it had been German air power that had caused Britain's acquiescence in the Munich Pact.[26] The US, which had hitherto neglected to develop its air forces, resurrected a programme to build almost 2,500 combat aircraft and set a target capacity to produce 10,000 aircraft per year. When it did enter the War the US established a 'National Roster of Scientific and Specialized Personnel' to identify 'practically every person in the country with specialized training or skill'.[27] Senior scientists understood the War as 'a battle of scientific wits in which outcome depends on who can get there first with best'.[28] Chemists held themselves 'aquiver to use their ability in the war effort'.[29] Mathematicians, engineers and researchers could point to the real impact of their contribution to the war effort. Vannevar Bush, the government's chief science advisor, told the President in 1941 that the US research community had 'already profoundly influenced the course of events'.[30]

The knowledge race captured the public's imagination too. The US government appealed to the public to contribute ideas and inventions for the war effort. While Vannevar Bush regarded tyros, individuals who circumvented established hierarchies to inject disruptive and irrelevant ideas at levels far above their station, as 'an unholy nuisance',[31] he and the military research establishment were open to the ideas of bright amateurs. The National Inventors' Council, 'a clearing house for America's inventive genius', reviewed inventions from the public that could assist the war effort.[32] It received over 100,000 suggestions,[33] and is distinguished, among other things, as being one of the many organizations and businesses that rejected the concept of the photocopier.[34] The Department of Defense released a list of fields in which it was particularly interested to receive suggestions including such exotica as 'electromagnet guns'.[35] In one startling example two ideas of Hugo Korn, a sixteen-year-old from Tuley High School in Chicago, were apparently given practical consideration. One was an airborne detector 'to spot factories in enemy country by infrared radiation'. The other was 'an aerial camera which would be used in bad weather conditions'.[36] During the First World War the Naval Consulting Board had performed a similar function, though out of the 110,000 proposals submitted to it all but 110 were discarded as worthless and only one was implemented.

< 18 >

Researchers during the War basked in public recognition of their critical importance. This new status, the President of MIT mooted, might 'result in permanently increased support of scientific research'.[37] As the end of the War drew near, political, military and scientific leaders paused to consider the transition to peacetime. The significance of the moment was not lost on Roosevelt. He wrote to Vannevar Bush in late 1944 asking:

> New frontiers of the mind are before us, and if they are pioneered with the same vision, boldness, and drive with which we have waged this war we can create a fuller and more fruitful employment and a fuller and more fruitful life . . . What can the Government do now and in the future to aid research activities by public and private organizations . . . so that the continuing future of scientific research in this country may be assured on a level comparable to what has been done during the war?[38]

In response Bush drew together the senior scientists of the nation to draft *Science: the endless frontier*, a report that established the architecture of the post-war research environment. At the core of its recommendations was a general principle of openness and cross-fertilization:

> Our ability to overcome possible future enemies depends upon scientific advances which will proceed more rapidly with diffusion of knowledge than under a policy of continued restriction of knowledge now in our possession.[39]

Though he argued for the need for federal funding, Bush was against direct government control over research.[40] While not directly involved in its establishment, Bush's emphasis on cross-disciplinary study, openness and a hands-off approach to funded research would percolate and become realized in RAND. *Science: the endless frontier* also proposed the establishment of what would become the National Science Foundation, an organization that was to play an important role in the development of the Internet many decades later.

Also considering the post-war world was General 'Hap' Arnold, the most senior officer in the US Army Air Force. He wrote that:

the security of the United States of America will continue to rest in part in developments instituted by our educational and professional scientists. I am anxious that the Air Force's post war and next war research and development be placed on a sound and continuing basis.[41]

General Arnold had a natural appreciation for military research. He had been a pioneer of military aviation at the Wright Brothers' flight school in 1911, where he and a colleague became the first US military officers to receive flight instruction. Despite a personal ambivalence towards scientists and academics, whom he referred to as 'long-hair boys',[42] he placed a priority on the importance of research and development. As he told a conference of officers, 'remember that the seed comes first; if you are to reap a harvest of aeronautical development, you must plant the seed called experimental research'.[43]

At the close of the Second World War Arnold supported the establishment of a new research outfit called 'Project RAND', an acronym as lacking in ambition as its bearer was blessed (RAND is short for 'Research and Development'). The new organization would conduct long-term research for the Air Force. Edward Bowles, an advisor to the Secretary of War on scientific matters, persuaded Arnold that RAND should have a new type of administrative arrangement that would allow it the flexibility to pursue long-term goals. It was set up as an independent entity and based at the Douglas Aircraft Company, chosen in part because of a belief that scientists would be difficult to recruit if they were administered directly by the military and because Douglas was sufficiently distant from Washington to allow its staff to work in relative peace.[44] RAND's earliest studies included the concept for a nuclear powered strategic bomber called the 'percojet', which suffered from the fatal design flaw that its pilots would perish from radiation before the craft had reached its target; a strategic bombing analysis that took account of over 400,000 different configurations of bombers and bombs; and a 'preliminary design of an experimental world-circling space ship'.[45] This was truly research at the cutting edge of human knowledge.

RAND was extraordinarily independent. General Curtis LeMay, the Deputy Chief of Air Staff for Research and Development, endorsed a *carte blanche* approach to Project RAND's work programme.[46] When the

< 20 >

Air Force announced its intention to freeze its funding of Project RAND in 1959 at 1959 levels, RAND broadened its remit and funding base by concluding research contracts with additional clients that required it to work on issues as diverse as meteorology, linguistics, urban transport, cognition and economics. By the time Paul Baran examined packet-switched networking at RAND the organization was working at levels both below and above the Air Force and with clients outside the military structure.

In 1958, a year before Baran joined RAND, a senior member of RAND's staff wrote in *Fortune* magazine that military research was 'suffering from too much direction and control'.[47]

There are too many direction makers, and too many obstacles are placed in the way of getting new ideas into development. R. and D. is being crippled by . . . the delusion that we can advance rapidly and economically by planning the future in detail.[48]

The RAND approach was different. As another employee recalled, 'some imaginative researcher conceives a problem . . . that he feels is important [and] that is not receiving adequate attention elsewhere'.[49] Before joining RAND Baran had been 'struck by the freedom and effectiveness of the people' there.[50] RAND staff had 'a remarkable freedom to pursue subjects that the researcher believes would yield the highest pay off to the nation'. One RAND staff member recalled 'anarchy of both policy and administration . . . [which] is not really anarchy but rather a degree of intellectual freedom which is . . . unique'.[51] The staff were given freedom to pursue their interests and indulge their eccentricities. 'We have learned that a good organization must encourage independence of thought, must learn to live with its lone wolves and mavericks, and must tolerate the man who is a headache to the efficient administrator'.[52] Though scientists at RAND may have been more politically conservative than their counterparts in academia,[53] many were oddballs who did not fit in: 'One man rarely showed up before two o'clock, and we had another who never went home.'[54]

Reflecting in 2003, Baran recalled a freedom for staff to pursue projects on their own initiative that has no contemporary comparison.[55] This was the environment in which Baran developed the concept of packet switching, a concept so at odds with established thinking about communications that the incumbent could not abide it.

< 21 >

Systems analysis, the RAND methodology, promoted the perspective that problems should be considered in their broader economic and social context. Thus by the time Baran joined RAND in 1959 the organization incorporated not only scientists and engineers, but also economists and, after some initial teething problems, social scientists.[56] This might explain why, though he wrote in the context of a sensitive military research and development project, Baran posed a remarkable question at the conclusion of one of his memoranda on distributed communications:

Is it now time to start thinking about a new and possibly non-existent public utility, a common user digital data plant designed specifically for the transmission of digital data among a large set of subscribers?[57]

From the outset Baran's ideas were broader than nuclear-proof command and control. His vision was of a public utility.

< 22 >

‹2›
The Military Experiment

Cold War though it may have been, its belligerents fought a hot war of technological gestures. In late 1957 it appeared to Americans as though the Soviets were winning. On 26 August 1957 the Soviets launched the Vostok R-7 rocket, the world's first intercontinental ballistic missile (ICBM). Two months later on 4 October 1957 a pulsing beep . . . beep . . . beep . . . from space signalled Soviet mastery in the space race. The Soviet Union had launched the first satellite, Sputnik, which circled the globe every 96 minutes at 18,000 miles per hour.[1] The beeps of its radio transmission were relayed to listeners on earth by radio stations. Visual observers at 150 stations across America were drafted in to report sightings of the object. *Time* magazine spoke of a 'Red moon over the US'.[2] Not only were the Soviets first to launch a satellite into space but, as the front page of *The New York Times* told Americans the next day, the Soviet satellite was eight times heavier than the satellite the US planned to put into orbit. If the USSR could launch so heavy an object into space what else could their rockets do? Then on 3 November the USSR launched a second satellite. This one weighed half a ton and carried a dog into the heavens. Soviet scientists hinted at plans for permanently orbiting satellites providing platforms for space ships. American scientists speculated on whether the next trick up the Soviet sleeve would be to detonate a hydrogen bomb on the moon timed for its eclipse on the fortieth anniversary of the October Revolution.[3] Four days after the launch of Sputnik II the President received the 'Gaither Report' from his Science Advisory Panel. Dramatically overestimating the strength of the Soviet missile force, it recommended $19 billion (1957 dollars) in additional defence expenditure.[4] The perception of a missile gap was so profound that in 1958 Senator John F. Kennedy could compare the supposed loss of American military superiority to the

British loss of Calais and surrender of any pretensions to power on the European continent in 1558.[5] The American sense of jeopardy was profound.

The US response, when it came, was underwhelming. On 6 December 1957 a Vanguard rocket was fuelled and prepared to launch America's first satellite into space. The first Soviet satellite had been the size of a beach ball. American's first attempt was the size of a softball. Size and weight mattered because the heavier the object the better the rocket, and the better the rocket the better the launching nation's nuclear missile capability. The US satellite weighed only four pounds compared to the half-ton Sputnik II. More significant was that the Vanguard launch was a catastrophic failure, exploding only a few feet above the ground. The world's media responded, as *Time* reported, with 'jeers and tears'.[6] The question, as one journalist put it the day after Sputnik I launched, was 'could the United States have launched a successful earth satellite by now if money had not been held back and time wasted?'[7]

Before Sputnik the various armed services had been fighting tooth and nail over research budgets, and the Secretary of Defense, Charlie Wilson, had cut research spending. After Sputnik, Neil McElroy, who took over the job of Secretary of Defense in October 1957, had a mandate to get things moving. He understood the importance of research. In his previous job as chief of Proctor & Gamble he had championed basic research. In 1957, the last year of his tenure, 70 per cent of the company's income came from products such as fluoridated toothpaste that had not existed a dozen years before.[8] McElroy's solution to the defence research problem was a new civilian agency within the Pentagon that combined the top scientific talent of the Army, Navy and Air Force, avoiding duplication and limiting inter-service rivalry over space and missile research. In February 1958 the Advanced Research Projects Agency (ARPA) was created over the heckles of the Joint Chiefs of Staff.

ARPA would be a different kind of research organization to what had gone before. It would not establish its own separate laboratories, nor would it be a vast organization like RAND. It would be a small operation that would issue contracts for research and development to other organizations. At the time that ARPA began to work on networking, its Information Processing Techniques Office had only two staff members, Bob Taylor and his secretary, who together administered a $16 million budget.[9] Like RAND, ARPA had a wide intellectual remit, and the scope to pursue long-term basic research. Indeed the establishment of NASA

< 24 >

in later 1958 forced ARPA to focus on long-term basic research rather than on practical rocket and space work. By the 1970s, ARPA had become a magnet for far-fetched research proposals. As a former IPTO director recalls, 'every brother and their crackpot friends told us about their projects that they wanted to do'.[10]

The Advanced Research Projects Agency pursues networking

Central to the story of ARPA's involvement in the Internet and to the development of computers in general was a remarkable character named J.C.R. Licklider. In 1962 ARPA's Director, Jack Ruina, recruited Licklider to work on two areas: command and control and behavioural sciences. Ruina was preoccupied with ARPA's work on ballistic missile defence and nuclear test detection and gave Licklider a wide degree of latitude to direct the command and control programme as he saw fit.[11] Licklider told Ruina that improving the usability of computer systems would lay the foundations for improved command and control.[12] He established a group of researchers who shared his interest in interactive computing, and named it, tellingly, the Intergalactic Computer Network. He asked this group to consider the big picture in computing:

> It seems to me to be interesting and important ... to develop a capability for integrated network operation ... Consider the situation in which several different centers are netted together, each center being highly individualistic and having its own special language and its own special way of doing things. Is it desirable, or even necessary for all centers to agree upon some language or, at least, upon some conventions for asking such questions as 'what language do you speak?'[13]

At the core of Licklider's thinking was an emphasis on collaboration. Licklider posited a future scenario in which a researcher at one research centre could find a useful computing resource over the network from a research centre elsewhere. This, in a world of incompatible machines and jealously guarded computing resources, was far-sighted talk indeed.

Though his first tenure at ARPA (he returned as Director of IPTO in 1974) was brief, Licklider inculcated within the Agency an enthusiasm for a new approach to computing in which the machines would be both networked and easy to use. In 1964 he chose as his successor Ivan

Sutherland, from MIT's Lincoln Laboratory. Sutherland had written the first interactive graphics system, 'Sketchpad', and was only 26 years old at the time of his arrival as Director of IPTO, where he would administer a budget of over $10 million. Sutherland's successor as IPTO Director was Bob Taylor, who had also worked on interactive computing before arriving at ARPA. Taylor's successor, Lawrence Roberts, had also worked on graphics and networking and was another of the cohort of technologists who had been inspired by Licklider at MIT Lincoln Laboratory to think of networking as the future.[14] Licklider's influence was felt further afield through his support of large research programmes in universities that stimulated the early computer studies departments and attracted the new generation of students to the new field.[15] Licklider had taken him to demonstrations where one could interact with a computer and move graphics on a screen. He also told him about 'time-sharing', a new approach to computing that allowed many different terminals to use the computing power of a single large machine.

Licklider had established the framework, but the person who first proposed that ARPA establish a significant networking project was Bob Taylor, head of IPTO from late 1965. His motive was purely practical. The Department of Defense was the largest purchaser of computer equipment in the world. ARPA itself was funding the installation of large computers at research centres across the country. Yet incompatibilities between the wide varieties of computers purchased prevented them from talking to each other, and unnecessary duplication of equipment was adding to this enormous expense. In Taylor's own office there were three separate and incompatible computer terminals linked to computers at different ARPA-funded centres. In a twenty-minute pitch Taylor proposed to the ARPA Director, Charlie Herzfeld, that ARPA could resolve the problem of duplication and isolation.[16] His proposal was simple: ARPA should fund a project to attempt to tie a small number of computers together and establish a network over which researchers using them could cooperate. If successful the network would not only allow different computers to communicate but it would enable researchers at one facility to remotely use programs on computers at others, thereby allowing ARPA to cut costs.[17] The network Taylor was describing would later be known as the 'ARPANET'.

Herzfeld, who had already been convinced by Licklider that 'computing was one of the really exciting things that was going on', allocated funds for the project immediately.[18] In December 1966 Bob Taylor

< 26 >

recruited a young researcher named Lawrence Roberts to run the project as IPTO chief scientist. Lawrence Roberts had been working on problems related to communication between computers[19] and had run an experiment connecting a machine in Boston to one in California the previous year.[20] Though Roberts was initially unwilling to join the agency, Taylor successfully used ARPA's budgetary influence on the Lincoln Laboratory to pressure the new recruit to come to ARPA.

In early 1967 Lawrence Roberts met with principal investigators from the various ARPA-funded research centres across the US to brief them on the proposed networking experiment. Remarkable though it seems in retrospect, the assembled leaders in computing research were not enthusiastic about the networking project that Roberts described to them. Networking was an unknown quantity and most could not conceive of its benefits. Moreover, they were concerned about the toll the project would take on their computing resources if they were shared across the network. Roberts took a hard line. He told the researchers that ARPA was:

> going to build a network and you are going to participate in it. And you are going to connect it to your machines . . . we are not going to buy you new computers until you have used up all of the resources of the network.[21]

Wesley Clarke, one of the fathers of microcomputing,[22] made a suggestion that went some way to placating the researchers. ARPA would pay for a small computer to be installed at each connected facility that would act as a middleman between ARPA's network and the facility's own computer (the facility's own computer was known in networking parlance as the 'host' computer). These middleman machines would be called 'Interface Message Processors' (IMPS). Dedicated IMPS at each site would remove the burden of processing from the facility's host computer. Before Clarke mooted this idea Roberts had apparently considered using a central computer based in Nebraska to control the ARPANET, which would, one might presume, have scuppered the all-important decentralized characteristic of the future Internet.[23]

There is a lack of clarity in the historical record about the level of influence that Paul Baran's ideas had on the ARPA project. Roberts appears to have been unaware of Baran's conceptual work at RAND on packet-switched networking until October 1967 when he saw a reference to

Baran in a paper that Roger Scantlebury, head of data communication research at the UK National Physics Laboratory (NPL), gave at a conference in Gatlinburg, Tennessee.[24] Baran was consulted the following month.[25] Roberts credited Baran's work as merely 'supportive'[26] in the conceptual rather than practical sense. The chronology of events that Roberts maintains on his website is explicit on this point: 'the Rand work had no significant impact on the ARPANET plans and Internet history".[27] For the sake of clarity it is worth noting, however, that Roberts did write to the Director of ARPA in mid-1968 saying that the ARPANET project would test 'a form of communications organization recommended in a distributed digital network study by the RAND Corporation'.[28] Moreover, Baran recalls that he had in fact met Roberts in February 1967, many months before Roberts indicates.[29]

Roberts was also influenced by a number of other networking and computer researchers. Among them was Leonard Kleinrock, who had written his PhD on how data could most efficiently flow across a network. Kleinrock had originally thought that his research would have an application in 'Post Office System, telegraphy systems, and satellite communication systems'.[30] Unaware of Paul Baran's military-themed work on distributed networking, Kleinrock developed many of the principles of packet switching necessary to implement such a network. The NPL in the UK also contributed ideas. At the Gatlinburg meeting in 1967, where Scantlebury had told Roberts of Baran's work, he also told him about the practical work that NPL had done on packet networking under the leadership of Donald Davies. The NPL team had become aware of Baran's parallel work on packet networking only the year before when a colleague at the UK Ministry of Defence alerted them to it. Yet the funding available to pursue the idea in the UK was dwarfed by the US effort over the coming decades. As Roberts recalled, NPL 'had the ideas, but they did not have the money'.[31]

Funding, however, was an issue. Despite the fanfare that greeted ARPA's creation, the establishment of the National Aeronautics and Space Administration (NASA) shortly afterward stole many of ARPA's most prestigious projects and decimated its budget.[32] From 1961 to 1963 ARPA rebuilt its funding and developed its reputation as a supporter of high-quality, high-risk research. Thereafter the Agency was better accepted within the Department of Defense and by the time of Charlie Herzfeld's tenure as director, from 1965–7, ARPA enjoyed the pinnacle of its rebuilt prestige within the defence establishment – but also witnessed the beginning of a new decline in its fortunes as Vietnam began to absorb American resources. Within ARPA, however, the process of funding new projects remained blessed by an absence of red tape. As Herzfeld said, 'ARPA was the only place in town where somebody could come into my office with a good idea and leave with a million dollars at the end of the day'.[33] One contractor working on the ARPANET remarked that it was ARPA's 'liberal view toward research funding . . . that allowed the internet to blossom the way it did'.[34] Yet the remarkable degree of latitude that ARPA enjoyed was not without limits. Lawrence Roberts recalls that funding was flexible at ARPA in the mid- to late 1960s to the degree that it could be excused or obscured when ARPA faced congressional oversight: 'We put projects in whatever category was useful and I moved projects back and forth depending on how it was selling in Congress'.[35]

In 1968 a new director of ARPA, Eberhardt Rechtin, signed off on an initial project to build a four-nodes network joining computers at the Stanford Research Institute (SRI), UC Santa Barbara, UCLA and the University of Utah, at a cost of $563,000.[36] This initial system would demonstrate whether a larger network with more nodes would work. The explicit goal of the programme was essentially the same as that which Bob Taylor had originally proposed the year before:

The installation of an effective network tying these [research centres] together should substantially reduce duplication and improve the transfer of scientific results, as well as develop the network techniques needed by the military.[37]

On 3 June 1968 ARPA issued a Request for Proposals to contractors to build the trial 'resource sharing computer network'. A small company called Bolt, Beranek and Newman (BBN) submitted the winning bid.

BBN had been originally introduced to computing by none other than J.C.R. Licklider, who had spent a period as its vice president before his tenure at ARPA. Leading BBN's bidding team was an engineer called Frank Heart. He summed up his approach: 'Get the very, very best people and in small numbers, so they can all know what they're all doing.'[38] The team included individuals who would play key roles in the future of networking and computing including Severo Ornstein, Will Crowther, Dave Walden and Robert Kahn. Individuals in Heart's team were free to be idiosyncratic, working long hours in rudimentary

<29>

offices at desks made from wooden doors with legs nailed on to them.[39] The systems they were building were unproven and the technologies theoretical to the point that many outside the project did not believe it would succeed.[40] IBM had said that such a network could not be built without a truly massive budget.[41] Indeed, even BBN hedged its bets, noting in its bid for the project that 'we take the position that it will be difficult to make the system work'.[42]

BBN, however, delivered the goods. The project progressed from award of contract to delivery of equipment in nine months, slightly ahead of schedule and within budget. On 29 October 1969 at 10.30 p.m., two of the IMP machines delivered by BBN to UCLA and the Stanford Research Institute made their first attempt to communicate with each other over 350 miles of leased telephone line. This was the first ARPANET transmission.[43] By December 1969 the fourth node had been connected. By April 1971 the network had expanded to include fifteen nodes. Yet though the network now connected the IMP machines at various participating research centres to each other, these were intended only to be middlemen between the network and the main 'host' computers at each research centre. Many facilities were slow to perform the extensive engineering and programming work required to link the IMP machines to their own host computers,[44] partly because of the considerable engineering challenge this posed and also because they did not yet fully appreciate the virtues of networking. In short, networking was slow to take off.

ARPA needed to generate interest in the idea of network. It had to show something tangible. On 24–26 October 1972 ARPA staged a large expo at the International Conference on Computer Communication at the Washington Hilton Hotel. A member of the BBN team, Robert Kahn, was tasked by Lawrence Roberts to organize the event. The expo took a year to prepare and featured sixty computer terminals arrayed in a vast hall where visitors could use them and connect to computers across the country on the ARPANET. Even naysayers visiting the demonstration began to understand that this 'packet-switching' technology was something real and practical.[45] ARPANET, as Dave Walden, one of the BBN team that had developed the IMPs, announced to a conference in 1975, had lain to rest the 'previously worrisome possibility that there might be no adequate solutions' to networking. 'Future network designers can use such techniques without fear of failure.[46] Yet though ARPA's functioning network was momentous, it was not an Internet yet.

< 30 >

<3>
The Essence of the Internet

The Internet is a loose arrangement of connected but autonomous networks of devices. Each device, a 'host' in networking jargon, uses a 'proto- col' to communicate with other devices on the network. These protocols tie together diverse networks and govern communication between all computers on the Internet. Not only are the protocols elemental to the Internet and how it works, but the unique collabora- tion between their designers was the formative event of Internet cul- ture. In as much as any single element of the whole can be, these protocols are the essence of the Internet. The remarkable manner in which a team of young collaborators developed these protocols set the tone for the future development of Internet culture. As their work on the protocols proceeded they began to establish the informal conven- tions that would characterize the tone of collaboration and discussion on the Internet thereafter. The process began in a bathroom, late on the night of 7 April 1969.

As BBN started building the IMPS for the ARPANET in 1969, an important piece of the network was missing: the software that would govern how computers would communicate. Graduate students at various facilities funded by the US Department of Defense Advanced Research Projects Agency (ARPA) had been given the task in 1969 of developing the missing communication protocols. They formed an informal 'network working group'. Finding themselves working in a vacuum, the students con- nected to ARPANET, who had been given the task in 1969 of developing the technical protocols, also began to establish the informal protocols that would influence interpersonal communications on the Internet in general.

Uncertain of their positions within the hierarchy of the ARPANET project, the students issued notes on their protocols under the title

<31>

'Request for Comments' (RFC). Steve Crocker, a graduate student who had received his bachelor's degree at UCLA only a year before, used the title Request for Comments to make the invitation to participate as open as possible, and to minimize any claim to authority that working on so crucial an aspect of the network as its protocols might imply. The first RFC document, which set the tone for the next half century of Internet culture and initiated the process to define the protocols that govern virtually all data exchange on the planet, was composed in humble circumstances. Its author recalls: 'I had to work in a bathroom so as not to disturb the friends I was staying with, who were all asleep.'[1] The tone in which the RFCs were typed was distinctive.[2]

Crocker was the de facto leader of the small group of six. He and two others of the group had been at the same high school in Los Angeles, Van Nuys High, and were graduate students of Leonard Kleinrock. (Kleinrock was under contract with ARPA to run the network measurement centre at UCLA.) Crocker was writing a document that outlined some broad ideas on how the students would pass around ideas through 'temporary, informal memos'.[3] Even as he drafted the document, the prospect of disapproval from far above in the academic hierarchy weighed heavily upon him:

> In my mind, I was inciting the wrath of some prestigious professor at some phantom East Coast establishment. I was actually losing sleep over the whole thing.[4]

Crocker was eager to open up the process to as many of his peers as possible:

> Closely related to keeping the technical design open was keeping the social process around the design open as well. Anyone was welcome to join the party.[5]

Vint Cerf, an early participant in the informal networking group (and now Vice President of Google), sums up the approach and context:

> Keep in mind that the original developers of the host level protocols were mostly graduate students. We adopted a humble and inclusive posture and a mantra that Dave Clark ultimately coined as 'rough consensus and running code' – that means we don't really

< 32 >

vote exactly, we just try to assess rough consensus among the group trying to agree on proposed standards.[6]

RFC 3, released in April 1969, elaborated on the character and objectives of the RFCs (note that the word 'Host' here refers to a connected computer):

> These standards (or lack of them) are stated explicitly for two reasons. First, there is a tendency to view a written statement as ipso facto authoritative, and we hope to promote the exchange and discussion of considerably less than authoritative ideas. Second, there is a natural hesitancy to publish something unpolished, and we hope to ease this inhibition.[7]

RFC 3 continues in the counter-hierarchical vein, establishing the principle that no text should be considered authoritative and that there is no final edit. This is a pivotal element of the 'perpetual beta' described in the next chapter. Also implicit was that authority was to be derived from merit rather than fixed hierarchy.

Crocker's RFC, though penned in humble circumstances, set the open, inviting tone of the next half century of Internet culture and initiated the process to define the protocols that govern virtually all data exchange on the planet. Since Crocker's RFC there have been almost six thousand RFCs published, which maintain an open, collaborative approach in Internet-engineering circles. The meritocracy of the RFCs was exemplified by a generation of delinquent programmers at MIT from the late 1950s to the late 1960s, who in turn created the 'hacker' culture that influenced much of what was to follow. The first fruit of the graduate students' labour was the NCP, the Network Control Protocols, which governed communications between machines on the Internet. The NCP, however, was merely the first protocol that allowed communications on the ARPANET. An 'internetworking' protocol that could tie different machines and networks together was yet to come.

Radio and satellite networks

San Francisco features disproportionately in the history of the digital age. Little attention, however, has been given to one of its acknowledged landmarks: a public house called Zott's. Zott's (named 'The Alpine Inn' since the mid-1950s) is a small, wood-panelled tavern and a historic focal point for the ne'er-do-wells of Silicon Valley. Its founder was Felix Buelna, a Mexican, who moved from Santa Clara in the wake of the gold rush when that area became crowded by would-have-been gold diggers in the mid-1800s. He built the inn on the site of a pony trail that had been used by rancheros and settlers to reach the coast. Buelna's inn was a place of gambling with a colourful clientele and, in the words of the US National Park Service's official survey, 'a long string of colorful owners'.[8] Regulars in the 1880s included the construction workers building Stanford University, whose entrepreneurs and technologies would propel the dot-com boom a century later. The inn also became the regular haunt of the new university's students. In 1908 the editors of the *Stanford Sequoia* lambasted their immoderate peers, writing that the student body had been 'held up to the world as a community composed largely of drunkards'.[9] In January the following year the president of the university wrote in vexed mood to the county supervisors requesting that they not renew the inn's liquor licence because it was 'unusually vile, even for a roadhouse, a great injury to the University and a disgrace to San Mateo County'.[10] Yet the humble wood-panelled structure remained a landmark through the twentieth century as the digital industry evolved around it. By early 2001 its car park accommodated the expensive sports cars of the young Silicon Valley millionaires.[11] It was fitting, then, that more than a century after its establishment Zott's should be the site for an important event in the history of the Internet.

On 27 August 1976 a van parked in Zott's beer garden. It was part of the Stanford Research Institute's (SRI) packet radio experiment, conducted under contract for ARPA. The SRI team removed a computer terminal from the van and placed it on a wooden table in Zott's beer garden. A wire connected the terminal to the van, and radio equipment in the van connected it to ARPA's new packet radio network, PRNET, which in turn was connected to ARPANET. The team at Zott's sent a message from their terminal across the PRNET and thence to a distant machine connected to ARPANET. This was one of the more momentous events to have happened in any beer garden: it was the first ever packet data transmission across two networks using the new 'internet' protocol.[12]

The discoveries that made this transmission possible arose as part of an earlier project at the University of Hawaii in 1970. Norman Abramson, the Professor of Electrical Engineering and Computer Science, had faced a difficult problem. He wanted to network the University of Hawaii's seven campuses. This posed three problems. First, the campuses were physically spread across four islands. Second, the leased telephone lines that connected ARPANET facilities to each other were too expensive for his budget. Third, the line quality of the Hawaiian telephone system was too poor to carry networking data. The answer, Abramson decided, was to use radio. Thus from 1970 ARPA began to fund Abramson's attempt to develop a packet radio network.

Radio signals travel differently to electric signals across telephone lines. While telephone signals travel from point to point in an orderly sequence, radio transmits indiscriminately to all receivers within its broadcast range. Signals broadcast by different nodes to the receiver at the same time can collide and be destroyed. Abramson's team developed an elegant solution to this problem: when any node sent a packet but did not receive confirmation of successful delivery from the receiving node it would wait for a random period and then resend the message. Since all nodes would wait a random period before resending, the odds of repeat collisions were slight. Thus the network would quickly correct itself when it lost packets. Using this method Abramson's team built a functioning network called the AlohaNet that linked Hawaii University's campuses to each other and to the ARPANET. This method of dealing with collision between messages was called the 'Aloha method', and ARPA used its example to build its own packet radio network, PRNET.[13]

The discovery of the Aloha method for packet radio networking was particularly timely since the political tides in which ARPA swam had become slightly more turbulent. In 1969 Senate Majority Leader Mike Mansfield had signalled his intention to cut $400 million from the defence research budget.[14] He was the author of Section 203 of the Military Procurement Authorization Act for Fiscal Year 1970, the so-called 'Mansfield Amendment', which stipulated that all funded research must have a 'direct and apparent relationship to a specific military function or operation'. Packet radio was just such a project. The power of massive, expensive mainframe computers could be relayed to the battlefield by networks of radio, cable and, as ARPA was beginning to prove, satellite.[15]

<35>

The launch of Sputnik in October 1957 had forced the United States to dramatically accelerate its space programme. Its first successful satellite, Explorer 1, entered orbit on 31 January 1958. The space programme had advanced considerably by the 1970s. Between January 1971 and May 1975, for example, a civilian programme launched a series of 'Intelsat IV' communication satellites from Cape Canaveral, each over forty times heavier than Explorer 1.[16] Yet though the space race had prompted this acceleration of US satellite technology, it would be the nuclear arms race that would in part create the conditions for the expansion of ARPANET to its first international node by satellite.

In 1957 the US had conducted the 'Rainier' test, its first underground nuclear detonation. The blast was detected by seismic devices across the globe and proved the value of seismology in nuclear detection.[17] The Limited Test Ban Treaty of 1963 banned open-air testing in favour of safer underground tests and made the speedy processing of seismic data critically important. In June 1968 the US and Norway concluded an agreement to cooperate in building a large seismic detection facility at Kjeller, near Oslo. The facility, called NORSAR, was built in 1970 and began sending seismic data to the US Seismic Data Analysis Centre in Virginia via the Nordic satellite station in Tanum, Sweden.[18] ARPA decided to 'piggy-back' on the original NORSAR satellite link, connecting the NORSAR facility to ARPANET[19] in June 1973. University College London (UCL) was connected to the ARPANET the following month via landline to NORSAR.[20] The ARPANET connection at UCL was used by researchers at centres across the UK working on diverse subjects including computer aided design and network analysis.[21]

International interest in packet-switched networking was growing. Robert Kahn, now at ARPA, believed that satellite networking could support the connection of US and international networks.[22] ARPA began to investigate the possibility of creating an Atlantic satellite network. In 1974 the UK Post Office agreed to cover the UK's costs for a satellite connection to the US, and in September 1975 ARPA initiated the SATNET Atlantic networking programme using civilian Intelsat IV earth stations in the US and the UK. In late 1977 the Norwegian Defence Establishment was also linked via a separate earth station in Tanum. By May 1979 ARPANET access from the UK was provided almost exclusively over SATNET and the landline connection via Tanum was removed at the end of the year.

Thus by the mid-1970s ARPA had built three functioning networks: ARPANET, PRNET and SATNET, using cable, radio and satellite. Now it remained to network the different networks.

By 1973 a new protocol was required to internetwork the ARPANET, PRNET and SATNET. After organizing the 1972 International Conference on Computer Communication at which the ARPANET was demonstrated in Washington, Robert Kahn had joined ARPA (now named DARPA) where, following some unrelated projects, he resumed his work on packet networking. In the spring of 1973 he approached Vint Cerf, one of the group of graduate students that had developed the NCP protocol for the ARPANET, and outlined the need for a new internetworking protocol that would allow computers to communicate together across cable, radio and satellite networks.[23] Cerf had just become an Assistant Professor at Stanford and ran a series of seminars to tease out the problem. He drew together a group of researchers who would later hold key positions in the networking and computer industries. Participants included Robert Metcalfe, who was representing the Xerox PARC research centre, and Gerard Lelann, who was visiting Cerf's lab from Cyclades, the French packet network project. Cerf's group continued the inclusive, open approach of drafting RFCs.

They were influenced by the example of Cyclades, which had adopted a centrifugal approach in which data transmission was not regulated by the equipment of the network itself but by the computers sending and receiving the data at its edges.[24] At the Xerox company's PARC research centre, Robert Metcalfe was working on something similar. Xerox had just unveiled a revolutionary new computer called the Alto. The Alto had a mouse, graphical display, a desktop and system of windows and folders for storing files. The machine was two decades ahead of its time and represented a paradigm shift in computing that the senior management of Xerox failed spectacularly to capitalize upon.[25] Metcalfe was working on a network to connect many Altos in an office, developing 'Ethernet' and Local Area Networking (LAN). He grew impatient with the consensus approach that Cerf, Lelann and others were taking and decided to move ahead on his own. In 1973 Metcalfe's PhD thesis had refined the Hawaiian Aloha method. He now applied these mathematical improvements to develop a system informally named Alto Aloha, which became PUP (PARC Universal Packet).[26] PUP adopted the same centrifugal datagram approach of Cyclades,

< 37 >

and its network was dumb to the extent that it was merely a system of cables. Unlike the ARPANET, where the IMP machines controlled many of the network's functions, the PUP network had no capability to control transmission or flow of data, or to verify delivery or repeat transmission of lost or partially delivered packets. Instead the software protocols running on the connected host computers would control the network. As a later PARC memo on the specifications of the PUP noted:

> Pup communication is end-to-end at the packet level. The inter-network is required only to be able to transport independently addressed Pups from source to destination. Use of higher levels of protocol is entirely the responsibility of the communicating end processes.[27]

This moved control over the operation of the network from the connecting infrastructure to the actual devices participating in the network themselves. This was a centrifugal approach, and it suited the requirements of the network of networks that ARPA had in mind.

The NCP (Network Control Protocol) that controlled communications on the original landline ARPANET was not appropriate for radio and satellite networking. Instead, a new internetworking protocol would give each connected 'host' computer a far greater degree of responsibility for control of the network. The new protocol, which would run on each host computer connected to the network, would not only establish connections between hosts, it would assume the functions that the dedicated Interface Message Processor (IMP) computers had performed: verifying safe delivery of packets, retransmitting them where necessary and controlling the rate of data flow. Simply put, to allow data to flow across a network that included landline, satellite and radio connections, a new protocol would take a much more flexible approach to communication control. In May 1974 Cerf and Kahn published an outline of the new Transmission Control Protocol (TCP):

> a simple but very powerful and flexible protocol which provides for variation in individual network packet sizes, transmission failures, sequencing, [and] flow control.[28]

< 38 >

This internetworking protocol is, in a technical sense, the essence of the Internet, and in its priorities and functions can be discerned the cardinal characteristics of the new medium. TCP is centrifugal by necessity, as one of its designers notes:

> We wanted as little as possible at the center. Among other reasons, we knew quite well that it's much easier to scale a system that doesn't have choke points in the middle.[29]

Some of the enthusiasm for the centrifugal approach of relying on the host computers themselves and abandoning the IMPs may have arisen from social rather than technical reasons. The IMP machines connecting host computers at each participating facility to the ARPANET were controlled by BBN, ARPA's main contractor, which gave BBN control over the network itself. From their central offices BBN engineers could remotely update, repair and monitor the use of IMPs across the network. Increasingly, researchers preferred the idea of a dumb network controlled by a community of computers using a common protocol without the IMP standing between the host and the network.[30] It is a small irony that the IMPs were originally introduced in 1969 not to control the network but to convince the ARPA-funded researchers that connecting to the ARPANET would not directly impose a burden on the processing power of their host computers. Support for the removal of the IMPs only five years later was a sign of how far networking had come.

Much as Paul Baran's original, decentralized network prioritized survivability over other considerations, the TCP prioritized robustness over accountability and control. Billing and accounting, which would have been foremost in the minds of commercial designers, were entirely absent from the ARPA internetworking protocol.[31] TCP was also heterogeneous by nature. It was designed so that machines on different networks using different technologies could seamlessly communicate as though they were on the same network. Various networks were bridged by so-called 'gateway' machines that maintained routing tables with the addresses of computers on their own local networks. TCP underwent several revisions, and following a meeting in January 1978 between Cerf and two researchers, Jon Postel and Danny Cohen, at the University of South California, it was split into two parts to streamline the functions of the gateway computers. TCP would handle communication between computers and an additional Internet Protocol (IP) handled internetwork connections between networks. The combination of TCP and IP would avoid the gateway computers from duplicating functions already performed by host computers within local networks. What remained was to make sure that internetworking actually worked in real world conditions.

Cerf, who had joined ARPA in 1976, oversaw a series of practical internetworking tests. A particularly ambitious test was conducted on 22 November 1977. As the SRI packet radio van drove along the California freeway, the radio equipment onboard broadcast data packets via PRNET to a gateway machine that connected to ARPANET. Travelling across the ARPANET by cable, the packets sent from the van reached a gateway machine on the East Coast of the United States that connected to SATNET. From this point the packets were relayed by orbiting satellite to Goonhilly Downs in the UK, and thereafter back via ARPANET to California. To monitor the fidelity of the network's transmission, a screen in the van generated patterns from the data it was receiving. Errors in the data transmission would be immediately clear from flaws in the pattern. Yet the system performed so well that whenever the signal was blocked by bridges and other objects that the van's radio could not penetrate, the pattern would only pause and then resume when the signal returned. There were no errors.[32] This test had spanned three networks and two continents. Cerf recalls, 'the packets were travelling 94,000 miles round trip . . . We didn't lose a bit!'[33] Another test put network computers aboard aircraft from the Strategic Air Command to simulate wartime conditions:

> airborne packet radio in the field communicating with each other and to the ground using airborne systems to sew together fragments of the Internet that had been fragmented by nuclear attack.[34]

Here was proof that internetworking was possible between radio, satellite and landline networks across the globe and under adverse conditions. An optimistic observer might have thought that now, after proof had been offered, the telephone companies would embrace TCP/IP and bring the Internet to the masses. Instead, however, the telephone industry rushed to develop its own standard. It was keen to maintain its central control over the network.

< 40 >

How the TCP/IP Internet suite of protocols differed from and eventually overcame the alternative put forward by the telephone companies says much about the character of the Internet and the nature of enterprises that are best suited to prosper upon it.

Centrifugal defeats centripetal (TCP v x.25)

ARPA's networking endeavours, like those at RAND previously, were totally at odds with the ethos of the telephone industry. The reason for this conflict extended back to the industry's very origins. In 1877 Alexander Graham Bell was granted a second patent for his telephone and formed the Bell Telephone Company. For a brief period only Bell Telephone and its licensees could legally operate telephone systems in the United States. Then, when his patent expired at the end of 1893, a glut of competitors rushed into the market. Between 1894 and 1904, over 6,000 independent telephone companies went into business in the country.[35] This had two effects. First, it dramatically accelerated the proliferation of telephone systems across the United States. Second, it resulted in a chaotic mess of incompatible telephone networks. Telephone subscribers might indeed find themselves newly connected, but they were also unable to use their telephones to communicate with people who did not happen to be on the same system they subscribed to. In the 1908 annual report of AT&T (as Bell was known from 1899 when it came under the ownership of its subsidiary, AT&T), the president of the company, Theodore Vail, warned that only through universal and consistent service could reliable telephony be assured.[36] The solution, AT&T argued, was monopoly. As its 1908 marketing slogan put it: 'one policy, one system, universal service'.[37] Vail's argument prevailed and in 1913 AT&T became a government-sanctioned monopoly under the regulation of the Federal Communications Commission (FCC).

From this point on, AT&T's control over the United States' telecommunications network was so absolute that, until the late 1960s, homeowners in the United States were even forbidden from modifying their telephone sets in any way. While Bell Labs, a research unit within AT&T, was a hive of innovation, the company had no strategic interest in transforming its network. AT&T was firmly wedded to the orthodoxies of central control and knew with the benefit of long experience that the circuit switching of telephone calls, the technology that Alexander

Graham Bell had patented in the late 1870s, worked as it was. Thus Paul Baran had been rebuffed in the mid-1960s when he approached AT&T with the opportunity to use the packet-switched networking concept he had developed at RAND. Even so, in 1968 ARPA had anticipated that the successful demonstration of four functioning nodes in a data network would convince a telephone company of the merits of digital networking. The original planning document for the ARPANET project included the optimistic objective of transferring the technology so that a utility could provide 'digital message transmission as a tariffed service'.[38] Yet even in 1975, after proof of concept and extensive testing of the packet-switched distributed network concept had been successfully conducted at the taxpayers' expense in the form of the ARPANET, AT&T refused to pursue the Internet idea.

Shortly thereafter, in the mid- to late 1970s, telecommunications companies in Europe, Canada, Japan and the US did begin to appreciate that the potential of digital packet-switched networks should no longer be overlooked. While some public data networks had been established in the late 1960s and early 1970s, such as the Broadband Exchange Service in Canada from 1969,[39] many telephone companies found the digital network revolution challenging. This was not least because they had been beaten to this conclusion by the computer manufacturers. While the ARPANET used open, non-proprietary standards to which any manufacturer's devices could connect, the commercial computer manufacturers began to offer proprietary equipment and networks that were incompatible with machines supplied by their competitors. Thus telephone companies would not be able to choose suppliers on the basis of competitive prices if they built a network using proprietary equipment from IBM, Digital Equipment Corporation (DEC) or some other supplier's technology. Thus, even as they became interested in data networks, the telephone carriers grew concerned that they might become in thrall to the equipment manufacturers.

The solution, the telecommunications giants realized, was to create an open standards network, the equipment for which could be produced by a plurality of suppliers, but over which they could retain the strict central control that they had always exercised over the traditional telephone and telegraph networks. Though they were keen to avoid monopolies in networking equipment, many of the telecommunications carriers were monopolies themselves. Outside the United States, telecommunications services were often offered either by regulated

< 42 >

monopolies along the AT&T model or by the so-called 'PPTS' (governmental ministries of posts, telegraph and telephone) or by nationalized companies. Within the US, as ARPA and the networking researchers it funded were veering off in the direction of multiple networks, decentralized control and open standards, AT&T remained fixed to the Vailian ideas that had helped to make it one of the largest corporations in the world. In the late 1970s, J.C.R. Licklider had cautioned that different networks would be unable to communicate with one another unless common standardized protocols were introduced.[40] This is indeed what began to happen.

Between the mid-1970s and the late 1980s, a pivotal period in the expansion of networking to the public, ARPA and its allies fought a standards war against the telecommunications industry.[41] Representing the interests of the telephone industry was the Consultative Committee on International Telegraphy and Telephony (CCITT), a body of the International Telecommunications Union (ITU). Within the CCITT a group began working on the question of standards in 1975. The resulting protocol, x.25, was adopted by the CCITT in September the following year. Despite their dawning awareness of data networks as an emerging market, the telephone companies had not fully made the leap to the concept of distributed networking that lay at the heart of Baran's work at RAND in the early 1960s. Nor had the telephone companies embraced ARPA's approach towards diversity. Foremost among Baran's considerations had been the need to provide a robust communications infrastructure using unreliable, redundant equipment. The telephone companies took the view that digital networks, like the analogue networks for telephone and telegraph before them, could only offer reliable service if every aspect of the network were controlled by the operating company.[42] The imperative for ARPA had been to enable 'a very broad class of interactions' between a diverse array of incompatible computers and networks that served different purposes.[43] Thus where TCP/IP enabled diversity, x.25 required consistency and conformity.

In contrast, TCP/IP, like the French network Cyclades, used 'datagram' packets. Datagrams are simple, elemental packets that can be combined as needed by host computers to scale up or down the level of complexity in their communications. x.25, however, was built to provide consistently high-quality communication in all cases – whether necessary or not – which made it inappropriate for many uses. This distinction between TCP/IP, which used datagrams, and X.25, which rejected them in favour of consistent and rigidly controlled communications, was an ideological division[44] between two generations of engineers, centripetal on one hand and centrifugal on the other, as much as it was technical. Vint Cerf, one of the chief architects of TCP, recalls that he had offered TCP/IP to the CCITT but had been rebuffed because the protocol had come from the Department of Defense, and because 'they thought they could not "sell" datagrams'.[45]

TCP/IP did not only accommodate different devices, but accommodated many different types of networks too. TCP/IP could be used inside a network, or to connect many networks, or both. Not so for the telephone companies. Their interest was in national public data networks. The diverse array of networks of varying sizes, architectures and purposes that TCP/IP could support, and which the Internet eventually became,[46] was beyond their view. According to Cerf, TCP/IP 'eventually won out because it was so general'.[47] Ultimately, homogenous X.25, the expression of the centripetal bent of the telephone industry, was defeated by TCP/IP, the open, diverse and untidy offering of the research community. As TCP/IP spread across the globe, communications began to take on the centrifugal character that had previously been the preserve of participants on the ARPANET. Moreover, new opportunities beckoned for underground, amorphous communities drawn together by common interest rather than proximity. The growth spurt that the early Internet enjoyed in the late 1980s was partly due to the ability of TCP/IP to work at both the macro and micro levels. This proved to be enormously fortuitous for the development of the Internet.

< 44 >

‹4›
Computers Become Cheap, Fast and Common

Even as Sputnik I soared into orbit in 1957 it was being tracked by a cutting-edge radar, the 'UHF Millstone', that had become operational that very month in the United States.[1] Millstone had an unprecedented 2.5 megawatt transmitting power and an 84-foot (25.6m)-diameter dish that stood on an 88-foot (26.8m)-high tower. The Soviet Union had won the race into space, but American technology was quietly progressing in a different but potentially more important direction.

In 1950, seven years before the launch of Sputnik, the US had started to investigate how computers and radars could be used together in a new and dramatically different way. In 1950 a group drawn from the US Air Force Scientific Advisory Committee chaired by George Valley concluded that the air defence system across the continental United States would stop only 10 per cent of Soviet strike forces.[2] This was particularly worrying due to two recent developments in Soviet technology. In August 1949 the Soviet Union had performed its first nuclear test, 'First Lightning', at the Semipalatinsk test site in Kazakhstan. Then during the Korean War, which lasted from June 1950 to July 1953, the US and USSR both fielded new jet aircraft, the US F-86 Sabre and Soviet MIG 15, capable of transonic speeds that made it impossible for radar operators to reliably interpret radar signals. Strategic bombers, presumably, would soon be equally difficult to detect. Air defence would have to change, and computers were the answer.

The Valley Group considered radical measures to buttress air defence. One was the idea of establishing an array of small radars dotted along the nation's borders that fed into a central computer system. Another was the establishment of a research laboratory at MIT that would study air defence solutions. Both recommendations proved pivotal in the development of the Internet. The Lincoln Laboratory at MIT would be a major force in the development of modern computing and networking and its early alumni include the emeriti of Internet history: Frank Heart, Kenneth Olsen, Wesley Clarke, Lawrence Roberts, Severo Ornstein, Robert Taylor and J.C.R. Licklider himself, who had been on Valley's air defence study group and on an MIT panel that deliberated over Lincoln's establishment.

The Lincoln Laboratory worked to realize the Valley Group's concept of a computer-connected, nation-spanning radar array. The SAGE (Semi-Automatic Ground Environment) program was initiated in 1954 to track and intercept high-speed enemy aircraft. To do so it would gather real-time information from an array of radars spread across the United States, instantly combine and analyse their data, and display the results on screens in such a way that human operators could quickly comprehend. Every part of this was revolutionary.

Building SAGE would demand a revolution in networking, computing and user interaction – the three fields of advance that would make the Internet possible. SAGE was a truly massive undertaking involving 7,000 programmers at various stages. Each of the 24 massive SAGE direction centres was linked by long-distance telephone lines to more than a hundred interoperating air defence elements, requiring system integration on a scale previously unimagined. SAGE drew data from sensors across North America including weather stations and ground and shipboard radar. Its real-time nature meant that the staff at the Lincoln Laboratory who worked on it became leaders in the field of high-speed computer communications.[3] Many went on to work at BBN on ARPA networking projects.

Approachable, usable computers

When it initially proposed a network of radars connected to a computer system, Valley's group had had no clear idea of how a radar and computer system might work together, or what kind of computer might be needed. Computers in the early 1950s were vast industrial tabulation machines, entirely unsuited to what the Valley group had proposed. IBM, for example, had run census-tabulating on an industrial scale for the US government from the 1880s. Its founder, Herman Hollerith, had filed his first patent on the 'art of compiling statistics'.[4] SAGE would demand systems that went far beyond mere tabulation. SAGE computers

< 46 >

would have to be agile and responsive, yet this was the precise opposite of the machines that represented the state of the art in the 1950s.

Since the equipment and the price of its operating time were at such a premium, large computers operated a system of 'batch processing' to receive instructions in an orderly manner. Instead of a single operator giving a series of commands directly to a computer, a queue of people with programs that required computer time submitted pre-planned sets of coded instructions in stacks of cards with holes punched in them. A priesthood of specialist administrators relayed the cards to the machine. A user, having never actually interacted with the machine directly, would receive the machine's printed responses to their stack of code cards some hours or perhaps days later. Here was a model of industrial-era computing in which the focal point was not the computer users themselves, but the machines and those who administrated them. This was totally unsuitable for the SAGE system. A new way of interacting with computers would have to be contemplated.

The answer, or at least the beginning of the answer, was an unusual computer called the Whirlwind. When it began life as a project of the US Navy it was intended to be a flight simulator, allowing a pilot direct control of the system.[5] This meant that it was one of the first interactive computers through which a user could directly operate the machine and observe its responses to instructions on a screen as they happened. Whirlwind was taken over by the Air Force and refined at Lincoln Laboratory in the early 1950s. The result was the AN/FSQ-7, known as Whirlwind II. IBM won a contract to build the 24 AN/FSQ-7s required for the SAGE system. When complete each AN/FSQ-7 weighed 250 tons, required a 3,000 kWh power supply, and included over 49,000 vacuum tubes.

From 1952–5, J.C.R. Licklider was part of the SAGE 'presentation group' at the Lincoln Laboratory.[6] His conundrum was how to present information in an understandable way to human operators so that they could respond in a direct, speedy manner. By 1963, when the SAGE system was operational, a user could look at a monitor on his terminal and observe the real-time tracks of multiple aircraft. Without typing a line of code or punching a single punch card operators could select various data on the screen with a handheld 'light gun' and assign fighter aircraft to intercept bogies. The SAGE computers represented a computing revolution.

SAGE stimulated a period of transition in computing in the mid-1950s to early 1960s. Wesley Clark and Ken Olsen, Whirlwind's designer and

< 47 >

engineer respectively, built two revolutionary computers at MIT Lincoln Lab. The TX-0 was completed in April 1956 and then work continued on the more powerful TX-2.[7] The TX machines were the first transistorized computers in the world and were interactive in a way that previous systems had not been. The TX-0 gave direct feedback to its operator through a circular glass display, indicator lights and a speaker that generated a tone depending on what instruction the machine was processing. Using a typewriter (flexowriter) a user punched instructions on to tape and fed them directly to the TX-0's reader. The user could observe the program running and see errors arising in real time.

In 1957 Ken Olsen and a colleague named Harlan Anderson left the Lincoln Laboratory and founded a company called Digital Equipment Corporation (DEC). DEC brought the revolutionary technology of the Whirlwind II and the TX to the commercial world. The company released the PDP-1, the world's first commercially available interactive computer, in 1960. It cost only $120,000, a fraction of the cost of contemporary IBM machines.[8] Thereafter computers continued to became smaller and cheaper. By 1965 DEC's more powerful PDP-8 cost only $18,000. These machines signalled the death of batch processing and heralded a future in which individuals would own their own, personal computers. Thus in the same years as Baran and Davies were working on packet networking at RAND and NPL, the computers that would connect to the networks they were conceiving of were undergoing their own metamorphoses.

Working down the hall from Wesley Clarke at MIT in the mid-1950s was J.C.R. Licklider. Licklider had become interested in cybernetics under the influence of Norbert Weiner and was attempting to develop electronic models of how the brain processes pitch. However, it quickly became apparent that two limiting factors were frustrating his work. First, the mathematics involved was so complex that Licklider could only tackle the problem with a very high-powered computer. Second, Licklider realized after auditing his use of time for a period in 1957 that he spent 85 per cent of his time on clerical work, 'getting into a position to think', and only 15 per cent on the actual problem.[9] When a chance meeting with Wesley Clarke introduced him to the TX-2 and interactive computing, the thought began to form in Licklider's mind of a division of labour between computer and man. Theirs would be a

< 48 >

symbiotic relationship: machines could perform clerical tasks better than humans; humans would be liberated to think and make decisions. The 85 per cent of time preparing to work would be drastically reduced. Licklider would soon be in a position to promote this concept.

Bolt and Beranek, two of the founders of BBN, knew of Licklider from their time working at MIT on psychoacoustics. In 1957 Licklider was recruited by BBN as Vice President. His arrival signalled a shift in BBN's focus. Licklider told Beranek that he needed a digital computer. Previously BBN had used analogue computers for acoustics work, and a digital computer in 1957 had a price tag greater than any other single piece of equipment that BBN had ever purchased for any project. Moreover, Licklider admitted that he had no specific purpose in mind for the machine. What convinced Beranek to approve the purchase was Licklider's view that 'if BBN is going to be an important company in the future, it must be in computers'.[10] He was correct. Just over a decade later BBN would win the contract to adapt the IMP computers for the ARPANET, and a few years later one of its engineers would invent e-mail. In a sign of how pivotal certain figures were in the small world of computing, it was the same Wesley Clark, the TX designer, who first introduced Licklider to interactive computers, who would propose that the ARPANET use the IMP machines.

Thus by the time Licklider arrived at ARPA in 1962, he was convinced of the importance of computing. Licklider shifted ARPA's computer work from war gaming and operational studies of command systems to a new focus on time-sharing research, graphics and networking,[11] and the name of his office changed from Command and Control Research to the Information Processing Techniques Office (IPTO). Thus, from the Whirlwind and SAGE, and then through ARPA's funding of relevant research programmes, a military need for air defence and command and control gave rise to a broader exploration of how humans and computers could better interact.

The world marvelled when the iPhone was released on 9 January 2007. Unthreatening, instantly understandable and attractive, the graphical user interface (GUI) of the iPhone brought not just connectivity to the people but also usability. Yet only four decades previously computers had been limited, alien things, kept at many removes from the average worker in an organization. As recently as 1975 the first generation of personal computers (PCs) were without video displays and reliant on a series of blinking lights to communicate with their users. Yet in 1965 Licklider proposed a vision of interactive computing:

> A man sits at a desk, writes or draws on a surface with a stylus, and thereby communicates to a programmed information processor with a large memory. It is the mental image of the immediate response, visible on the oscilloscope, through which the computer acknowledges the command and reports the consequences of carrying it out.[12]

Even as he wrote, the systems that he described were just beginning to seem feasible. Douglas Engelbart, a far-sighted engineer at the Stanford Research Institute, was reading Norbert Wiener and Ross Ashby on cybernetics and believed that human intellect could be augmented by using computer technology.[13] Engelbart had established the Augmented Human Intellect Research Center to study computer tools that would give users 'a useful degree of comprehension in a situation that was previously too complex'.[14] He sought new ways of 'conceptualizing, visualizing, and organizing working material, and ... methods for working individually and cooperatively'.[15] He gave his team their own dedicated computer consoles, most unusual in the era of batch processing, and instructed them to conduct every aspect of their work on the computer and to create the tools they needed as they went. The result was the 'oN-Line System' (NLS). The NLS was truly revolutionary. It introduced for the first time the mouse, word processing, video conferencing, the use of multiple windows for different programs, and collaborative documents. All were incorporated within an intuitive and easy to understand GUI. Engelbart demonstrated the NLS before an audience of thousands at the Fall Joint Computer Conference in 1968. The crowd was stunned. Engelbart's demonstration became known as 'the mother of all demos'. The modern computer was beginning to emerge.

Spacewar! and Sketchpad

At the end of the 1950s the Research Laboratory of Electronics (RLE) at MIT buzzed with disruptive, innovative people. Here among the dropouts and eccentrics a new culture began to develop. Theirs was a culture totally at odds with the bureaucratic mindset of IBM and the

< 50 >

centripetal, controlling inclinations of the telephone companies. They referred to themselves as 'hackers'. While the rest of MIT used the term 'hack' to refer to elaborate pranks, a 'hack' denoted a smart innovation that solved an engineering problem in the slang lexicon of the members of MIT's Tech Model Railroad Club (TMRC). The TMRC was a focal point for obsessive technical innovators. The club boasted an impressive railway board under which the club's Signals & Power Subcommittee had rigged a staggeringly complex array of equipment. In 1954 a control system was built that allowed control of five trains at once across thirty different sections of the rail system simply by adjusting the voltage and polarity of the electricity passing through the rails.[16] This astoundingly complicated system had been built using electro-mechanical relays, telephone equipment and sundry parts sourced by the club's covert 'Midnight Requisitioning Committee' who purloined necessary parts from across MIT.[17] Many of the members of the TMRC were also working at the Research Laboratory of Electronics, and viewed computers in the same way as they viewed the model rail network in their clubroom: something to be obsessively studied and perfected.

In 1959 the RLE took delivery of the TX-0 computer, gifted to it from the Lincoln Laboratory. This machine was the first user-usable computer that the students associated with the laboratory had ever had at their disposal. Feedback came not hours or days later from the hands of an administrator, but immediately and directly to the user from the computer itself. This was the dawn of interactive computing. In the era of the IBM mainframe and batch processing, it was a breath of fresh air that fed the growth of a new and vibrant computing culture. The arrival of this interactive computer prompted emergence of a wave of user-driven innovation that would eventually define much of the culture of personal computing. In contrast to the bureaucracy that surrounded the IBM 740 at MIT, the TX-0 and the PDP-1 computer that followed it were 'set up as a do-it-yourself operation'.[18] Since graduate students with legitimate work to perform on the TX-0 had preferential time slots, the hackers used the machine at unsocial hours. They often worked through thirty-hour days in obsessive bursts of coding.[19] As John McKenzie, who directed the RLE, reported, 'Practically all of the system software mentioned was done on a voluntary basis by users not on the TX-0 staff at the time their programs were written.'[20]

The TX-0 and the PDP-1, remarkable though they were for their interactivity, were modest computers nonetheless. Technology at this

<51>

remedial level required that programming did the most with the amount of available computer resources available. Hackers prided themselves on creative efficiency, on their ability to hack and reduce the number and length of instructions to a minimum. This produced two defining characteristics that prevail on discussion forums on the Internet today: first, a Darwinian meritocracy,[21] and second, a desire to understand and optimize code that precludes any concept of completion. No program was ever finished because it could always be refined. Both were illustrated by twelve-year-old Peter Deutsch, whose father was an MIT professor and who regularly spent time at the RLE Lab working on the TX-0. Deutsch was a gifted programmer who gained the respect of the hackers. As the chronicler of the hacker scene, Steve Levy, notes, 'by virtue of his computer knowledge he was worthy of equal treatment'.[22] When Professor Jack Dennis created an assembler program for the TX-0 his code was then pulled apart and improved by the hackers.[23] This in itself defied standard assumptions of academia about who should be allowed to improve on whose code. Yet more remarkable still was that one of the hackers was a twelve-year-old who happened to pass his free time at the laboratory. The culture evolving around these new machines had almost entirely jettisoned the established hierarchy. This ethos would spread as MIT staff moved to other institutions, such as the Stanford AI Lab (SAIL), from where it would make a significant impact in the development of mainstream culture through Google, Yahoo and other Internet companies.

In 1962 the hackers produced one of the world's first computer games, called *Spacewar!* Inspired by a diet of trash space adventure books and Japanese monster cinema that relied on a 'determined avoidance of plot, character, or significance',[24] the game displayed duelling black and white spacecraft that two players could control. Each was commanded using the world's first computer game joysticks, built from spare parts at the TMRC clubroom.[25] This was the dawn of a whole new era in computer interactivity, and it occurred six years before Engelbart's public demonstration of the mouse. The next year, in 1963, interactive computing had a further breakthrough. A young computer scientist named Ivan Sutherland, who would shortly be recruited by Licklider as his successor at ARPA, was wrapping up his PhD thesis at MIT's Lincoln Laboratory. Sutherland understood that normal computer use was 'slowed down by the need to reduce all communication to written statements that can be typed'. Until now, he argued, 'we have been writing letters to rather than conferring with our computers'.[26] Sutherland was using the TX-2, the TX-0's big brother, to develop 'Sketchpad', a graphical design program that allowed the user to draw directly on to a display screen with a light pen. The PhD thesis in which he described this program would be regarded as one of the most important theses ever written in computing.[27]

These developments, the computer game *Spacewar!*, the graphical program Sketchpad, and Engelbart's oN-Line System, lay the foundations for computers that could be used by average human beings. Some of Engelbart's staff went on to work at Xerox PARC and Apple Computer where they carried their knowledge of the GUI and interactive computing to a commercial audience. In the mid-1970s Xerox created a graphical user interface with mouse and icons for its Alto experimental computer, and finally released the Alto's commercial off-shoot, the Xerox Star, in 1981. The first consumer computer with a GUI was the Apple Macintosh of 1984. Other personal computers such as the Atari and Amiga, and some IBM PCs running DOS, had GUIs from 1985. The first version of Microsoft's Windows was released in November 1985.

Yet though computers were becoming increasingly usable, before the 1980s they were not yet 'personal', nor were they cheap or compact. This too was about to change.

Computers for the masses

The invention of the transistor at Bell Labs in 1947 liberated computing from the large, unreliable vacuum tubes on which the first digital computers were based. The new technology, however, still required engineers to hand-solder thousands of transistors, wires and other components together to make complicated devices. Then in 1958 an engineer at Texas Instruments named Jack Kilby did something that would revolutionize not only computing, but the production of all electronic devices on the planet. He constructed a small transistor and circuitry on a single piece of germanium, an element similar to silicon, drawing their circuits on the metal itself by a process of diffusion. This device, built from only one material, was the world's first integrated circuit. Kilby realized that the difficulty and expense of building small electronic devices such as hearing aids and calculators would be reduced by an order of magnitude if their circuitry were built, as his patent describes, 'using only one material for all circuit elements'.[28] His invention prompted dramatic miniaturization and sophistication of electronics, and a precipitous price drop. Then, a little more than a decade after Kilby's breakthrough, a young company called Intel used the integrated circuit technique to build the world's first microprocessor in 1971. It crammed an entire computer on a single piece of silicon the size of a postage stamp.

Intel was founded by Robert Noyce (an engineer who had also invented the integrated circuit at almost exactly the same time as Jack Kilby) and a colleague named Gordon Moore.[29] Even though Intel marketed its '4004' microprocessor as a 'micro-programmable computer on a chip',[30] the incumbents in the computer industry, known as the 'Big Bunch', dismissed it as a device to control traffic lights and cash registers.[31] BUNCH was an acronym for the computing giants of the pre-PC era: Burroughs, Univac, NCR Corporation, Control Data Corporation and Honeywell. The 4004 represented the beginning of their end. Though postage-stamp sized, it delivered the same processing power as the US Army's ENIAC computer, which had been known as the 'giant brain' when it was introduced in 1946.[32] The ENIAC had been the largest electronic apparatus on the planet. Its system of 17,468 vacuum tubes could perform ballistics calculations in a mere thirty minutes that would have taken twelve hours to perform using hand calculators.[33] Now the Intel 4004 marked the beginning of a centrifugal trend that would transfer computing power from a few massive, industrial computers descended from the ENIAC to thousands of small computers in the offices and homes of amateur enthusiasts across the United States.

The moment of change came when the 'Altair 8800' was announced on the cover of the January 1975 edition of *Popular Electronics*. The Altair was the first so-called personal computer (PC) and was built around Intel's 4004. The Altair was small enough to fit on a desk and cost only $397 (over $1,500 in 2009 terms). Before building the Altair, its creator, Ed Roberts, had sent a close friend a message speaking of

> building a computer for the masses. Something that would eliminate the Computer Priesthood for once and for all. He would use this new microprocessor technology to offer a computer to the world, and it would be so cheap that no one could afford not to buy it.[34]

The *Popular Electronics* feature announcing it began with the words, 'The era of personal computing in every home . . . has arrived.'[35] Indeed it had.

Thereafter, a tide of microprocessors hit the market. In 1975 MOS Technology released the 6502 processor, of which the 6510 variant would eventually power the popular 'Commodore 64'. In 1978 Intel released the 8086 processor that would power IBM PCs running Microsoft DOS. The following year Motorola released the 68000 processor that powered Apple, Amiga and Atari computers. Thus by the late 1970s there were three manufacturers competing to sell microprocessors to an eager community of amateur enthusiasts. The arrival of the Altair equipped with Intel's 4004 signalled the end of the Big Bunch's hegemony in the computer industry.

Its impact was not necessarily clear at the outset, however. The machine itself did not look particularly impressive. It was encased in a blue box with lights and switches on the side. The user programmed and interpreted it by way of the switches and lights. It had no monitor, no keyboard, no mouse. Yet although its outward appearance belied its revolutionary nature, geeks in the know took note. At Harvard University, a Bill Gates and Paul Allen were whipped into such a frenzy by the release of the Altair that they developed a version of the BASIC programming language for the machine before they ever actually saw a physical Altair up close.

MITS, Ed Roberts's company, had staked its future on selling a mere two hundred Altair computers. When the Altair was released it sold thousands. To capitalize on the unexpected frenzy, the company organized the World Altair Computer Convention at the Airport Marina Hotel on 26–8 March 1976. Yet as the convention opened Ed Roberts was dismayed to find that a competing firm was advertising a piece of additional hardware that would expand the Altair's functions at a lower price than the component he was selling himself. One of the defining characteristics of the Altair was that it was technically open to expansion and could accommodate expansion boards to add new capabilities.[36] The openness of the Altair had bred competition and MITS, introducing the personal computer era, had become the first victim of 'cloned', or copied, PC hardware. The competing expansion board was designed by a man called Bob Marsh, who was a regular at a new gathering called the Homebrew Club.

The Homebrew Computer Club had been established a few months after the release of the Altair. It was a regular and informal gathering where computer enthusiasts in Silicon Valley could meet and share ideas. The club was a hybrid of elements from the radical student movement, the Berkeley community computing activists and electronic hobbyists. Hippy groups in California had been quick to recognize the computer as a device of empowerment. As early as 1972 a group called the People's Computer Company published an impassioned call on the pencil-drawn cover of its first newsletter:

> Computers are mostly used against people instead of for people; used to control people instead of to free them; Time to change all that – we need a . . . People's Computer Company.[37]

The following year, a hippy group called Loving Grace Cybernetics started a social experiment called 'Computer Memory' that brought an early form of social networking to the residents of Berkeley, California. The group installed computer terminals with display screen and keyboard at the entrance of a popular record store and other locations in the city. The terminals were connected to a computer system that allowed users to leave messages for other visitors to read. This, the hippies believed, 'harness[ed] the power of the computer in the service of the community'[38] and created an 'an information flea market'.[39] Much like the People's Computer Company a year before, this experiment in social computing was intended to liberate computing 'from the constricted grasp of the few to its rightful place as the wealth of the information-sharing community'.[40]

The Homebrew Club was established by two individuals who had been involved in the Personal Computing Company. Posters for the Homebrew Club announced:

> You might like to come to a gathering of people with likeminded interests. Exchange information, swap ideas, talk shop, help work on a project, whatever . . .[41]

Attendees would show their handiwork, which could be expansions to add new features to an Altair, implementations of a new microprocessor, or entirely new systems. Much like the informal networking group of graduate students who developed the ARPANET protocols, attendees at the Homebrew Club were part of an environment where the overriding theme was collaborative. As Steve Wozniak, the inventor of the first Apple computers, recalled, the 'theme . . . was "Give to help others".'[42] Peers would judge each other's hardware and hacks on the elegance of their design, efficiency and stability. Much as the hackers at the MIT RLE had gloried in their efficient code, Homebrew regulars showed off their hardware hacks and passed around software and schematics. Within a few months the Homebrew Club had a regular attendance of hundreds and met at the auditorium of the Stanford Linear Accelerator.

Steve Wozniak introduced Apple's first computer at the Homebrew Club as though it were a new hack:

> The Apple I and II were designed strictly on a hobby, for-fun basis, not to be a product for a company. They were meant to bring down to the club and put on the table . . . and demonstrate: Look at this, it uses very few chips. It's got a video screen . . . Schematics of the Apple I were passed around freely, and I'd even go over to people's houses and help them build their own.[43]

The personal computer came of age in 1977 when Apple released the Apple II at the West Coast Computer Faire. Where PCs had previously been sold in parts for enthusiasts to assemble, the new Apple II could be bought as a ready-made unit. It was a computer for consumers, easy to install and use. Unlike some PC manufacturers who had opted to keep the inner workings of their systems secret, Apple released a reference manual that detailed the entire source code and schematics of their machine.[44] It could be easily adapted to fit different needs and was easy to programme software for. What happened next was entirely unforeseen by Apple.[45] Apple's computers became platforms for spontaneous development by their users.

In the spring of 1978 a Harvard MBA student named Dan Bricklin mulled over the idea of

> a magic piece of paper where I could change the number at the beginning of a set of calculations and have all of the other numbers automatically update themselves.[46]

Together with a friend, Bob Frankston, Bricklin developed and started to market a new software for financial accounting on the Apple II called VisiCalc. This became a huge hit among small businesses that could not afford to pay for time-sharing on remote mainframes or to lease their own minicomputers. A new market for personal computers began to emerge as a new type of consumer began to purchase personal computers to run VisiCalc and other software rather than to hack and tinker with the computer itself at Homebrew and other clubs. The Apple II had become an unexpected commercial success simply by being a platform on which new applications could be developed.

Attendees at the Homebrew Club meetings had known themselves to be in the vanguard of a revolution. Following the success of the Apple II and VisiCalc, the personal computer revolution became apparent even to IBM, the bastion of industrial computing. Its entry into the PC market signalled that the market had arrived, and the manner of its entry would prompt the market to explode.

On 12 August 1981 IBM started to sell its first PC, called the '5150', and began a process that would permanently undermine its dominance of computing. The company was entering the PC market in a hurry. To do so it abandoned the normal development process that had been used at IBM for decades. Instead of developing proprietary hardware and code within IBM, a small team would build the new system using technology already built and tested by other manufacturers. The company went further yet. Following the spirit of the personal computing age it decided to make the architecture of its machine entirely open. Seeking to capitalize on the creativity of the users and the hobby culture that surrounded the new personal computing market, IBM published the source code for its entire PC system. Then, in November 1980, it signed a deal with a tiny software company called Microsoft to supply 'DOS', a piece of software to manage IBM's PCs and interpret users' inputs (in other words, an 'operating system'). Under this deal Microsoft would also be allowed to sell DOS to IBM's competitors. This allowed IBM to appeal to potential customers who had already used existing applications on other computers running Microsoft's BASIC programming software. In its press release to announce its first personal computer, IBM told consumers that its partnership with Microsoft would 'provide users with the opportunity to transfer hundreds of widely used applications to the IBM Personal Computer with minimal modifications'.[47]

< 58 >

However, though the IBM–Microsoft deal would enable IBM to rush its first PC to the market without having to design a new operating system from scratch, it would also ultimately cause the ruin of IBM as a computer manufacturer.

Within ten months of the launch of IBM's first PC, a competitor, Columbia Data Products, launched the 'Multi Personal Computer 1600' using almost exactly the same hardware as the IBM machine and supplying it with the Microsoft DOS operating system. This was the first so-called 'IBM-compatible PC'. In other words, it was a clone. IBM had let the genie out of the bottle. The release of additional clones onto the market stimulated fierce competition,[48] driving the price of the IBM-compatible PCs downwards and making their manufacture an increasingly marginal activity. Yet even as PCs became more affordable and IBM's fortunes began to wane, Microsoft's revenues grew. Bill Gates's deal with IBM had made the physical computer into a common commodity, an item that could be bought from any manufacturer, while Microsoft capitalized on the resulting boom in sales of PCs equipped with its operating system. IBM began a precipitous decline and Microsoft a spectacular rise. By 1992, twelve years after the deal, Microsoft's market value had grown from virtually nothing to equal IBM's. Before the end of the decade Microsoft's market value was twice that of IBM.[49] IBM had been ranked number one in the top companies by market value in 1990 and 1980 (and number three in 1970). Its fall was so dramatic that by 2000 it was not even included in the top ten.[50]

IBM's adventure in personal computing did, however, prevent its established competitors from building their own PC empires and generated sufficient revenues in the short term to support the research and development necessary to dominate the mainframe business in the long term. For Apple, the cloning issue proved instructive. Though it owed its commercial success to VisiCalc, which was a result of its openness to users' innovations, Apple ultimately managed to avoid IBM's fate by refraining from absolute openness. While its platform was open to software that could make the computer more valuable to users, the secrets of its hardware were jealously protected and manufacturers of clones were sued.

The commoditization of IBM-compatible PC, though disastrous for IBM, was an enormous boon to prospective computer users. The lowering price of computer hardware was compounded by continuous

<59>

advances in technology. In 1965 Intel co-founder Gordon Moore had observed that low-cost electronics had increased in complexity

> at a rate of roughly a factor of two per year . . . Certainly over the short term this rate can be expected to continue, if not to increase.[51]

This understanding, known as Moore's Law, suggested that computers would become increasingly common and ever smaller. Components in fact advanced at a rapid pace from the late 1960s. The capacity of hard drives increased at 35 per cent per year between 1967 and 1995, and the speed of Intel's microprocessors rose 20 per cent each year from 1979 to 1994.[52] To understand the pace of change, consider William Gibson's 1984 book, *Neuromancer*. The book is famed for coining the term 'cyberspace',[53] a fictional computer environment in which one could navigate 'a graphic representation of data abstracted from the banks of every computer in the human system',[54] a sort of tangible Internet. Yet despite Gibson's bold vision of the future his expectation of future development of computing hardware was astonishingly limited when measured against what actually happened. For example, the novel's protagonist lives in a far-distant future where technology has advanced almost beyond recognition. Yet he is betrayed for the sake of memory chips totalling 3 megabytes of random-access memory (RAM). The person who stole the RAM chips from his computer is later killed for the same 3 MB of RAM. In real life, contrary to Gibson's expectations, computers grew so powerful so quickly that less than a decade after *Neuromancer* was published most new computers already had more than 3 megabytes of RAM installed in them.[55] That Gibson considered 3 MB a trove worth killing for in the bold future he conceived shows the galloping pace of technological change. By 2010, even many lightweight, portable computers were sold with a thousand times the amount of RAM than the characters in *Neuromancer* had killed and died for.

In the 1960s an IBM computer had occupied a quarter of an acre of air-conditioned floor space, required sixty operators to input instructions and provide maintenance, and cost $9 million.[56] From the early 1980s the all-in-one PC began to create a new market of potential computer buyers. IBM's press release for its first ever PC said the machine was

< 60 >

intended to be used by 'just about everyone', including 'the first-time or advanced user, whether a businessperson in need of accounting help or a student preparing a term paper'.[57] Another brochure advertised the machine's ease of use, even by laypeople:

You don't have to be a computer expert to learn how to use your IBM Personal Computer. You – or any member of your family – can do it with just a little time and practice.[58]

These were truly personal computers: all-in-one systems that required little assembly, cost between 500 and 2,000 dollars and had all the parts necessary to allow the user to operate them for whatever purpose they intended. The old centripetal model of mainframe computing became a niche rather than the norm. On 5 February 1984 *The New York Times* reported that:

The nation's computer industry should pass a remarkable milestone this year: for the first time, the value of desktop, personal computers sold in the United States – computers that were almost unheard of only eight years ago – will overtake sales of the large 'mainframe' machines that first cast America as the leader in computer technology.[59]

Only a quarter of a century later, in June 2008, Gartner reported that the number of PCs in use had reached one billion worldwide.[60] When one considers that the global population of humans is approximately 6.7 billion, the PC has become pervasive to the degree that there is more than one computer for every seven people on the planet. The power that the hippies and the Homebrew enthusiasts had craved was now distributed in the hands of consumers. The networks would soon follow.

<PHASE II>
EXPANSION

The Hoi Polloi Connect

The computer, long the preserve of large corporate headquarters and elite government research facilities, was now within the grasp of amateur enthusiasts operating from their bedrooms and garages. They would be at the forefront of the next wave of innovation, one that would transform human communications and commerce. Yet for the revolution to begin, computer users at home had to be able to connect their machines to the phone lines. This would be a challenge.

Since the late 1870s, the emerging telephone industry had rigorously pursued a centripetal strategy. Anticipating the competition that would greet the expiry of Bell's second patent in 1894, Theodore Vail, the company's president, decided to maintain Bell's technology lead. He established an experimentation unit in 1879 to continue research and develop new patents. He also bought options on patents where necessary, and thereby gained control over the loading coil that enabled long-distance connections. By 1900, the Bell system controlled approximately 900 patents.[1] In parallel with Bell's technology race, it embarked on a land grab across the US. In 1880 Vail established a corporation to take control of every local company providing service in towns and cities and the long-distance lines through which the exchanges were connected, thereby giving Bell control of every aspect of the telephone network across the United States.[2] The company sought investors and local partners while taking care to maintain control over the emerging network. By 1910 Bell was in a position to buy the long established telegraph monopoly, Western Union, which had rejected the opportunity to buy Bell's patents 35 years earlier.

To stave off the prospect of government intervention, the company signed the 'Kingsbury Commitment' in 1913, committing it to make certain concessions, including divesting itself of Western Union, while at the same time securing its long-distance and urban monopolies.[3] Finally, the Federal Communications Act of 1934 officially enshrined Bell's monopoly, permitting new entrants to compete only if it were judged by the government to be in the public interest. By 1939 one observer could write that Bell was 'the largest aggregation of capital ever controlled by a single company in the history of private business enterprise'.[4] This was the Goliath that stood between home computer owners and networking.

The telephone network opens, the grassroots networks form...

Bell operated a monopolistic, universal service. Its control extended even to the very telephone sets in American homes and offices, which were leased to, rather than owned by, its subscribers. AT&T would not permit subscribers to connect any device to its network other than the specific telephone set it provided. The home user was prohibited from attaching 'foreign' devices to the phone network. AT&T had sold modems, devices that provide an interface between digital computers and the analogue phone system, since 1962. Yet in the absence of competition from other manufacturers these were expensive, bulky, slow devices, unsuited to the budgets or needs of the homebrew generation. The prospects of amateur enthusiasts using their home phone line to venture online appeared slim.

Then, in the late 1960s and '70s, AT&T's rigidly centralized control over the public telecommunications network began to break down. Two landmark cases signalled the opening of the network to new, innovative uses. The first case related to the 'Hush-A-Phone', a plastic mouthpiece that could be clipped on to the receiver of a telephone to block the sound of a person's voice from others nearby while amplifying it to the receiver. AT&T claimed that this innocuous device threatened to damage its continental network. A sensible person might think this heady stuff for a small plastic cup with a hole at both ends. Nonetheless, the FCC agreed with AT&T's argument. On appeal, however, the DC Circuit Court of Appeals was less impressed and forced the FCC to reverse its decision. The terms of the Court of Appeals' decision highlight the outlandishness of AT&T's original claim:

> To say that a telephone subscriber may produce the result in
> question by cupping his hand and speaking into it, but may not

< 66 >

do so by using a device which leaves his hand free to write or do whatever else he wishes, is neither just nor reasonable.[5]

Yet while Hush-A-Phone eventually won the day the episode proved that AT&T would jealously guard its network against any innovations or foreign attachments, no matter how trivial. Indeed the Hush-A-Phone had made so small a commercial impact that AT&T had not known of its existence for over two decades, and apparently only became aware of it when an AT&T lawyer happened to spot it in a shop window.[6] Innovators of all sizes beware. Such an environment was not fertile ground for an Internet of modem-using homebrew geeks.

Deregulation of the network gathered momentum a decade later when another innovative device and AT&T's heavy-handed response to it further eroded the monopoly's position. The 'Carterfone' was a radio device that could be attached to a standard telephone set to extend the network beyond the fixed telephone lines. Its inventor, Thomas Carter, had built it to allow him to make telephone calls while working on his ranch. Having patented the device in 1959 he began to sell it to oil companies where the radio could allow workers to stay in contact while operating across the vast oil fields.[7] AT&T argued, with justification, that the Carterfone violated FCC Tariff Number 132, which stated:

> No equipment, apparatus, circuit or device not furnished by the telephone company shall be attached to or connected with the facilities furnished by the telephone company, whether physically, by induction or otherwise.[8]

As a result, AT&T warned its subscribers, they would be penalized if they connected a Carterfone to their handsets. A legal battle ensued. Carter filed an antitrust case against AT&T and the matter was ultimately referred to the FCC. On 26 June 1968 the FCC found that the long-standing restriction on what equipment was permitted to be connected to the US telephone network

> has been unreasonable, discriminatory, and unlawful in the past, and that the provisions prohibiting the use of customer-provided interconnecting devices should accordingly be stricken.[9]

The legal battle to secure this judgement, however, had been long and arduous. In the words of the FCC Commissioner who worded the opinion, Thomas Carter was a 'very stubborn Texas cowboy who was willing to sell off his cattle ranches to help pay the lawyers to take on AT&T during a dozen years of litigation'.[10] Nonetheless, the network was opening to more innovative uses. Finally in 1975 the FCC adopted Part 68 of Title 47 of the Code of Federal Regulations, which allowed consumers to attach whatever device to the network they wished, with the proviso that the device should not damage the network.[11] The network was now open to the homebrew generation.

Among their ranks was Ward Christensen, a young man so excited by the prospect of finally being able to own one of the new 16-bit personal computers that he recalls having 'pinups of 16-bitters on my walls' in the mid 1970s.[12] When the first modem for use with PCs was released in 1977[13] Christensen wrote a program called XMODEM to allow his machine to communicate across the phone system via a modem. Christensen released XMODEM freely among his friends in the homebrew community and it was quickly adapted to work on other many other types of PC that ran on different operating systems. Thus by the end of 1977 the phone system was open, inexpensive computer and modem equipment was commercially available and the software to allow them to communicate was in circulation free of charge.

The following year Christensen and a friend named Randy Suess invented a piece of software called the Computer Bulletin Board System (BBS).[14] The hardware was relatively simple. Built from commonly available parts, a circuit board would power up when the modem received a phone call, and load the software for the BBS from a floppy disk so that it could respond to users' commands delivered over the phone line. When the user hung up, the device shut itself down and awaited the next call.[15] Though simple, the BBS was a significant development. This remedial system of bulletin boards hosted on personal computers is the forerunner of contemporary web forums. The BBS allowed amateurs to set up their own boards, offering files, news and opinion to whomever cared to dial in. Since it could also store files that had been uploaded to it by external users, it provided a means to proliferate software, including pirated software. The new social phenomenon captured the imagination of a new generation of PC users. One married couple decided to start a BBS and become 'sysops',

< 68 >

BBS System Operators, after watching the 1983 film *WarGames* in which a high-school student breaks in to a US defence system using a home modem. Through their BBS the couple 'made many new friends. We have callers from all over the country.'[16] Yet for all this the BBS was a very limited system that could not accommodate more than one user at a time.

Yet from 1984 onwards a new system called FidoNet allowed BBSs to call each other and pass files and messages from board to board. It turned isolated BBSs into nodes in a global system. FidoNet's creator, Tom Jennings, was a punk activist with anarchist leanings who eschewed employment at leading software firms in favour of the life of an itinerant hacker.[17] He saw FidoNet as 'a non-commercial network of computer hobbiests [*sic*] ('hackers', in the older, original meaning) who want to play with, and find uses for, packet switch networking'.[18] BBS had started as a local phenomenon and users made local calls to BBSs in their area. By exchanging the files between distant and local BBSs, FidoNet extended the BBS into a regional and global phenomenon. In late 1985 a new feature called EchoMail was introduced to FidoNet by Jess Rush, a sysop, which allowed users anywhere on the FidoNet to broadcast messages to common discussion groups.[19] Now, ten years after the discussion lists on the ARPANET, the public had a means of participating in similar discussions across wide geographical distances. The BBS brought a simple form of networking to a wide community and caused an explosion in social computing. In 1987, three years after Tom Jennings developed FidoNet, there were 6,000 bulletin boards in operation; three years later, 24,000; and by 1992 there were 45,000.[20]

The ARPANET research community was aware of the homebrew and BBS scene but had little interest in it. The focus within the ARPA research community was on large computers whereas the focus among BBS users was on PCs.[21] Yet the popularity of the bulletin boards was creating a population of modem-using PC owners who would be the first to adopt the Internet and the World Wide Web when they became available to consumers. Moreover, in some regions of the globe where Internet is not widely adopted, the BBS mechanism of dialling up to retrieve and set messages in a batch has continued to provide a means of affordable connectivity.[22]

Private networks of the jet age and the centrifugal trend within businesses

While the US military was beginning to consider how to use networking in the 1960s, the private sector was beginning to provide commercial subscribers with access to centralized computing power. Perhaps the most remarkable examples of private-sector networking arose from another technology of the globalizing world – the jet engine. The jet age of the mid- to late 1950s witnessed the arrival of a new generation of aircraft propelled by jet engines. Airliners such as the de Havilland Comet, Boeing 707 and Tu-104 carried more passengers further, quicker and cheaper. As *Popular Mechanics* breathlessly informed readers, 'New and almost staggering speeds in transportation' beckoned.[23] In some cases journey times were cut in half. Much of the world could now be reached from any airport within a day. Destinations previously distant became local. While the number of passengers flying with the International Air Transport Association (IATA) airlines had been 20.3 million in 1949, within six years it more than doubled to 51.7 million.[24] Despite the growth in the number of reservations made for this glut of passengers, many airlines still relied on a reservations system called SITA that dated from 1949. SITA mainly used a system of manual transmission of perforated tape records. In 1962 a study found that details of a single booking could take one and a half hours to be relayed via SITA from the desk of an agent meeting a customer to the national control office and back to the agent's desk.[25] In some European offices the delay could be over twenty hours. In short, the logistics of the propeller age could not accommodate the explosive growth in the number of passenger bookings of the jet age.

In 1963, a year after the review, SITA convened a symposium at which airlines, agents and technical experts met to discuss the problem. By 1969 SITA had developed what its history calls the world's first worldwide packet-switching network dedicated to business traffic.[26] By 1971 the system provided interactive data exchange between terminals at different offices. In parallel with SITA's network, American Airlines had signed an agreement with IBM in 1957 to develop SABRE, a computerized reservations system. IBM proposed a system based on its experience with the SAGE air defence system. Development costs were enormous. The first experimental system went online in 1960, and SABRE was operational by 1965. The SABRE system connected 1,500

< 70 >

terminals across the United States and Canada to one central computer site, and provided information on every American Airlines flight for a year in advance, including reservations, name of ticket holder, itinerary and contact details.[27]

It is important to differentiate these developments from those at RAND and ARPA during the same period. While the ARPANET attempted to connect incompatible machines based at a diverse range of facilities owed by different groups, commercial networks such as the SITA and SABRE systems used standard equipment across their entire networks and had the benefit of a single, unified chain of responsibility. Or put another way, ARPANET was heterogeneous and the SITA and SABRE airline reservations systems were not. Moreover their functions were limited to commercial necessity whereas ARPANET was a test bed for networking research. Yet though they were not cradles of innovation, commercial networks like the SITA and SABRE systems showed the pace of advances in networking in the years after the SAGE air-defence project.[28] Indeed, Lawrence Roberts, the manager of the ARPANET project, left ARPA to work on Telnet, a commercial packet-networking service. What these private networks lacked was the openness and centrifugal character that came to define the Internet. Private-sector services would, however, begin to provide networking services to home PC users with modems from the late 1970s onward, creating a population of home networkers who would be in the first wave of users when the Web became available in the early 1990s.

CompuServe, among the first widely popular subscription services used in the home, had initially begun to offer time-sharing services to corporations in 1969 and to consumers from 1978. Its consumer business under the name MicroNet allowed PC users to dial in to access CompuServe's mainframe machines, which had previously been used solely to provide services to corporate clients. Home users could now store and run files on the mainframe and leave messages for other users, similar to the BBS systems. Access to MicroNet was initially expensive but as the mass market of home users began to eclipse the small market of corporate users CompuServe reoriented itself towards the home user, dropping the name MicroNet for its consumer service in the process. CompuServe was joined by competitors America OnLine (AOL) in 1989 and Prodigy in 1990, both of which offered their subscribers access to a corralled selection of content and messaging services, but not to the Internet at large. The growing popularity of the Web

<71>

in the mid-1990s eventually forced these services to give their sub-scribers access to the entire network. Ultimately they became, in effect, mere Internet Service Providers, offering a connection to the Web rather than being valued as destinations in their own right. Remarkable though the selection of content and programs that any one subscription service could offer had appeared in the late 1980s, it could not compete with the virtually unlimited array of content on the Web.

Computing within large organizations was a microcosm of the centrifugal trend in the wider world. Businesses were slow to grasp the importance of the computer. (With the exception of a single article on 'Office Robots', which appeared in *Fortune* in 1952, the business press would ignore computing until the mid-1960s.[29]) Nonetheless, from the 1950s internal power shifts within large organizations began to create a new appetite for business computing in some circles. According to one perspective, industrial computing in large organizations accelerated between 1957 and 1963 because financial executives valued the control these new systems gave them over financial records, not because the machines reduced the operating costs of the organization.[30] Through the 1960s the centralizing nature of computerized data processing enabled financial executives to extend their influence within their organizations. From the late 1960s executives of other departments at last began to understand that their positions were threatened by the financial executives' monopoly on computerized information across their organizations.[31] The power of a central mainframe computer could be shared with these other executives and their departments, but only through time-share systems they operated over slow telephone lines. The competing departments therefore often began to outsource their computing requirements to external suppliers, or, better yet, to buy smaller computers of their own. In the years between 1975 and 1981 increasingly inexpensive computers became available to staff at ever-lower levels of responsibility within the organization, thereby eroding the central control of the financial executives.

The release of the VisiCalc spreadsheet for the Apple II revealed something previously unknown. Corporations that had previously used external contractors such as Wang and IBM for word processing, and Tymshare and GE Time-Sharing for financial calculation, could now give these tasks to their own employees to perform at their own PCs.[32] Throughout the 1980s the purchase of PCs at virtually every level

<72>

of organization marked centrifugal shift from, in Paul Strassmann's words, 'the dominance of computer experts to the defensive enthusiasm of office workers' who were eager to learn how to use the computers for themselves.[33]

With a PC appearing in every office, organizations were moving from one single mainframe to which all data was fed, to a network of many PCs that everyone could use. Local Area Network (LAN) allowed organizations and universities to network the new generation of PCs. At the same time the TCP/IP protocols allowed LANs to connect to each other, and were freely available in the 1980s. Early in the decade a group at MIT developed TCP/IP for PCs running Microsoft's DOS operating system and gave the source code away freely with the only stipulation that MIT's authorship should be acknowledged.[34] Thus by the mid-1980s it was possible to buy equipment to connect small personal computers to the Internet. The growth of LAN at universities and other large organizations would produce an explosion of Internet connections. While a little over 200 computers had been connected to the Internet in August 1981, within two years that figure had more than doubled, and within four years the number of connections had increased nine-fold.[35]

‹6›

Communities Based on Interest, not Proximity

Individuals like to be networked. Since the beginning of human experience, the tyranny of geography dictated with whom one hunted, warred against and procreated with. Hunter-gatherer bands were drawn together by the pursuit of local resources. Tribal allegiances were tied to kinship and common belief and all human relations were determined by the narrow constraint of proximity. Though distances had contracted since cave dwellers first rolled a tree trunk as a wheel, no invention had yet liberated the social animal from the constraints of geography. Neither rise of empires nor advances in communications or lengthening of trade routes lifted the yoke of geography from human relations. The journey time between New York and Boston had fallen from 5,000 minutes by overnight express stagecoach to a mere 300 minutes by motorcar in the century and a half before 1950. This, however, was only a slight loosening of proximity's hold.[1] Yet, in the years of the mid-1950s to mid-1960s, a decade before networking took its first experimental steps, a careful observer could discern the first signs that humanity was about to liberate itself from the grip of geography. They appeared in the form of a blind, five-year-old boy named Joe Engressia.

Killing geography

In 1957 Joe Engressia first realized that he could control the phone system and make long-distance phone calls at no cost by whistling a specific pitch down the phone line. The AT&T phone network used twelve combinations of six audio tones as control signals. Engressia's whistles through the mouthpiece were interpreted as the phone company's own control tones. Engressia was one of a scattered group of technologically curious youngsters across the United States who spent their free time experimenting with controlling the phone system. These kids called themselves 'phone phreaks'. Many were blind and were to some extent socially isolated among kids their own age. It was the phreaks, however, who first liberated themselves from reliance on their proximate peers. Theirs would be a community drawn together by the attraction of common interest rather than the strictures of geography.

In 1968 Engressia was caught by the phone company and disciplined by the University of South Florida where he was enrolled. The ensuing media coverage made him a figurehead for isolated communities of phone phreaks sprinkled around the country. He started to receive phone calls from phreaks across the US. Many of the kids who phoned Engressia sought a wider community of kids like themselves, lonely and isolated. Through the phone network they could meet other similarly gifted and disadvantaged kids. An exposé in *Esquire* in 1971 cited one example: Ralph, a pale, overweight, pimply sixteen-year-old boy who lived in a California suburb. His parents, according to the reporter, did not understand what Ralph and his friends were doing with the phone, or whether it was legal, but because he was blind they were content that he had found a hobby that kept him busy.[2] In fact what Ralph was doing was entirely illegal. He and three other phreaks were attempting to establish a permanently open line into which phreaks across the nation could tap. Previously a permanently open line, nicknamed the '2111 Conference', had allowed isolated kids to join a conversation with phone phreaks across the country.

The phreaking phenomenon had spread quickest among blind children. First, they were sensitive to sound and perhaps better suited to the auditory aspect to learning the tones that operate the phone system. Second, some blind kids went to winter and summer camps specifically for blind children, from where the secret spread among their peers who then returned to various scattered towns. Phreaking spread beyond the blind community by way of John T. Draper, known by his nickname 'Captain Crunch'. Crunch had learned from one of the blind young phone phreaks that the toy plastic whistle given free with 'Cap'n Crunch' breakfast cereal made the precise 2,600-cycle tone required to seize control of the telephone network.[3] He, along with members of the MIT hacker community and the Homebrew Club, spread phone phreaking beyond the blind community.

By the 1980s the community was so defined and self aware that it had established norms and conventions to which its members loosely

< 75 >

adhered. One such convention, according to two phreaks called 'Taran King' and 'Knight Lightning', was that 'real phreaks can think up a creative name'.[4] As another guide said in a mock Ten Commandments style,

> Use not thine own name when speaking to other phreaks,
> for that every third phreak is an FBI agent is well known . . .
> Let not overly many people know that thy be a phreak,
> as to do so is to use thine own self as a sacrificial lamb.[5]

Since the criterion for admission to this community was the capacity to phreak the phone system, all participants shared a common interest in learning more about the phone system. It was both the enabler and focus of their community. Within the community those with the most refined mastery of the phone system enjoyed elevated prestige. A medium that allowed this, even in so primitive a way as the phone system did, was powerful. Yet something much more powerful than a jerry-rigged phone system was coming.

In 1960, J.C.R. Licklider, the visionary behind networking, and Robert Taylor, the manager at ARPA who set the ARPANET project in motion, made a pretty far-fetched prediction. Startling, in fact. They predicted that:

> In a few years, men will be able to communicate more effectively through a machine than face to face . . . We believe that we are entering into a technological age, in which we will be able to interact with the richness of living information – not merely in the passive way that we have become accustomed to using books and libraries, but as active participants in an ongoing process, bringing something to it through our interaction with it, and not simply receiving something from it by our connection to it.[6]

In an era when computers were simply giant data processors and users were kept at a respectful remove by a bureaucratic priesthood of computer administrators, this was heady stuff indeed.

Yet even as Licklider and Taylor wrote the change was beginning to occur. Cambridge Professor John Naughton recalls noticing the emergence of a sense of community among students using Cambridge's time-share computer in the late 1950s. Because they could directly operate the machine and were simultaneously connected to the same computer from different terminals, the time-share students were able to swap electronic messages and socialize in a manner inconceivable to students toiling under the batch-process system. Naughton, meanwhile, was still using the old batch-processing system. He and his peers 'didn't even recognize each other except as members of the same queue' for processing time.[7] The ability to leave messages for others on the same machine, even without networking, transformed the computer from a processor of instructions into a communications device. Robert Taylor at ARPA had also observed that people using time-sharing at research centres were forced to speak to one another and pondered, 'couldn't we do this across the country?'[8] It was clear that interactive and shared computer systems were more socially constructive then their bureaucratic, centralized predecessors.

From the early 1960s, screen to screen messages became common on time-share systems. In early 1971 an RFC was circulated that proposed using the ARPANET to swap messages between connected facilities. This proposal seems not to have advanced beyond the assumptions of the ink age, proposing a 'mechanism to receive sequential files for immediate or deferred printing', rather than making the leap to sending a message composed on a screen at one facility to be read on a screen at a different facility or even from teletype to teletype.[9] Then, in late 1971, human communications took their first steps beyond the ink age. At BBN an engineer named Ray Tomlinson was working on a protocol for sending files across the network. He made a mental leap and realized that the file transfer protocol he was working on, called CPYNET, could also carry messages as files across the network if he incorporated it into an existing time-share message program called SNDMSG. The adjustments were 'a no brainer'. Tomlinson sent the world's first e-mails to his group announcing his discovery. If they intended to use it, he told them, they should use an '@' sign to designate when the recipient was based at a different host computer elsewhere on the network.[10] Thereafter a series of programs refined the e-mail idea and implemented it on different computers. Messages could now be sent from one screen on the East Coast of the United States to another on the West Coast in no time at all. This, unsurprisingly, was a big deal.

E-mail consumed two-thirds of the bandwidth connecting ARPANET facilities almost as soon as it was invented. Leonard Kleinrock,

<77>

who directed the ARPANET Network Measurement Centre at Stanford University, monitored the rise of e-mail first hand:

> The point at which it became abundantly clear to me that people-to-people communication was the dominant form of traffic carried by the Internet was in mid-1972 shortly after email was introduced to the internet . . . Email traffic took over the traffic very quickly. Prior to that, the traffic was mainly file transfers and remote use of computers by researchers who logged on to machines that could be accessed through the net.[11]

One of Tomlinson's colleagues joked that he could not tell his boss what he had done 'because email wasn't in our statement of work'.[12] E-mail was a completely unplanned addition to the ARPANET, and came as a surprise to both ARPA and BBN. As a BBN retrospective report on the ARPANET reflected in 1981, 'the largest single surprise of the ARPANET program has been the incredible popularity and success of network mail'.[13]

Within a few years of its invention, e-mail had evolved into more than simply a medium for one to one correspondence. It became a medium for group discussions. In 1975 an e-mail distributed among a large community of recipients started the first discussion group, 'Msg-Group'. In one of the first postings to the group Steven Walker suggested a set of principles that have characterized much of Internet discussion ever since:

> I would encourage a FORUM-type setup if its not to difficult to setup, realizing that many (myself included) will have little time to contribute. I worry that such arrangements tend to fragment the overall group but maybe thats good if the fragments report in now and then.[14]

So was born the discussion list, an ever-lengthening conversation with many participants discussing topics of common interest. Science fiction, a natural subject of interest for a community of computer scientists, became a popular topic of ARPANET chatter: a discussion list called 'SF-Lovers', became the most popular list on ARPANET. So popular in fact that the frequency and bulk of messages sent to the SF-Lovers discussion list consumed so much of the network's bandwidth

< 78 >

that managers at ARPA had to shut the list down for a period of months.[15] Remarkably, considering that the network was funded by the Department of Defense with the intention of sharing of expensive computer resources for research, SF-Lovers' moderator successfully argued that the list was providing valuable experience dealing with large lists and should be reinstated. Thus did a military-sponsored network become a tool for informal human chatter.

E-mail stripped away the accumulated layers of formality that had been observed in correspondence of the ink age:

> one could write tersely and type imperfectly, even to an older person in a superior position and even to a person one did not know very well, and the recipient took no offense. The formality and perfection that most people expect in a typed letter did not become associated with network messages, probably because the network was so much faster, so much more like the telephone.[16]

Strict hierarchies were flattened, and the barriers between individuals at different levels of an organization's hierarchy were minimized. Staff at ARPA now found that they could easily contact the Director, Stephen Lukasik, by e-mail. Similarly, Lawrence Roberts used e-mail to bypass principal investigators and communicate directly with contractors below them. As e-mail spread throughout facilities connected to ARPANET, the rapid-fire e-mail exchanges between people at different levels of the academic hierarchy established new conventions of expression. The smiley face [:-)], for example, made its debut in the early 1980s. On discussion boards where academics sent each other informal messages it was difficult to delineate the humorous from the serious. In September 1982 an e-mail discussion at Carnegie Mellon produced a misunderstanding that arose from a warning that mercury had been spilt in the facility.[17] When some interpreted the warning as a joke, Scott Fahlman suggested that in future a smiley :-) should be used to denote intentional humour.

'Familiarity', as Aesop taught in his fables, 'breeds contempt'. Many years later in the early 1990s a young computer programmer named Linus Torvalds would spar with a superior on a discussion group. The exchange began when Alan Tanenbaum, a professor of computing and operating systems expert, criticized an early version of Torvalds's new and groundbreaking operating system, Linux. By any orthodox

<79>

reckoning, Tanenbaum was Goliath and Torvalds was David. Tanenbaum was a tenured professor, an acknowledged expert in operating systems design, and the author of the very piece of software for which the Usenet group was named. Yet Torvalds, a second-year undergraduate too shy to lift his hand in class and who had not known anything about the operating system Unix until a year previously, felt comfortable aggressively retorting to Professor Tanenbaum's challenge on the 'minix' discussion group. Tanenbaum posted a message under the heading 'Linux is obsolete'.[18] The next day Torvalds posted a blistering retort. He accused Tanenbaum of making 'excuse[s] for the limitations of minix' and added 'sorry, but you loose: I've got more excuses than you have, and linux still beats the pants of minix in almost all areas'.[19] Only online could Torvalds, a shy programming upstart, challenge a professor of computing. Torvalds, certain in his improvements on the Professor's work, felt no need to observe his status in the academic hierarchy.

Chatter changed the network and brought the true potential of networking into focus for ARPANET participants. The first issue of ARPANET's official newsletter included the observation that 'with computer networks, the loneliness of research is supplanted by the richness of shared research'.[20] Lawrence Roberts who had cajoled ARPA-funded facilities to participate in the ARPANET now found that 'they started raving about how they could now share research, and jointly publish papers, and do other things that they could never do before'.[21] BBN's 1981 report describes the impact of the network on the computer research community in the US:

It has become more convenient for geographically separated groups to perform collaborative research and development. The ability to easily send files of text between geographically remote groups, the ability to communicate via messages quickly and easily, and the ability to collaboratively use powerful editing and document production facilities has changed significantly the 'feel' of collaborative research with remote groups.[22]

As the 1970s drew to a close a wider community of computer users not connected to ARPANET began to partake in the joys of networked communication. In 1979 three graduate students developed a way to transfer updates of message files between computers that ran the Unix operating system.[23] Unix computers, which were widely used at US university computer science departments, could dial each other using a jerry-rigged modem, find updated files and copy them. This system was called 'Usenet' and allowed many users to subscribe and contribute to specific topics of discussion and upload or download new contributions whenever they wished. Its creators believed the system would be used by between fifty and a hundred computers and would receive one or two posts a day on the narrow subject of Unix computing.[24] In reality Usenet proved to be enormously popular, drawing together far-flung individuals to discuss specific topics of interest. Here was an entirely user-driven, 'pull' style of content delivery, as opposed to the 'pushed' of the one-to-many broadcast and print media. Its creators called it the 'poor man's ARPANET'.[25] Now both ARPANET and Usenet users had a medium through which they could find others of similar interests, much as the phone phreaks had done.

Though it revolved around science fiction storylines, the informal chatter on trivial issues across the breadth of the ARPANET was something momentous and novel. Never before had such a conversation been possible between so many in which all were free to contribute. The pinnacle of participatory democracy, the Athenian *Ecclesia* (Assembly), had a quorum of 6,000 for certain decisions, and could accommodate debate among a number of prominent speakers. However, poor Athenians were unable to attend without the loss of a day's earnings. On the online discussions on ARPANET, and eventually Usenet and BBSs, debate was not limited to the articulate, prominent few, nor did one have to be in physical attendance or observe hierarchical mores. Every participant in the online conversation could speak as well as listen. As the *Cluetrain Manifesto* alerted readers in 1999, 'the Internet is enabling conversations among human beings that were simply not possible in the era of mass media'.[26]

Virtual but intimate

Gunpowder, originally thought by the Chinese to be a dust to preserve life, ended up having a radically different, quite opposite, application. Powerful and disruptive technologies often have unforeseen consequences. It is remarkable to think that the ARPANET, according to its original objectives, was a failure. Yet it was. The purpose of the ARPANET had simply been, in the words of RCA's audit of 1972, to ensure that

< 81>

'resources available to one member are equally available to other members of the community without . . . regard to location'.[27] Frank Hart, the ARPANET project manager at BBN, reflected in 1990 that that objective had 'never been fully accomplished'.[28] Yet something grander, more profound, had occurred.

As Licklider and Taylor predicted in 1968,

> life will be happier for the on-line individual because the people with whom one interacts most strongly will be selected more by commonality of interests and goals than by accidents of proximity.[29]

What Licklider and Roberts could not have foreseen was the level of intimacy that online communities would elicit. The most important of these, measured by its impact on online culture, was a subscription-based community called The Well. It began life in 1985 as the brainchild of Stewart Brand and Larry Brilliant. Brand was a founder of the influential *Whole Earth Catalog* and had assisted Douglas Engelbart in his groundbreaking demonstration of the NLS in 1968. He provided the software and hardware to run the system. His partner, Larry Brilliant, was concerned with using The Well as a social experiment, and was charged with drawing the diverse array of people who were involved in his *Whole Earth Catalog* as The Well's initial participants. The idea was to establish a communal space where subscribers could talk about topics of common interest. The service was arranged into various 'conferences', where people with common interests could converse using simple text. In mid-1987 the number of members of The Well had reached 2,000. By the end of the year The Well had made its first profit. It proved that people were willing to pay to socialize online. Moreover, participants formed a close, intimate community despite the technical limitations of the computers they used to connect.

In 1985, when The Well was established, PCs were very limited machines with black and white displays. They had no built-in hard drives. Mice were such a novelty that reviewers of the Apple Macintosh in 1984 were amazed to find one attached to the machine.[30] The speeds at which participants connected to The Well prohibited any picture or video content. In 1985 the latest, most expensive modem was capable of speeds of 9.6 Kbps and cost between $700 and $1,000.[31] To put that in perspective, the hardware built into the first-generation iPhone was

< 82 >

capable of connecting to the Internet at 3.6 Mbps, almost four hundred times as fast as the fastest modem in 1985. Yet from such humble platforms could rich relationships be formed between members of online communities. Stewart Brand believed that the 'intensity and intimacy' of online communication should have come as no surprise. A historical parallel, according to Brand, were 'the correspondences and the books of past intellectuals'.[32] Other media such as broadcasting and publishing precluded intimacy whereas 'a letter has intimacy and eloquence because it's addressed to a known audience of people the author respects, whose opinions he or she cares about'.

Life and death was shared in intimate detail online. The birth of the first baby of a Well member was celebrated in 1986; the first marriage between two members occurred in 1988; and the first death of a member, Blair Newman, was mourned in 1990.[33] By 1995, the community had become so intimate that Tom Mandel, dying of cancer, bid his peers on The Well farewell with a depth of emotion rarely expressed in public:

> I'm sad, terribly sad, I cannot tell you how sad and grief stricken I am that I cannot stay to play and argue with you much longer. It seems almost as if I am the one who will be left behind to grieve for all of you dying . . .[34]

The strength of his prose proved that intimate online relationships between users were possible even with remedial computers and slow networks.

The intimacy of The Well was a sign of things to come, yet though it is the most potent example of the intimacy of early communities it is not a most perfect one. Due in part to the technological limitations of its bbs system it was localized in San Francisco.[35] Also, its members were not anonymous and the service held events where they could meet in person. Indeed, when San Francisco was struck by an earthquake in October 1989 The Well was used by many as a way to communicate and share information, and many of its members were devotees of the San Francisco band The Grateful Dead. Yet, though it was vested in San Francisco, The Well exhibited many of the characteristics that came to typify the later anonymous, geographically distributed online communities that would follow in later years.

Intimate, and powerful too

Attempting a calculation of something as vast yet ethereal as the value of a network is as hopeless as wondering whether a million angels may fit upon a needle's point. Yet the evolution of these calculations reveals something of the evolving understanding of networks. In the era before digital networks, David Sarnoff, the founder of NBC, stated that the value of a broadcasting network was determined by the number of its viewers. By virtue of the media with which it dealt, Sarnoff's Law conformed to a limited, centripetal logic. It was a simple calculation of one-to-many broadcast reach and was rendered obsolete by computer networks. Somewhat more apt was the idea of 'network effects'. In 1908 Theodore Vail, AT&T's president, had told shareholders that the value of a telephone network 'increases with the number of connections':[36]

> a telephone – without a connection at the other end of the line – is not even a toy or a scientific instrument. It is one of the most useless things in the world. Its value depends on the connection with the other telephone – and increases with the number of connections.

A network was not simply worth how many people it could reach from a single point of broadcast, but how many users of the network could be reached by other users on the same network.[37]

A more recent expression of this idea is Metcalfe's Law,[38] coined by George Gilder in 1993 after Bob Metcalfe, the founder of 3Com and inventor of Ethernet. Gilder, defending the model of dumb, unreliable networks in the TCP/IP model versus a new generation of telecommunications-industry centralized, guaranteed reliable networks in the model of x.25, spoke of the merits of the Ethernet model. He used a graph that Metcalfe had apparently used in the 1980s to persuade customers to build sufficiently large local area networks (LAN) 'large enough to exhibit network effects – networks larger than some "critical mass"'.[39] Metcalfe suggested that computer networks had a greater value than could be gauged by the standards of broadcast or telephone networks. While an individual might only ever contact perhaps a hundred or so different people on a network of thousands, the value of the network is measured by the potential to contact many more. Metcalfe's Law is a loose definition that states that the value of a telecom-

< 84 >

munications network is proportional to the square of the number of users of the system. Metcalfe told prospective purchasers of his LAN equipment that the number of connections to a network could reach 'a critical mass of creativity after which the benefits of a network grow larger than its costs'.[40] This has broader implications when multiple networks are involved, as David Reed, one of the early contributors to the TCP protocol, writes:

> Because Metcalfe's Law implies value grows faster than does the (linear) number of a network's access points, merely interconnecting two independent networks creates value that substantially exceeds the original value of the unconnected networks.[41]

Metcalfe's Law referred to networks in the early years of internetworking, when simple functions such as e-mail and file transfer represented significant new capacities for organizations. However, in the years since Metcalfe's Law additional services have become common on the Internet. Discussion groups, social networking, chatrooms with many participants all represent an additional layer of service. Thus there should be an additional law to describe these new services on the Internet 'because it facilitates the formation of groups in a way that Sarnoff and Metcalfe networks do not'.[42] David Reed spent much of his career working on networked group applications and has expanded Metcalfe's Law with the Group Forming Law, also known as Reed's 3rd Law. From Reed's perspective 'group forming is ... the technical feature that most distinguishes the Internet's capabilities from all other communications media before it'.[43] Reed's 3rd Law observes that the value of networks that allow their participants to form groups and collaborate on common goals scales in a far more dramatic way.[44] Group-forming networks such as online communities and discussion groups, argues Reed, scale not linearly, as Sarnoff's broadcast networks did, or by the square number of the total number of participants as Metcalfe's Law suggests, but exponentially.

> If you add up all the potential two-person groups, three-person groups, and so on that those members could form, the number of possible groups equals 2^n. So the value of a GFN increases exponentially, in proportion to 2^n.[45]

< 85 >

This is because 'any system that lets users create and maintain groups creates a set of group-forming options that increase exponentially with the number of potential members'.[46] Thus where N equals the number of participants in the network the value of a network conforming to Sarnoff's Law is simply N; yet the value of a network conforming to Metcalfe's Law is $N(N-1)$ or N^2; and the value of a network conforming to Reed's 3rd Law is 2^N. Furthermore, Reed says, 'the exponential, 2^N, is a sneaky function. Though it may be very small initially, it grows much faster than N^2, N^3 or any other power law'.[47]

In 1962 Douglas Engelbart, the inventor of the mouse and much else besides, had imagined a time when many people of different disciplines could work on a common problem using many computers and shared data.[48] This became a reality from the mid-1980s onwards as PC owners with modems began to dial in to communities of common interest and give and seek advice from their peers. These were a new breed of 'Netizens':

There are people online who actively contribute towards the development of the Net. These people understand the value of collective work and the communal aspects of public communications. These are the people who discuss and debate topics in a constructive manner, who e-mail answers to people and provide help to new-comers, who maintain FAQ files and other public information repositories, who maintain mailing lists, and so on. These are people who discuss the nature and role of this new communications medium. These are the people who as citizens of the Net, I realized were Netizens.[49]

The Netizens' forebears were the original six members of Steve Crocker's RFCs mailing list who worked together on the ARPANET's protocols, and the hackers and homebrew community who freely shared information in the service of compulsive optimization of code and hardware. By 1994 a Well regular, Howard Rheingold, described Usenet newsgroups in terms that approximated Engelbart's vision:

Newsgroups have constituted a worldwide, multimillion member, collective thinktank, available twenty-four hours a day to answer any question from the trivial to the scholarly. If you have a question about sports statistics, scientific knowledge, technical lore –

anything – someone has the answer. This magical knowledge-multiplying quality comes from the voluntary effort of many people who freely contribute expertise.[50]

The networks naturally lent themselves to the stimulation and formation of communities. As one of the founding fathers told his colleagues, 'our best success was not computing, but hooking people together'.[51]

<7>

From Military Networks
to the Global Internet

The story of the Internet's first decades pivots around the difficulties of a willing government to gift a revolutionary technology to a private sector unwilling to accept it. Twenty-first-century observers would be baffled by the inability of the telecommunications giant, AT&T, to grasp the potential of the Internet. AT&T could have taken over control of ARPANET and gained a head start in the new digital dispensation. Yet on two separate occasions it rejected the opportunity to develop the Internet: first, when RAND had approached it with only a concept of how digital packet networking could work in the 1960s; and second, when ARPA presented working proof of the ARPANET in the mid-1970s. It would scarcely seem possible knowing what is now known about the Internet that a company could have rebuffed the opportunity to gain an early mover advantage.

This, after all, was the company whose employees still revered Alexander Graham Bell as both corporate founder and inventor of the technology that created their industry. Having been gifted with the early mover advantage once by its founder, AT&T was blind to the potential of the Internet, much as the telegraph giant Western Union had been blind to the promise of the telephone when offered Bell's patent in the 1870s. When Alexander Graham Bell and his financier, Gardiner Hubbard, offered to sell the patent for the telephone to Western Union in 1876, Western Union's experts concluded that:

Messer Hubbard and Bell want to install one of their 'telephone devices' in every city. The idea is idiotic on the face of it. Furthermore, why would any person want to use this ungainly and impractical device when he can send a messenger to the telegraph

<88>

office and have a clear written message sent to any large city in the United States?[1]

Now almost exactly a century later, AT&T's astonishing lack of interest in running the ARPANET meant that ARPA had to search for an alternative party to do so. Ironically, it turned to the Defense Communications Agency (DCA), whose involvement had been regarded as the kiss of death for packet networking only a decade before.

Military administration

DCA had become convinced of the importance of packet-switched digital networks in the interim, and concluded an agreement with ARPA in 1975 to take over day-to-day responsibility for the operation of the ARPANET for a period of three years. After this three-year period ARPA expected to have found a private sector company to assume responsibility, yet in reality DCA's administration of ARPANET would last until 1983. Thus was the hand of military administration thrust into the community of computer scientists – not a cold and steely mitt perhaps, but certainly something different to the informal and often haphazard procedures that had held sway under ARPA.

In July 1980 Major Joseph Haughney, the manager that the Defence Communications Agency had assigned to oversee the ARPANET, explained why controls would be tighter:

Now that the network has grown to over 66 nodes and an estimated four to five thousand users, flexibility must be tempered with management control to prevent waste and misuse . . . We just want to ensure that we can verify proper resource utilization and prevent unauthorized penetrations.[2]

DCA attempted to prevent unauthorized access, limit leisurely use of the network and control the sharing of files. At one point an exasperated DCA officer warned ARPANET not to participate in a chain letter that had been widely circulated across the network. This was a waste of network resources for which DCA would hand out severe penalties 'up to and including the possibility of removing entire facilities from the net if appropriate'.[3] Sparks such as these were inevitable at the juncture of cultures so different as the computer research community and the military. Nor were they without precedent. The Second World War Army Air Force General 'Hap' Arnold, though himself a historic figure in the development of US military research and development, referred to the techies as 'long-hair boys'.[4] Had DCA continued to administer the ARPANET for a period of decades, the culture of the Internet might have been marked less by the long-haired eccentrics and more by hierarchical, disciplined military convention.

DCA's administration, however, proved to be temporary. In 1983 the network was split into two. The military facilities that had been connected to ARPANET were now segregated within a new, secure network called MILNET. ARPANET and MILNET were both connected through gateway machines using TCP/IP, but these gateways could limit access from ARPANET to MILNET if necessary. With the separate MILNET pursuing rigorous operating procedures under DCA's watchful eye, ARPANET was free to continue as a research network where invention trumped order. So much the better for the Internet.

The longer-term consequence of DCA's tenure as manager of the ARPANET was that the protocols that today knit together the Internet, TCP/IP, were imposed as standard across the entire network. Most facilities connected to the ARPANET were reluctant to devote the effort required to convert from the first ARPANET protocol, NCP, to the new internetworking protocol, TCP/IP. They did not need to change from the ARPANET's original NCP protocol because they were not networking with other networks beyond the ARPANET. Moreover, TCP/IP would be difficult to implement, as NCP had initially been, and would inevitably undergo further adjustments as the technology matured. Despite this reluctance events that were about to unfold within DCA would see the Agency make TCP/IP mandatory for all connected, entrenching the internetworking protocol and establishing a basis for the later expansion of the Internet.

What follows, the reader is warned in advance, is a steady flow of acronyms. DCA decided to develop a second generation of its 'automatic digital network' (AUTODIN), which had from 1966 provided communications with US military bases around the globe. AUTODIN II would become DCA's military communications network while ARPANET would be maintained as a space separate for research and testing. TCP/IP would connect the two networks through gateway machines. To allow DCA to use TCP/IP in this capacity, the Secretary of Defense made the protocol a military standard in 1980. This meant that when the AUTODIN

< 90 >

II project ran into serious difficulties the TCP/IP protocol was available as an alternative option for wider use in military networking. In April 1982 Colonel Heidi Heiden, who had been appointed by the Assistant Secretary of Defense for Communications for Command and Control to report on the matter, recommended to a Department of Defense review board that the proposed Defense Data Network (DDN) should be based on the ARPANET. TCP/IP became not only the bridge between ARPANET and AUTODIN II but the standard across both ARPANET and the new DDN. The military was adopting TCP/IP and stragglers would be cut off.

Two months later a DCA newsletter circulated on the ARPANET announcing the decision on the DDN and admonished the facilities that had not yet ordered the equipment required to make the switch from NCP to TCP/IP.[5] In March 1981 Major Haughney had already announced that the deadline for every node to cease using NCP was January 1983.[6] After a number of setbacks the entire network adopted TCP/IP, the internetworking rather than networking protocol, in June 1983. The foundations for the Internet had been laid.

The next step

Much had changed in the two decades since ARPA initiated the ARPANET. In the beginning, when Lawrence Roberts had met with the principal investigators of the research centres funded by ARPA in early 1967, few had been enthusiastic about networking. Yet ARPA had forced the project through and access to the ARPANET proved to be of enormous value to the facilities that had the privilege of being connected. Participation was open only to ARPA contractors since the network was intended to support US government work rather than to compete with commercial offerings.[7] While other networks existed, such as the proprietary DECNET and the physics research network MFENET, the ARPANET and its exclusivity created demand among America's young computer science departments. As the eighties dawned and ARPANET's first decade of operation began to draw to a close, those without access jealously regarded their connected peers.

One of those who felt that demand most keenly was Lawrence Landweber, a professor at the University of Wisconsin. Landweber approached the National Science Foundation (NSF) with proposals for a computer science network. His second proposal, in which ARPA cooperated, was approved by the NSF in January 1981.[8] NSF committed to support the project for five years after which the network would need to pay for itself. The new Computer Science Network (CSNET) connected to ARPANET using TCP/IP and was novel in a number of respects. First, the central role played by NSF marked the beginning of a transition from military to civilian use of the Internet. Second, the network was open to all computer researchers in the United States and eventually beyond. Annual fees ranged from $5,000 for university to $30,000 for industry facilities in contrast to the $90,000 price of a single IMP (the machine that each facility connected to ARPANET was required to install).[9] CSNET not only prompted an explosive growth in the number of people with connections to the Internet but also proved that those without ARPA support were willing to pay for the service. Moreover, CSNET contributed to an open approach to Internet billing across networks. Robert Kahn at ARPA made an agreement with Landweber that CSNET subscribers would not be charged for traffic that crossed the ARPANET – an agreement, according to Landweber, that 'broke new ground with respect to the principle of access and openness'.[10] Centres with limited budgets could connect to CSNET using a telephone dial-up system called Phonenet.

The same year that Landweber's proposal for CSNET was accepted, two academics from Yale and the City University of New York began to develop an alternative network for academics in the humanities. Using the remote spooling communications system (RSCS) that the IBM machines in their respective universities operated, the two established a connection using a leased line and modems to pass messages back and forth between their mainframe computers in May 1981. They named the network 'Because it's there' (BITNET), in reference to the IBM equipment that was ubiquitous in academic facilities. After some development BIT-NET could run on some DEC and Unix machines. Over a ten-year period from 1982, it provided a cheap and efficient means for academic institutions around the world to connect to one another. By 1991, shortly before its popularity declined, BITNET connected 1,400 organizations in 49 countries, including the EARN European research network.[11] A new system called 'Listserv' performed functions similar to the message groups on the ARPANET, circulating group e-mail discussions to a list of discussion participants. The BITNET operated similarly to Usenet using low-bandwidth leased telephone connections from one node to another.[12] In 1989 BITNET merged with CSNET to create the

Corporation for Research and Educational Networking (CREN). From 1993, BITNET began to decline as superior alternatives became more readily available.

Three years after its agreement to support CSNET, in 1984, the National Science Foundation initiated a programme supporting supercomputing research at American universities. Research centres in the same region would be linked by regional networks, connected in turn to a high-speed national 'backbone' network. In addition, any university could connect to the new national high network, NSFNET. This was an important choice on the part of NSF. Both NASA and the Department of Energy would have preferred that NSFNET include only government research centres.[13] The new NSFNET essentially continued the work of CSNET in expanding connections among academic institutions. It also used TCP/IP, which meant that the internetworking protocol would now be implemented on all connected machines, whether mighty supercomputers or humble PCs.[14]

In 1987 the Michigan Educated Research Information Triad (MERIT), a body with an acronym worthy of its intentions, was commissioned to build NSFNET. The ARPANET would act as a temporary backbone for NSFNET traffic while work was in progress. The MERIT NSFNET backbone became operational on 24 July 1988. Its introduction enabled further growth of Internet connections. At the end of 1987 over 28,000 machines were connected to the Internet. Two years later almost 160,000 were online.[15] Traffic on the backbone doubled every seven months.[16] Between 1989 and 1991 MERIT upgraded the backbone to handle far higher data speeds, from 1.5 Mbps to 45 Mbps. J.C.R. Licklider had lamented that the ARPANET project in the early 1970s had been 'forced to taper off without really attacking the problems of use by non-programmers'.[17] This was now being corrected. The massive expansion of the community of users connected by NSFNET tested networking in a new way, connecting a plethora of new systems and users of varying degrees of expertise and experience. The internetworking protocol was put through its paces. Gradually MERIT administrators ironed out problems as they arose.

As NSFNET grew, another momentous event occurred. ARPA's mandate was to support new technologies and it was keen to unburden itself of a network that started operation in 1969 and was now 'slow and expensive'.[18] The ARPANET was an order of magnitude slower than the NSFNET backbone. It was decommissioned on 28 February 1990. So ended the military era of the Internet. In its place, a rapidly expanding and increasingly reliable civilian network was growing. Across the US and beyond, connections to NSFNET began to grow exponentially. In a single year the number of connected machines doubled. By October 1990 almost a third of a million computers were connected. The next year the figure doubled again. Just short of 620,000 computers were online by October 1991. In October 1992 over one million computers were connected. By October 1993 more than two million computers were connected to the Internet.[19] E-mail traffic was gradually surpassed by new and more sophisticated information-finding services such as Gopher, Archie and Veronica. The stage was now set for a 'killer ap' to use on this new Internet, something that people other than specialist computer scientists could use, something revolutionary.

The end of the beginning

For a brief moment during the 2000 presidential election in the United States the history of the Internet became an issue of much debate. Al Gore, the Democratic Party's candidate, came under attack because, it was reported, he had claimed to have invented the Internet. According to one estimate, more than 4,800 television, newspaper and magazine items made reference to the purported claim during the campaign.[20]

In the 1980s Gore had been among a cohort of so-called 'Atari Democrats', a group of Democratic Party politicians who believed that computing held the prospect of future prosperity. Gore raised the idea that the US, despite its early-mover advantage in networking, was losing this edge as other countries developed their own national networks. In 1986 Gore, then in the Senate, sponsored a bill requiring the Office of Science and Technology Policy (OSTP) to undertake a study of the challenges and opportunities for networking and computing research including supercomputers at university and federal research centres. In response, Gordon Bell, one of the senior figures at DEC, chaired a committee on computing and digital infrastructure of the Federal Coordinating Council on Science, Engineering and Technology. The resulting report, released in November 1987, contained the main features that would appear in the 1991 High Performance Computing and Communication Act. These included the need to connect the networking efforts of NASA, Department of Energy, NSF and ARPA; and to establish a 1.5-Mbps network that would connect between two and three

<94>

hundred US research institutions, and in the longer term, to develop a 3-gigabyte (Gbps) network within fifteen years.[21] The 1991 Act was informally known as the Gore Act, and it set the conditions for the next phase of the Internet.[22]

Nine years later, however, Gore's work returned to haunt him. The controversy during the 2000 presidential election arose from an interview that he participated in with the television programme, CNN *Late Edition*, on 9 March 1999. Had any one of the writers of the almost 5,000 pieces on the incident consulted the transcript of Gore's statement they would perhaps have learned that he had never, in fact, used the word 'invent' at all. The transcript reports that Gore said: 'During my service in the United States Congress, I took the initiative in creating the Internet.'[23] Vint Cerf and Robert Kahn, two individuals uniquely placed to comment on the matter, defended his record. Gore, they said, 'deserves significant credit . . . No other elected official, to our knowledge, has made a greater contribution over a longer period of time'.[24]

A global Internet

In 1851 the first international submarine cable was laid across the English Channel, and the first transatlantic transmission occurred seven years later.[25] The first message transmitted along the Atlantic Ocean floor, from Queen Victoria to President James Buchanan, read, 'England and America are united. Glory to God in the highest and on Earth, peace, goodwill toward men.' Though brief, the transmission took thirty hours.[26] (For reasons that Tom Standage relays with no small humour, the transatlantic cable that had relayed the message had failed within a month.)[27]

Far less ceremony attended the first international connection of the ARPANET to the NORSAR seismic array near Oslo in 1973. The year before, at the public demonstration of the ARPANET at the Washington Hilton Hotel in October 1972, a group of researchers had taken the first steps towards formal international cooperation on the Internet. They formed the International Network Working Group (INWG), initially comprising ARPANET researchers, representatives from the National Physics Laboratory (NPL) in the UK, and from the French Cyclades networking project. NPL and ARPA already had a history of cooperation on networking. Donald Davies at NPL had invented packet-switched networking at almost the same time as Paul Baran had at RAND, and NPL contributed ideas to the ARPANET project from the beginning. It had been NPL's Roger Scantlebury, attending a conference at Gatlinburg in 1967, who introduced Lawrence Roberts to Paul Baran's neglected work on packet networking. In addition, the team at Stanford working on the TCP protocol from the spring of 1973 included a member of the French Cyclades network team. The new INWG agreed to operate by an informal agreement of standards and the first draft of the TCP protocol developed at Cerf's laboratory at Stanford was reviewed by the group in September 1973. The INWG would go on to have regular meetings on both sides of the Atlantic and grow from an initial group of 25 participants to include several hundred participants on the mailing list by the 1990s.[28]

A number of other international cooperative bodies emerged. In 1981 the International Cooperation Board (ICB) was established to coordinate work on SATNET, ARPA's satellite network. The ICB expanded into a forum for NATO members to cooperate on networking research. In addition, International Academic Networkshop (IANW) meetings were held annually from 1982 to 1989 and brought together researchers from the US, Europe and eventually Asia-Pacific countries. At the IANW meeting at Princeton in November 1987 a new body was established called the Coordinating Committee for Intercontinental Research Networks (CCIRN). The CCIRN involved Canada, the US, Europe, the Internet Advisory Board (IAB), ICB and, from 1992, representatives of the AsiaPacific, Africa from 1995 and Latin America from 1997. CCIRN produced a further offshoot called the Intercontinental Engineering Planning Group (IEPG). A torrent of acronyms though all this is, it demonstrates the gathering pace of international cooperation on networking.[29]

Since the late 1960s, private proprietary networks such as the SITA airline reservation system had spanned the globe. Thereafter networks using various protocols including BITNET, TCP/IP, X.25 and DEC's 'DECNET' proprietary system proliferated. Many countries, including several European countries, Canada, Brazil, Japan and Australia were developing internal networks, many of which used X.25. Much as ARPANET had, these networks tended to serve specific academic and research purposes. Scientific collaborations required interconnectivity and international traffic. International connections evolved in the form of networks like the High Energy Physics Network (HEPNET), which used DEC's DECNET protocol; the European Research Network (EARN), which

< 96 >

used BITNET; and the NASA Science Internet (NSI), which used DECNET and TCP/IP.[30] European networks also began to consolidate and inter-network under the coordination of various bodies (the Réseaux Associés pour la Recherche Européenne (RARE) coordinated the development of X.25 networks and the Réseaux IP Européens (RIPE) coordinated TCP/IP). A European backbone project called EBONE 92 began to build a NSFNET-style network to which other networks could connect.[31]

E-mail connectivity across the Internet was the first global, cross-network, cross-platform connectivity. In 1983 CSNET began to provide a gateway for e-mail from international affiliated networks to ARPANET. Thereafter e-mail gateways enabled networks of different protocols to swap e-mail. Some nations with particularly limited connectivity were able to use the remedial FidoNet service to collect e-mail from the Internet.

By the 1990s networks of various types were beginning to proliferate, and TCP/IP was increasingly playing a larger part in allowing them to intercommunicate. What was emerging was a global Internet, a new global commons. A natural question was, how would this be governed?

The norms of nerds

On 12 February 1812 Lord Byron, perhaps the most outrageous and dis-reputable of the English poets, took the floor at the House of Lords to make his maiden speech. A bill had recently been introduced that would impose a death penalty to quell the Luddites, the textile artisans who were rioting in opposition to the industrial revolution and wreck-ing mechanized looms.[32] Byron made his maiden speech in defence of the artisans and decried industrialization. It might seem odd then that Byron's daughter should be in the *avant garde* of the next wave of dis-ruptive technologies – computing. Odder still, considering the stereo-type of programmers: Byron himself was a promiscuous bisexual, the most flamboyant figure of the romantic movement, constantly in debt, and ever surrounded in scandal. Yet his only legitimate daughter was a mathematical genius and would be remembered as history's first computer programmer.

Mathematics, it is fair to say, was not among the many passions that convulsed Byron's short life. In *Don Juan*, Byron's famous long poem, he used the character Donna Inez to portray the cold, mathematical bent of his wife, Anne Milbanke, which he had found so insufferable. In his eyes her 'favourite science was . . . mathematical; her thoughts were theorems; she was a walking calculation'. When she legally separated from him, Milbanke privately cited a number of sins including incest with his half-sister, Augusta Leigh, after whom Milbanke and Byron's daughter, Ada, had been named, and who, confusingly, it is speculated may have borne him a third child. As he lay dying of a fever in 1824, Byron's letter to his separated wife rested, unsent and unfinished, upon his desk. He had written to thank her for sending him a letter describing Ada, whom he did not know. His daughter, Byron had read, was a budding mathematical genius.

Eleven years after the death of her father, Ada first met Charles Babbage, who between 1837 and 1871 worked on his 'analytical engine', a hypothetical machine that could be used to perform various calculations and which anticipated features that would appear again in the first generation of computers a century later. An Italian mathematician, General Menabrea, published a *Sketch of the Analytical Engine Invented by Charles Babbage, Esq.* in 1842. Ada translated the text into English. The notes she appended to her translation were longer than Menabrea's original text and included a detailed description of how an operator could calculate the Bernoulli numbers, a sequence of numbers relevant to number theory in mathematics. This description has been cited as the world's first computer program, and Ada, daughter of the Luddites' defender, as the world's first programmer.

There had always been something very different about programmers. In the 1960s, Richard Greenblatt, one of the MIT hackers, had been so consumed by late-night coding sessions that he regularly slept, unwashed, on a camp bed at the laboratory.[33] He was not unique. Three decades later, Po Bronson described the twenty-something millionaire founder of Yahoo!, David Filo, lying asleep under his desk under his computer (until the accumulating junk forced him to lie elsewhere).[34] The dot-com fairytale story of the late 1990s was different to the norm: rags to riches certainly, but then to rags again by choice and compulsion. Even the former hedge fund analyst and Amazon founder, Jeff Bezos, spent his first years at the company working at a desk made out of a door with legs nailed to it, just as the initial BBN team had done when they worked on the ARPANET tender in 1968.[35] BBN, previously an acoustics consultancy with conservative employees, had become an increasingly eccentric place when it entered into the computer business.

< 98 >

Programmers observed no particular work hours, arrived in T-shirts and fed on a diet of Coke and pizza. As one of the company's founders recalls, 'dogs roamed the offices'.[36] Similarly, the MIT Whirlwind project at Lincoln Lab, whose computers prompted the hacker golden era, was home to more than a few eccentrics. Wesley Clark and Bill Fabian left the Lincoln Laboratory for the most bizarre of reasons: they wanted to bring a cat into the lab, which Lincoln would not allow. Rebelling against the no-cats-in-the-laboratory policy, they left to go 'somewhere where cats were tolerated'.[37] The BBC's obituary of Jon Postel, one of the original network working group that developed the protocols for the ARPANET, and a key figure in Internet administration until his death in 1998, recalled a day in the early 1970s when Postel was due to work on some Air Force systems.[38] Arriving on the tarmac with customary informality, Postel was informed by Air Force personnel that he would not be permitted to board the plane until he had put on shoes.

These people, pioneers of the digital era, observed different norms. As they remade the world in their image, established certainties would be displaced. The Internet would be governed in a new, unorthodox way. As *Time* reported, 'the rules that govern behavior on the Net were set by computer hackers who largely eschew formal rules'.[39] Baran's distributed network idea in the early 1960s had naturally lent itself to a less hierarchical, less centralized ethos. Similarly, the protocols of the ARPANET and then the Internet, and the manner in which they were developed by the informal network working group, set an open, collaborative tone for the governance of the Internet and Internet standards generally. Following Steve Crocker's first request for comments (RFC) document in April 1969, the purpose of the RFCs were further elaborated in RFC 3: 'we hope to promote the exchange and discussion of considerably less than authoritative ideas.'[40] RFC 3, foreshadowing the idea of the 'perpetual beta' three decades later, established the principle that no text should be considered authoritative, that there was no final edit. Also implicit was that authority was to be derived from merit rather than fixed hierarchy. A later elaboration of this principle was:

We reject kings, presidents and voting.
We believe in rough consensus and running code.[41]

Though it began as a mailing list for six people, the informal working group that had worked on the initial NCP protocols for the ARPANET

<99>

in 1969 evolved into formal groups. A heavily acronymed succession of bodies took over the role of the graduate students' informal networking group. In 1979 Vint Cerf, then program manager at ARPA, set up the Internet Configuration Control Board (ICCB), which drew together ARPANET researchers and ARPA management to guide the strategic development of the network and protocols, a process that had been solely dominated by ARPA up to that point.[42] In January 1983 Cerf's successor, Barry Leiner, reorganized the ICCB as the Internet Activities Board (IAB).[43] In 1989 the IAB consolidated its growing number of technical task forces into two separate entities: the Internet Engineering Task Force (IETF), which focused on short-term practical issues, and the Internet Research Task force (IRTF) that focused on long-term issues. In 1992 the Internet Society was established to provide an organizational umbrella for the IETF and the Internet Architecture Board, which provides broad oversight of the IETF and of standardization. Despite the formal layers of boards and task forces, the openness and collaborative spirit of the original six-person working group that exchanged the first RFCs in the late 1960s appears to have been maintained.[44]

Reflecting on the development of the IETF, where most of the important work on new Internet standards and engineering problems is conducted, Steven Crocker believes that the process has remained open despite growing in complexity since his first RFC:

> The IETF working groups are open to anyone, again without cost. The physical meetings have a cost, but it's not required that someone attend the physical meetings. Everything is available over the net, and decisions are not firm until people on the net have had a chance to weigh in.[45]

The IETF operates under Dave Clarke's core rule of 'rough consensus and running code' rather than formal voting.[46] It has no formal members, no legal existence and its participants are volunteers. It does, however, have a hierarchical structure, including a chairperson and working groups whose own chairpersons have authority to govern the work of their groups. Indeed, a working group chairperson can exclude the inputs of disruptive participants, though no participant may be prohibited from reading or attending the working group discussion and participants can appeal.[47] In some cases closed design teams can work on a particular aspect, but their work is subject to approval by the

< 100 >

relevant working group of various interested parties. The IETF is 'a large, open community of network designers, operators, vendors, users, and researchers'.[48] Participation, despite the necessary development of a structured process, remains open to all.

RFCS continue to be central in the development of new standards for Internet technologies. 'Any individual', according to the rules set forth in RFC 2418, can request a time slot to hold a preliminary brainstorming meeting about a new topic of interest to determine whether there is sufficient interest and expertise within the IETF to establish a working group on the topic.[49] Should the group proceed to produce a document, known as an 'internet draft', it is reviewed by senior figures within IETF called Area Directors. The Area Directors can send the draft back to the working group for further work. The next stage is to announce a 'last call' on the document, which gives all individuals with an interest the opportunity to submit their input. The proposal is then sent to the Internet Engineering Steering Group, made up of the IETF chairperson and the Area Directors, for review. A last call for comments is issued and then the proposal is finally published as an RFC or sent back to the working group for further refinement. Despite the strictures of the process, IETF standards are *de jure* rather than de facto in the spirit of the 'running code' maxim, and become true standards only when they become widely used. Furthermore, the standards issued as RFCS remain open to further refinement in subsequent RFCS.

The IAB, the IETF, the Internet Society, all the bodies developed from the original group of graduate students who worked on the NCP in 1969, were technological rather than political in nature. They were necessarily international in outlook. To the extent that its governance was vested in engineers, the standards of the Internet were international. However, a lingering point of controversy surrounded one facet of Internet governance – the United States' continued control of the Internet's Domain Name System (DNS). From the early period of the ARPANET and until his death in 1998, Jon Postel, one of the members of the original Network Working Group and the editor of the group's RFCS, had volunteered to keep track of the numeric address codes of the machines on the network. From 1983, he established the Internet Assigned Numbers Authority (IANA) at the University of South California to regulate the assignment of Internet addresses as the number of connections started to increase. The same year the Domain Name System was introduced to act as a phone directory for the increasing number of IP addresses and names of machines connected to the Internet.[50] Anticipating the commercialization of the Internet, the NSF issued a solicitation in 1992 for bidders to perform 'network information service management', which would include issuing URLs of websites (i.e. the name rather than numeric IP of a website: www.yahoo.com instead of its IP address 209.131.36.158). A company called Network Solutions was selected to provide the domain name registration service contract from 1 January 1993 to 30 September 1998.[51] It would work with the Internet Assigned Numbers Authority (IANA), and Jon Postel remained in charge of issuing new top-level domain names (i.e. .com and .biz). A review of Network Solutions' operations in December 1994, immediately before the commercialization of the Internet in January 1995, recommended to the NSF that fees be charged to registrants for the service.[52] Nine months later, Network Solutions then made their charging proposal. Network Solutions would have a monopoly on domain name registration, and moreover would report to no overseeing authority from 1998 onwards when its agreement with NSF elapsed. This was an untenable situation. From October 1996 a network community-organized effort developed a new body called the International Ad Hoc Committee (IAHC) to consider a new approach to top-level domain names (like .com, .uk, etc.). In February 1997 the IAHC reported with a range of proposals on top-level domain governance, including on the choice of registrars and measures to resolve disputes over domain names. The IAHC plan was endorsed by IANA, the Internet Society, the World Intellectual Property Organization, the International Telecommunication Union and the International Trademark Association. Yet it faced considerable opposition. Vint Cerf recalls that the international aspect of the IAHC plan 'ignited a firestorm among some members of Congress (who somehow thought that the US still "controlled" the Internet) and led to Ira Magaziner's involvement'.[53]

Ira Magaziner was a senior advisor to President Clinton. In 1997, prompted by Magaziner, the Clinton administration committed to privatization in its 'Framework for Global Electronic Commerce'. The following year, in January 1998, the US Department of Commerce proposed a new non-profit corporation that would take over control of the Domain Name System. The following June, it published a statement of policy that outlined the rationale for privatization:

< 102 >

A private coordinating process is likely to be more flexible than government and to move rapidly enough to meet the changing needs of the Internet and of Internet users. The private process should, as far as possible, reflect the bottom-up governance that has characterized development of the Internet to date.[54]

The following November, the new corporation, called the Internet Corporation for Assigned Names and Numbers (ICANN), was established with the stipulation in its articles of incorporation that it 'shall operate for the benefit of the Internet community as a whole'.[55] The US government had been specific about its wish to have the new corporation physically based in the US, but acknowledged the need for international consensus. ICANN signed a memorandum of understanding with the US Department of Commerce to study future options for DNS management. The next month, in December 1998, ICANN signed an agreement with the University of Southern California in which it assumed the functions that had been fulfilled until the death of Jon Postel, only two months before, by Postel and the IANA.

Controversy, however, began to surround ICANN from mid-2005. In late 2003, the US Department of Commerce agreed an extension of the memorandum of understanding with ICANN until September 2006. However, on 30 June 2005, the Department signalled a new direction:

The United States Government intends to preserve the security and stability of the Internet's Domain Name and Addressing System . . . and will therefore maintain its historical role in authorizing changes or modifications to the authoritative root zone file.[56]

The US intended to maintain nominal authority over ICANN. Two years previously, in December 2003, the UN held a World Summit on the Information Society in Geneva where a working group on Internet governance (WGIG) was established. The WGIG reported in July 2005 that Internet governance should be the preserve of no single government and mooted various mechanisms whereby ICANN would come under the authority of an intergovernmental body. This was to be discussed at the second World Summit on the Information Society, at Tunis in November 2005. After a shift in the EU's position on the question, the US found itself isolated, as *The New York Times* reported: 'A figurative ocean separates the American position – that the Internet works fine

<103>

as it is – from most of the rest of the world.'[57] The establishment of a five-year Internet Governance Forum was agreed to debate the issue.

Then, with comparatively little ceremony, the US Department of Commerce and ICANN signed a joint affirmation on 30 September 2009 that replaced unilateral US oversight with intergovernmental oversight by the Governmental Advisory Committee (GAC). Eleven years after its establishment ICANN had become independent.

<104>

<8>

The Web!

CERN is the European Organization for Nuclear Research and the world's largest particle physics laboratory. In the 1980s and early 1990s it was home to a dizzying array of incompatible computers brought by thousands of researchers travelling from different countries. It represented all the diversity of the computing world within one self-contained environment. A contractor named Tim Berners-Lee developed a piece of software called 'Enquire' in the 1980s to map relationships between the various people, programs and systems he encountered there. Enquire marked the first step in his invention of the World Wide Web.

Arranging knowledge

Berners-Lee named the Enquire program after his favourite childhood book, a Victorian text for children called *Enquire Within Upon Everything*. His early attempt to order information, though particular to data at CERN, recommenced the search for a new method of ordering and exploiting information that had haunted Vannevar Bush at the close of the Second World War half a century before. In the months before the nuclear detonations at Hiroshima and Nagasaki, Bush, the US government's Chief Scientific Advisor, was keen to remind his countrymen of the promise rather than simply the peril and potency of science. He wrote an article in *The Atlantic*:

> The applications of science have . . . enabled [man] to throw masses of people against one another with cruel weapons. They may yet allow him truly to encompass the great record and to grow in the wisdom of race experience.[1]

<105>

He and visionaries such as Ted Nelson and Douglas Engelbart who came after him both sought to develop tools that could allow human beings to better cope with the weight of information bearing down on them.

Bush's solution was a device called the 'Memex', a hypothetical mechanical apparatus that would, Bush hoped, provide speedy retrieval and cross-referencing of information cards. A user researcher could cross-reference items of information with other items of information at the touch of a button to weave relationships between documents. This 'mesh of associative trails' would mirror the leaping connections that the brain makes to bind different bits of information together in a usable context:

> The human mind ... operates by association. With one item in its grasp, it snaps instantly to the next that is suggested by the association of thoughts, in accordance with some intricate web of trails carried by the cells of the brain.[2]

The concept that Bush described in 1945 was wildly ambitious in the age of paper and pen.

In 1960 an eccentric Harvard graduate student named Ted Nelson invented 'hypertext',[3] a system that did on computer what Bush's 'associative trails' attempted mechanically. Phrases and words in a hypertext document could be linked to additional information. A user, reading a hypertext document on a computer screen, could click various links within documents to pursue particular veins of information. Ted Nelson used hypertext as part of a wildly ambitious system called Xanadu in which documents would have multiple versions that could easily be compared and could be read out of sequence according to reader's line of interest rather than the printed flow of text. The Xanadu idea so was revolutionary that it took three decades before it began to bear fruit.

Berners-Lee, conscious of the work of Bush and Nelson before him, came to realize the potential of a system that would allow a loose arrangement of ideas and data unconstrained by hierarchies or categorization. Enquire had merely been a tool that allowed Berners-Lee to draw links between different data on his own machine, beyond which it could not link.[4] In 1990 he embarked on a new project that would give researchers complete freedom in choosing what format their documents took. It would be a world wide web (www) of information. Irrespective of the type of data, its format or computing platform, any data on the Web such as a text, image or movie file could be called up from a web server by a simple URI (universal resource identifier):

> Its universality is essential: the fact that a hypertext link can point to anything, be it personal, local or global, be it draft or highly polished.[5]

He developed a hypertext language called HTML based on a pre-existing language called SGML that was widely used on IBM machines at CERN, and started developing a client program, meaning a browser and editor with which users could create and view HTML files, in October 1990. By December 1990 he had established a server to host HTML web pages and a web browser to view web documents. The www, one of the most important advances in human communications history, had been invented. Surprisingly in retrospect, almost nobody cared.

A distinct lack of interest in the revolution

The early days of the www were marked by a distinct lack of interest. Berners-Lee's proposals for a web system at CERN were twice shelved.[6] As a result his work on the Web proceeded without formal approval and he worked with the hazard of being ordered from above to cease.[7] When he did create the www system, people within CERN were slow to use it. Berners-Lee had developed the web client program on a 'NEXT' computer, a cutting-edge workstation created by Steve Jobs of Apple fame.[8] In the absence of web-client software for other types of computers, the Web remained tethered to the NEXT platform which, despite its qualities, would never become a mainstream device. An intern was drafted in by Berners-Lee and Cailliau at CERN to write a rudimentary browser that could work on any system, even the old teletype display systems that displayed one line of text at a time. When this simple line-mode client was complete the www became viewable on every computer at CERN – though only one line at a time. Berners-Lee and Cailliau convinced the manager of CERN's gargantuan telephone directory to write the telephone directory for CERN on the Web in HTML so that a hard copy was no longer required for each of the ten thousand people associated with CERN.

<107>

Then in May 1992 a student at Berkeley named Perry Pei Wei released a browser for the www on Unix. This was a major step because Unix was the operating system of choice within the computer science community. The program required prior instillation of Pei Wei's own programming language called Viola before it could run, but it finally allowed users of Unix machines to view the www not just in line-by-line mode but in colour, with graphics, animations and the ability to point and click on links in www pages using a mouse. Wei's browser was built primarily as a means to demonstrate his Viola programming language and he had chosen to create a www browser because he saw in the URL addressing system of the www an elegance and flexibility that surpassed the web's contemporary alternatives.[9] The month after Pei Wei's browser was released a team of students at the Helsinki University of Technology completed another Unix www browser called 'Erwise'. Berners-Lee travelled to Finland to try to convince the students to develop their browser into a program that could not just view but edit web pages too, but further development of Erwise was abandoned upon the students' graduation. Tony Johnson, a physicist at the Stanford National Accelerator Laboratory (SLAC), developed another Unix browser called 'Midas'. The same year the small team at CERN produced a basic browser for the Macintosh platform, called 'Samba'. Thus by the end of 1992 users on Macintosh, NEXT and Unix systems could, with some effort, view the Web with a degree of point and click functionality. Eventually, in March 1993, Tom Bruce at the Legal Information Institute at Cornell released a browser called 'Cello' for the PC. A PC version had been a long time coming. Windows at that time had no built-in support for the TCP/IP Internet protocols and was difficult to write web software for.[10] It had taken over two years for early browsers for all the major computing platforms to appear. Now in early 1993 the stage was finally set for a dramatic uptake in www use.

In 1995 investors marvelled at the largest initial public offering (IPO) in history when Netscape, a www browser company then less than two years old, went public.[11] This was remarkable, not only because of the scale of the IPO, but because just a few years previously Berners-Lee had had to beg uninterested students, companies and researchers to develop web software. Earlier in the life of the www, in 1991, the CERN duo discovered Grif, a company that had produced a SGML hypertext editor, 'Grif', which ran on Unix and PCs but had no Internet functionality. The program could edit hypertext documents with graphics and different

< 108 >

fonts. When Berners-Lee approached Grif and offered to give them his software for free so that they could incorporate it with their own and release a www browser/editor he was rebuffed. The company simply did not see the value of the www. Grif later did produce a browser and editor called Grif SymposiaPro but it was too late to seize a major share of the market in the intense 'browser war' that followed the release of Netscape and the Microsoft alternative, Internet Explorer. Grif, like the Helsinki students who abandoned Erwise, believed that the web was a curious but limited technology.

Only in 1992 did a new team whose members understood the potential of the web begin to work on a new browser. A student and staff member at the National Centre for Supercomputing Applications (NCSA) decided to develop a browser for Unix. What set their effort apart was that the student, Marc Andreessen, was keen to attract as many users as possible to his browser. He adopted what Tim O'Reilly would later call 'the perpetual beta' approach, acting on feedback and bug reports from users on Usenet news groups. The first release of the NCSA browser, called 'Mosaic', arrived in February 1993. In April 1994 Andreessen left the NCSA to set up Netscape with Jim Clark. Only sixteen months later Netscape's historic IPO alerted Wall Street that something new and entirely unexpected was happening on the strange new 'information superhighway'.

Death of a Gopher

www was not the only popular Internet service in the early 1990s. In 1994 file transfer protocol (FTP), Wide Area Information Servers (WAIS) and Gopher were among those regularly used. All were eventually displaced or incorporated within www. The demise of Gopher, a quicker but far more basic information service, is instructive. Though the www had initially been neglected at CERN, at least it had not been strangled. Yet the team developing Gopher at the University of Minnesota worked against stiff internal opposition. Despite the widespread success of the Gopher system, the first Gopher Conference was held not at the University of Minnesota where Yen's team was based but at the University of Michigan due to strife at Minnesota. A political struggle raged within the university's computer department during the 1980s and early 1990s. On the one hand, the dominant, long-established mainframe specialists resisted the transition to smaller, cheaper,

<109>

personal computing. On the other, the microcomputer specialists argued that users needed more control of their systems, that networks were the future and that the university must devote resources to their field of work. This was a dispute between pioneers of the emerging centrifugal trend and the centripetal establishment. Professor Shih-Pau Yen, who led the development of Gopher, was only able to maintain the project by threatening to resign and by proving that the external sources were paying its costs.[12] Yen maintains that his team were so poorly resourced that they used old computers with black and white displays in the age of www with images, colour fonts and animations.

To raise funds for continued development, Yen's team decided to charge a fee for commercial use of its server software. Gopher would continue to be free for the vast majority of users. The charge was interpreted as a betrayal by the wider community of Gopher users and contributors. The defensive tone of the Gopher team's messages to the online community shows the fierce opposition they encountered. A lengthy explanation of the rationale behind the fee concludes with the line, 'Please don't abuse the Gopher Development team :-)'[13] The opposition was understandable, Yen concedes, because Gopher was the basis of an ecosystem: though his team had produced the server, Gopher client programs for each different computer platform required the contributions of programmers among the user base.[14] The charge also gave commercial Gopher developers pause for thought. Those thinking in the longer term were unwilling to continue working on a platform for which they might some day be subject to fees. Gopher was a victim of the centripetal establishment's antipathy at the University of Minnesota and of the convention growing among users that communal or co-developed software should be without cost.

CERN learned from Gopher's example. It officially declared in April 1993 that the www software could be freely used by anybody.[15] Previously, Berners-Lee's request to freely release the intellectual property rights to the www under a new form of licence known as 'GNU' had not convinced his superiors. In 1993 Berners-Lee decided that some mechanism to maintaining the qualities of the Web was necessary. For the first few years of its existence the Web was 'defined by nothing more than specifications stored on some disk sitting around somewhere at CERN'.[16] Something more concrete was needed. When the early developers of www software met in early 1994 for a 'www wizards' workshop', Berners-Lee proposed the idea of a consortium to oversee the

< 110 >

future direction of the Web. The www Consortium, known as 'w3c', was formed to promote interoperability and standardization of web technologies.

Open-source: the hacker renaissance

At roughly the same time as the Web was gaining popularity a revolution was occurring within software development that would produce the systems on which most websites would run, and would influence a new approach to property that would make collaborative projects like Wikipedia possible. At the centre of the revolution was Richard Stallman, one of the last hackers remaining at MIT in the 1980s. Like all revolutions, it started with a gripe. The facility where Stallman worked had taken delivery of new computers whose manufacturers demanded that their users sign non-disclosure agreements prohibiting them from swapping code and building on each other's work. From Stallman's perspective:

> This meant that the first step in using a computer was to promise not to help your neighbor. A cooperating community was forbidden. The rule made by the owners of proprietary software was, 'If you share with your neighbor, you are a pirate. If you want any changes, beg us to make them.'[17]

The proprietary control exercised by the manufacturers was a return to the centripetal approach of the old mainframe companies. This was precisely what the hackers had reacted against in the 1960s and '70s. In Stallman, known by his colleagues as 'the Last Hacker',[18] was refined the hacker ethos that a program's source code should be open to modification. His anger about proprietary-controlled software would prompt a hacker renaissance.

He viewed rigid ownership of software as 'obstruction' of the hacker's necessary labour[19] and in 1983 founded the free software movement as 'a movement for computer users' freedom'.[20] Stallman resolved with the obstinacy of a purist to build a new operating system that hackers could use as they saw fit. He would base his design on Unix, the operating system created in the early 1970s at Bell Labs by Ken Thompson and Denis Ritchie. The terms of AT&T's regulated monopoly prohibited it from entering the computer software market, and so Unix was made cheaply available to academic and research organizations. Unix had become a popular focus for users to hack improvements. Following AT&T's divestiture at the end of 1983, Unix was marketed commercially.[21] His would be a 'Unix-like' system, compatible, but not the same. The acronym for his suite of software would be GNU, which stands for 'GNU's Not Unix'. In September 1983 he began to seek collaborators to work on the project on Usenet groups:

> I cannot in good conscience sign a nondisclosure agreement or a software license agreement. So that I can continue to use computers without violating my principles, I have decided to put together a sufficient body of free software so that I will be able to get along without any software that is not free. I'm looking for people for whom knowing they are helping humanity is as important as money.[22]

By the end of the 1980s Stallman and his collaborators had almost completed an entire suite of GNU software. What remained to be developed was the 'kernel', the most elemental part of an operating system that communicates on behalf of other software with the computer's hardware. Though incomplete, GNU set the stage for a remarkable further development.

In 1990 a second-year undergraduate at the University of Helsinki began working on a hobby project. His name was Linus Torvalds and he was building small programs to learn about Unix and explore the features of his new PC. He also wanted to be able to read e-mail news groups more easily. By mid-1991 he realized that the development of a full operating system was the logical next step to his endeavours. The system he was developing was based on 'Minix', a variant of Unix geared towards the educational market that was free to copy. Three months later he had a usable kernel.[23] In August 1991 he posted a message to a Usenet group where discussion focused on Minix and asked for feedback and contributions for his project to design a free operating system.[24]

> I'm doing a (free) operating system (just a hobby, won't be big and professional like gnu) for 386(486) AT clones. This has been brewing since april, and is starting to get ready. I'd like any feed-

<112>

back on things people like/dislike in minix, as my os resembles it somewhat (same physical layout of the file-system (due to practical reasons) among other things).[25]

A colleague of Torvalds who shared an office with him at Helsinki University recalls Torvalds's excitement when a few dozen people downloaded Linux in the first few days after he made it available.[26] With such meagre expectations, Torvalds found himself only seven years later in 1998 on the cover of *Forbes*.

In October 1991 Torvalds released Version 0.02, a working kernel.[27] Because it was based on Minix, and thus compatible with Unix, Torvalds's kernel was also compatible with the suite of programs developed in Stallman's GNU project from the mid 1980s. Collaborators began to answer the call for assistance he had posted on Usenet. They included people who had contributed code to the GNU project and to another project called Berkeley Unix Distribution. Torvalds began to use the GPL (GNU General Public License) created by Richard Stallman to license release of Linux. The GPL, which 'guarantee[s] your freedom to share and change free software',[28] became a sort of 'written constitution' for the Linux community.[29] The Linux project began to grow in complexity. Version 0.001, released by Torvalds in 1991, had ten thousand lines of code and a single user, Torvalds himself; version 0.99, released in 1993, had 100,000 lines of code and was used by twenty thousand people.[30] At this point Torvalds began to delegate code review to a core group of five. In 1994 version 1.0 contained 170,000 lines of code and had 100,000 users. By 1998 the number of users had grown to 7.5 million, and Linux, now at version 2.1.110, had 1.5 million lines of code contributed and tested by approximately 10,000 programmers. One rough estimate of the accumulated effort on Linux from 1991 to 2007 when counted as hours of work done hit the $1 billion mark.[31]

This scale of collaboration was possible because of the Internet, much as Licklider and Roberts had envisaged in 1968 when they mooted that the 'interconnect[ion of] separate communities' would 'make available to all the members of all the communities the programs and data resources of the entire super community'.[32] The community that emerged from the wide collaboration on Linux was a loosely governed structure over which Torvalds watched as benevolent dictator and moral authority. His lieutenants have ownership of parts of the project. They are, he claims, selected by the community according to merit:

The programmers are very good at selecting leaders. There's no process for making somebody a lieutenant. But somebody who gets things done, shows good taste, and has good qualities – people just start sending them suggestions and patches. I didn't design it this way. This happens because this is the way people work. It's very natural.[33]

He, however, maintains approval over final decisions on major new modifications to Linux and acts as a coordinator.

Alerting readers to the advent of open-source in 2003, *Wired* published a feature on the phenomenon that delivered the message in no uncertain terms: 'Open source is doing for mass innovation what the assembly line did for mass production.'[34] The involvement of such a large community of developers in proposing, testing and refining contributions to Linux made the system adaptable but solid. As Eric Raymond observed, the result of many eyeballs was to make complex problems shallow:

> Given a large enough beta-tester and co-developer base, almost every problem will be characterized quickly and the fix obvious to someone. Or, less formally, 'Given enough eyeballs, all bugs are shallow.' I dub this: 'Linus's Law'.[35]

Moreover, the centrifugal model of software development enabled by the GPL licence meant that Linux could be modified to fit different requirements and variations have been written to operate on computers of every conceivable type, from tiny electronic devices to massive supercomputers. The combination of the Linux kernel, the GNU suite and a graphical user interface adapted from a project called xfree86 proved so successful that the computer industry took notice. In the late 1990s, firms with an interest in establishing a competitor to Microsoft in the operating system market began to support Linux.

Linux provided an example of the free software that Stallman had described. From 1998 IBM began to support and invest in Linux. In the same year Netscape, the most popular web browser, began an open-source project so that users could collaborate on improvements. From mid-1995 the open-source model of collaborative, free and open software development was adopted for another important project. Building on NSCA web server software, collaborators in the 'Apache' project created a free, open-source web server. Within a single year the Apache web server became the dominant software keeping websites everywhere available on the Web, and remains so to the present day.[36] The Apache web server, combined with the Linux operating system and two other open-source technologies, the MYSQL database and PHP web application language, are one of the dominant forces on which content on the www relies. Much of the Web, therefore, relies on open-source software and the collaborative effort of thousands of volunteers.

Growth and order

On 25 July 1994 the front cover of *Time* magazine announced 'the strange new world of the Internet'. The Internet was of course only new to those who had not known of it previously. What was new was the www, which put a user-friendly face on the network. Also new was an explosion in the number of connected networks, thanks to the initiatives of the National Science Foundation. Over the six years of the NSF MERIT backbone the number of connected networks rose from 240 in 1988 to 32,400 in 1994. Between 150 and 300 networks joined the Internet each week.[37] In 1992 traffic on the network grew at 11 per cent each month, and six thousand networks were connected, two-thirds of them in the US.[38] By October 1994 3.8 million computers were connected to the Internet. By July 1995 6.6 million were online. The www increasingly became the focus of interest. One indicator of the growing fascination with the www are the data on the number of visitors to Berners-Lee's own CERN server, info.cern.ch, where the www software and information about web servers around the world were available: a hundred hits in the summer of 1991, a thousand in the summer of 1992, ten thousand in the summer of 1993. The rate doubled every three to four months and increased tenfold annually.[39] As Berners-Lee recalls, 'in 1992 academia, and in 1993 industry, was taking notice'.[40] In April 1995 the Web became the dominant service on the Internet, surpassing even the File Transfer Protocol (FTP) that was used to transfer large files.[41] This was phenomenal since the Web had become accessible on all the major computing platforms only two years before with the release of the PC browser, Cello. Interest in the Web accelerated the growth of Internet connections. In July 1995 6.6 million computers were connected to the Internet. That number doubled in one year to 12.8 million. By July 1997 19.6 million computers were connected to the Internet.[42]

<115>

Users quickly found novel ways to use the Web. Among these was the web cam. It had been invented at the University of Cambridge Computer Laboratory as a matter of utmost practicality. The fifteen researchers working in the Lab's Trojan Room placed a small camera in the snack area of their building beside the communal coffee pot. The researchers in the Trojan room kept a small black and white video display of the coffee pot permanently visible in a window on their screen so that they could avoid making the trip to get coffee until somebody else had gone to the trouble of refilling the pot. The system, initially operable on the local network, was extended to the Web in 1995. Web cams quickly became common on the Web, providing a novel means to view the mundane from across the globe. Web users could view traffic congestion in foreign cities, with the image updated every minute or so. More exciting in a voyeuristic sense was when a student at Dickinson College in the US named Jennifer Ringley began to provide stream images from a camera in her dorm room in 1996. For the next seven years millions of Internet users could observe her unscripted daily existence at her site JenniCam.org. The heady combination of nail painting, tending to pets and occasional nudity generated a mass audience and appearances on primetime TV chat shows.

Though it may have seemed at the time as if the power to publish to the www would revolutionize human communications, there was something necessarily limited about the first wave of www websites. The power to publish websites to a global audience was spoiled by the rudimentary categorization and search technologies available at the time. The first generation of websites from the early 1990s to about 2002 shared a number of limitations. This was the 'I go get Web' where the user sought Web gems among the deluge.[43] Even before the invention of the www it had become clear that tools would be needed to sift through the mass of data available on the Internet. The first search tool was called 'Archie', released in 1990 by Alan Emtage, a graduate student at McGill University. Archie allowed users to narrow down the scope of their search for files to specific servers. It searched FTP servers, indexed their contents and allowed users to search for specific files. Archie was limited in that the user had to enter the precise filename of a specific item rather than entering an approximate phrase. One had to know what one sought in advance. Archie would then direct the user to the appropriate FTP server, and the user would then have to manu-

< 116 >

ally peruse the server's folders to find the file. The remarkable thing was that, even to the creator of Archie, the first tool in what would become a multi billion-dollar industry that revolved around searching for things on the Internet, the need for search services was not foreseen:

> It was only after we made it known that we had the database and got lots of requests to search it that we realized that there was a need for this kind of service.[44]

In 1993 a search tool for the Gopher system called 'Veronica' brought the user directly to the item on the relevant Gopher server, but still searched only for items by precise title. Also in 1993 Matthew Gray at MIT developed 'www Wanderer', perhaps the first 'web crawler'. Wanderer was an automated software known as a 'bot' that travelled from website to website gathering data on the number of sites as it went. In 1994 Brian Pinkerton was working on a browser for the NEXT OS and released 'WebCrawler'. Informed by his experience working on information management at NEXT, Pinkerton made WebCrawler index all text within the documents it found.[45] The crawler and indexer were the core components of a new generation of search engines that could return relevant results without being given precise research requests. Finally, the Web was coming to a point where the newcomer could find material with relative ease.

In the same year as WebCrawler appeared four other search engines were established: AltaVista, Lycos, Excite and Yahoo! Yahoo!, one of the most popular sites on the Web, began life under the surprisingly unassuming name 'Jerry and David's Guide to the Web'. Procrastinating in the fourth year of their PHD in 1993, Jerry Yang and David Filo focused their attention on fantasy league baseball.[46] Yang created a crawler program that would seek out any available data on baseball players from FTP and Gopher resources. Upon the release of Mosaic, Yang spotted an opportunity for further diversion from his PHD work and started to browse the new www compulsively. He established a list of the interesting sites as he browsed. They put the growing list on the Web in 1994. Yahoo! had a friendly and easy approach totally at odds with standard business practice. For example it included links to its competitors' sites to allow users to check for further results.[47]

AltaVista was initiated within DEC which, though it had led the microcomputer revolution, had failed to adjust to the PC era. Although

AltaVista was one of the most popular destinations on the Web in 1996, DEC was in its death throes. AltaVista, strangled of support, was repeatedly sold to a succession of new owners.[48] Ironically AltaVista's founder, Louis Monier, was an alumnus of Xerox PARC, the scene of the most egregious cases of an early technology innovator neglecting next-generation development from within its own ranks. Another entrant, Lycos, was developed at the Carnegie Mellon University and supported by ARPA. It pioneered the examination of links between sites to gauge their search relevance. Excite, like Yahoo!, was started by graduate students at Stanford. It pioneered free e-mail and personalization, allowing users to filter the content they wanted to see according to their personal preferences. Web searching was blossoming into a vital business. From the late 1990s it would come of age in the form of Google.

An unassuming Sergey Brin wrote on his PHD profile page at Stanford in 1999:

> Research on the web seems to be fashionable these days and I guess I am no exception. Recently I have been working on the Google search engine with Larry Page.[49]

The previous year he and his colleague Larry Page presented a paper announcing their new search engine, Google. They argued in much the same vein as Vannevar Bush had half a century previously that 'the number of documents in the indices has been increasing by many orders of magnitude, but the user's ability to look at documents has not'.[50] The duo had begun to work together in 1996 on an unexplored element in the relationship between websites: back links. Though each website contains code outlining its outgoing links to other sites, it was not possible to know what other sites had incoming links back to it. By developing 'BackRub', a system to determine the incoming 'back links' between sites, Brin and Page could determine which sites were most cited by other sites. The most cited sites would be given higher 'page ranks', appearing first in the search results and their backrub would be more important to other sites.

> Google works because it relies on the millions of individuals posting websites to determine which other sites offer content of value. Instead of relying on a group of editors or solely on the frequency with which certain terms appear, Google ranks every web page

< 118 >

using a breakthrough technique called PageRank™. PageRank evaluates all of the sites linking to a web page and assigns them a value, based in part on the sites linking to them. By analyzing the full structure of the web, Google is able to determine which sites have been 'voted' the best sources of information by those most interested in the information they offer.[51]

The system not only judged the relevance of websites to search queries on the basis of their own text but also on the basis of third-party descriptions found beside the outgoing links of other sites.

The backrub system proved to be enormously effective, returning more relevant results to search queries than any of its competitors. Thus when Yahoo! offered to buy Google for $3 billion, Google rejected the offer. Indeed such was Google's popularity that in June 2006 the *Oxford English Dictionary* added the word 'google' as a verb. The name Google, which Page and Brin chose in 1997, was inspired by the mathematical word 'googol', which denotes a massive number: one with a hundred zeros. The enormity of the googol, according to Google, 'reflects their mission to organize a seemingly infinite amount of information on the Web'.[52]

<9>
A Platform for Trade and the Pitfalls of the Dot-com

The first item ever sold on eBay was a broken laser pointer. Startled that someone had bid for the broken item eBay's founder, Pierre Omidyar, contacted the bidder to ask whether he understood that the laser pointer for which he had bid $14.83 was in fact broken? The bidder responded: 'Yes, I'm a collector of broken laser pointers.'[1] It was late September 1995. Omidyar realized that he was onto something big.

By the end of the next year the value of all goods sold on eBay had reached $7.2 million. eBay proved that the Internet was 'a marketplace so massive, and so diverse, that nothing is beyond commodification'.[2] It might have seemed as if the network had been designed for this express purpose. In reality this was the opposite of the truth. The Internet became a global marketplace without any explicit plan to make it so. Indeed, until the very beginning of 1995 commercial activity on the Internet was expressly forbidden under the National Science Foundation's Acceptable Usage Policy.

Yet change had been in prospect from the beginning of the decade. Indeed, from many decades before. In 1968 Paul Baran described a system in which shoppers at home would be 'electronically conveyed through a huge general purpose store carrying almost every imaginable product'.[3] By the 1990s a wide variety of private, commercial and academic networks spanned the globe and much of the Internet was run or had been built by the private sector. The NSFNET backbone, for example, received less than a third of its funding from the NSF, and NSF-supported regional networks received less than 50 per cent.[4] Government contracts granted to build and operate NSFNET and its regional networks had stimulated expertise and competition within the private sector. Two privately funded Internet carriers spun off from the government – UUNET and PSI. Three commercial Internet Service Providers, PSINet,

<120>

Alternet and CERFnet, joined to form CIX in 1991. Since TCP/IP had not been designed to facilitate accountability and billing the three companies transported each other's traffic free of charge through a common router. Thereafter CIX attracted additional networks, within and beyond the US. The private, commercial networks were proliferating.

There could perhaps have been no clearer sign that commerce was about to hit the networks than the advent of the first commercial spam in April 1994. A married couple of lawyers, Carter & Siegel, sent an advertisement for their advisory service on the US immigration green card lottery to the hundred or so various alt.culture Usenet newsgroups, each of which catered to readers with an interest in a different country. Next they hired a programmer who, in one night, coded a piece of script that would automate the process of sending the 'Green Card Lottery' notice spam to sixty thousand groups. The couple used the script, and ninety minutes later millions of people across the globe received their first spam.[5]

Thus by November 1990, when stakeholders met to discuss the commercialization of the Internet, there had already been 'regular requests for access by commercial services' to the NSFNET. The group concluded that:

> Offering the NSFNET backbone at no cost , , , inhibits private investment in backbone networks [and] constrains the Market for commercial TCP/IP services.[6]

In 1993 the NSF took steps to privatize the operation of the Internet. NSF published a plan for the change in May 1993: ISPs would operate their own networks and gateways would interconnect them. NSF's own networking activities would be limited to a high-speed research network. By this time, in 1993, the Internet included ten thousand networks.[7] In accordance with the plan, the prohibition on commercial activity on the NSF backbone was rescinded on 1 January 1995. Finally, on 30 April 1995, MERIT closed the NSFnet backbone. US-government ownership of the Internet, which had applied since the first two nodes had communicated across ARPANET in 1969, ended.

The irony for those who had argued during the Cold War that defence research and development expenditure was 'crowding out' and distorting the US economy was that government-funded research on networking and computing during the Cold War ultimately planted the

< 121>

seeds for the e-economy after the Cold War. The Internet, funded by government since the beginning, would produce a bear market such as Wall Street had never seen.

dot Tulip

From 1634 to 1637 a wave of enthusiasm and investment swept the Dutch Republic. The object of the investors' interest was the tulip. In Turkey, the tulip was becoming an important element of court culture, to the extent that the Sultan of the Ottoman Empire appointed a Chief Florist to his court.[8] By the time tulip bulbs had made the long and costly journey from Constantinople to Harlem they were more than simply a decoration or gardener's diversion. The tulip gave off a whiff of the exotic East. It became the collector's item of the Dutch urbane. *Extraordinary Popular Delusions and the Madness of Crowds*, a book written in the 1840s which was probably not entirely accurate, depicts a pervading mania:

> In 1634, the rage among the Dutch to possess [tulips] was so great that the ordinary industry of the country was neglected, and the population, even to its lowest dregs, embarked in the tulip trade. As the mania increased, prices augmented, until, in the year 1635, many persons were known to invest a fortune of 100,000 florins in the purchase of forty roots.[9]

According to the same account, which may in this reference be farther yet from accuracy,[10] a single bulb of the rare *Sempre Augustus* species of tulip was traded for enormous quantities of mixed goods including two lasts of wheat (a last equals approximately 1,800 kg), four lasts of rye, four fat oxen, eight fat swine, twelve fat sheep, two hogs-heads of wine (approximately 380 litres), four tuns of beer (a tun is over 750 litres), two tuns of butter, one thousand pounds of cheese, a complete bed, a suit of clothes and, to top the collection off, a silver drinking-cup. Another trade for a single bulb of the rare Viceroy species, according to the same account, was 12 acres of building land.[11]

Apocryphal or not, these tall tales resonate with the 1996–2000 dot-com bubble. In March 2000, as the dot-com stocks began to look increasingly vulnerable, Ron Baron, a prominent money manager, apparently circulated copies of *Extraordinary Popular Delusions and the*

< 122 >

Madness of Crowds among his employees.[12] The Dow Jones database of news articles returns 433 articles between 1999 and 2001 containing the phrase 'tulipmania' or 'tulip mania'.

The analogy was not yet evident in the mid-1990s. Optimism was rampant. In 1995, *Fortune* told business readers, 'Finally here's something about the Net to pique your interest. Real money. Real fast.'[13] Silicon Valley's most famous venture capitalist, John Doerr, spoke of 'the single greatest legal creation of wealth in the history of the planet'.[14] The July 1997 cover of *Wired* announced that the combination of technological advance and commercial opportunity had started a revolution:

> We are watching the beginnings of a global economic boom on a scale never experienced before. We have entered a period of sustained growth that could eventually double the world's economy every dozen years and bring increasing prosperity for – quite literally – billions of people on the planet. We are riding the early waves of a 25-year run of a greatly expanding economy that will do much to solve seemingly intractable problems like poverty and to ease tensions throughout the world.[15]

Conventions governing business, growth and investment seemed to have been turned on their heads. Starting with Netscape's IPO in 1995, dot-com stocks began a steep rise. At the end of 1996 the NASDAQ index was at just over 1,291. By July 1998 it had climbed to 2,000 points. The clamour for shares in dot-com IPOs drove the NASDAQ index ever higher. In September 1999 VA Linux Systems made its IPO. It offered its shares at $30 per share and by the close of trading the same day they had risen to $239.25 a share. This was a one-day leap of 698 per cent.[16] On 11 March 1999 the NASDAQ index rose above 3,000 points, and climbed above 4,000 points on 29 December 1999. Finally, on 10 March 2000, the NASDAQ peaked. Its value was over 500 per cent of what it had been on the day of the Netscape IPO five years previously, and it had risen 75 per cent in the preceding four and a half months alone.[17] To understand the scale of the upset in the markets, consider Cisco Systems, a company that builds networks and networking equipment. By 2000 it was ranked the third most valuable company in the United States by market value, having risen 689 places in the ten years since 1990. It was beaten to top place only by the energy companies General Electric and Exxon.[18]

<123>

The collapse, when it came, was rapid. In mid-2000 the bull market collapsed and a bear market took over. Not only did the young dot-com companies begin to fail, but established technology giants such as Intel were forced to announce big layoffs. By November 2000, only nine months after the NASDAQ's peak, CNN dubbed the collapse a '$1.7 trillion lesson'.[19] The lesson would get harsher yet. By March 2001 the NASDAQ had fallen from 5,000 to 2,000 points. By October 2002 its value was a quarter of its March 2000 value, having fallen from $6.7 trillion to $1.6 trillion.[20] What happened, and why, having experienced this, might any sensible person be optimistic for the future?

The collapse had been foreseen by a shrewd few. In early December 1996 Alan Greenspan, the Chairman of the US Federal Reserve, attended a dinner in his honour at the American Enterprise Institute. After the guests had finished eating, Greenspan rose to make a long speech on the challenge of central banking in a democratic society. In the last few paragraphs of his speech Greenspan injected words of caution. He accepted that sustained low inflation and lower risk premiums were driving up stock prices. Yet at the same time he noted the growing distance between investors' expected returns and how much those stocks were actually earning. Greenspan asked:

> How do we know when irrational exuberance has unduly escalated asset values, which then become subject to unexpected and prolonged contractions as they have in Japan over the past decade?[21]

Greenspan's warning about irrational exuberance was forgotten as stocks continued to soar. With spectacular IPOs such as Netscape's in 1995 being eclipsed by the seven-fold one-day leap during the VA Linux Systems IPO it was a reasonable bet that investor expectations had grown far beyond probable returns. In early 2001, as the NASDAQ faltered, Warren Buffet made clear his belief that the exuberance had been irrational:

> Nothing sedates rationality like large doses of effortless money. After a heady experience of that kind, normally sensible people drift into behavior akin to that of Cinderella at the ball. They know that overstaying the festivities – that is, continuing to

<124>

speculate in companies that have gigantic valuations relative to the cash they are likely to generate in the future – will eventually bring on pumpkins and mice. But they nevertheless hate to miss a single minute of what is one helluva party. Therefore, the giddy participants all plan to leave just seconds before midnight. There's a problem, though: They are dancing in a room in which the clocks have no hands.[22]

On the other hand, there was perhaps a kernel of rationality driving the dot-com fiasco, much as there had been some logic to the tulip bubble. The most highly valued patterned tulips were necessarily rare. They grew only from bulbs infected with the mosaic virus. The virus caused their colourful, patterned petals but it also reduced their capacity to reproduce. Thus the infected bulbs most in demand for their beauty were also rarest because of their inability to reproduce.[23] Moreover, demand for the tulips extended beyond the Netherlands to cities like Paris whose elite were enthusiastic consumers. The follies of the dot-com era too had mitigating factors. It was undeniable that those who moved quickly with good ideas enjoyed spectacular success. Amazon had beaten Barnes & Noble, the high street giant, by dominating the Internet before Barnes & Noble awoke to its potential.

eBay provided the most dazzling example to investors trying to adjust to the new balance between profit and risk in the dot-com world. eBay started life as 'AuctionWeb' on 4 September 1995. By the end of the following year 41,000 users had traded $7.2 million worth of goods on site. In 1997 (when the site was renamed eBay), 341,000 users traded goods worth $95 million. By the end of 1998 eBay's gross merchandise volume had reached $740 million and registered users numbered 2.1 million. The figures continued to rise, reaching $2.8 billion and 10 million registered users by the end of 1999 and $5.4 billion and 22 million users by the end of 2000. In 2001, despite the dot-com collapse, $9.3 billion worth of goods were traded by 42 million registered users. This mind-boggling growth continued thereafter: in 2002, $14.9 billion and 62 million users; in 2003, $23.8 billion and 95 million users; in 2004, $34.3 billion and 135 million users; in 2005, $44.3 billion and 181 million users; in 2006, $52.5 billion and 222 million users.[24] By 2007 the total value of sold items on eBay's trading platforms was nearly $60 billion. eBay users across the globe were trading more than $1,900 worth of goods on the site every second.[25] Anticipating statistics like these,

<125>

investors were ready to bet significant quantities of capital on ideas that sounded less far-fetched than eBay had been.

As the dot-com boom gathered pace in the late 1990s, it became increasingly difficult to spot and act on opportunities before competing investors. Whereas in the pre-dot-com era a company required a minimum of four quarters of profitability to attract funding, these rules were forgotten in the dot-com frenzy. Some investors were newcomers who had never known the rules to begin with: Goldie Hawn had established her own start-up and an investment group called Champion Ventures was established for retired athletes by former 49ers American Football players. Investment decisions that normally would have taken weeks or months were now taken in ever-shorter periods – in some cases, over the course of a telephone call. The CEO of one start-up recalls:

I made a call to a friend of mine, Ron Conway of Angel Investors, and he jumped on it immediately. The next morning we had our money – the $700,000 seed money.[26]

Word of mouth within Silicon Valley's tightly knit financing community began to carry the weight of authority. Prominent investors who valued each other's opinions or felt a duty to back each other's investments lent a momentum to individual decisions, good or bad. In 1999 venture capital investments reached their historic peak of $48.3 billion.[27] Rationality, in Buffet's words, had been given its sedative dose.

Much changed yet more the same

Rationality was under siege. The scale of the change promised by dot-com hype was difficult to encompass. How much would the world change as a result of the new and direct contact that sellers and buyers across the globe could now enjoy? The publishing industry was one of the first to experience disintermediation. At the 1997 Book Expo America, Amazon employees had been greeted as heroes by independent publishers who for decades had been in thrall to the distribution giants.[28] Examples like this proved that the Internet threatened established incumbents with oblivion and that small upstarts could find opportunities in the digital age. Just what these opportunities were, however, was not clear in the mid-1990s.

< 126 >

Chief among the reasons why so many stumbled in the dot-com bubble was that the Internet was an entirely unknown quantity. Investors had not yet discerned what the Internet had changed and what it had not. In fact, a great many of them had fundamentally misunderstood the Internet. Even in 1996, many Internet users were so inexperienced with browsing the Internet that they contacted Amazon's customer support to learn how to use the scroll bar on their web browsers to scroll down to the bottom of the Amazon page.[29] This was no different for investors. Ron Conway, known as the 'Godfather of Silicon Valley', was something of a Luddite. A writer who followed him daily noted that an assistant was tasked with printing out his e-mails and handing them to him on paper.[30] The prevailing mantra of the mid-1990s was 'the 'Net changes everything'. This was no doubt compelling to investors with little experience of the Internet. The Net *could* change everything. Productivity would soar. Business would be different. To some it seemed as if the laws of nature no longer mattered. Physics, however, asserted itself with a vengeance.

Weight was still weight, and distance still distance. The Internet only made an impact on digital communication, not physical delivery. As Negroponte had said, the secret in the digital economy was to move electrons, not atoms.[31] Many of the dot-com companies failed because they lost money in delivering physical items over long distances. SwapIt.com, for example, operated on the premise that users would post second-hand items to the company and receive credits with which they could buy other users' second-hand items from the site. The company had to do all the physical storing and sending.[32] SwapIt, which could have been a centrifugal user-to-user system in the vein of eBay, relied instead on the old centralized model of a distribution to and from a central depot.

One of the most damaging misjudgements of the Internet was that it changed the conditions of business so completely that previous experience was obsolete. Impetuous entrepreneurs relied on vision over experience and attempted to develop entirely new businesses from scratch in established sectors in which they had no experience. This had worked for Amazon, but few others. A company called Webvan, for example, sought to revolutionize grocery retail. It was the brainchild of Louis Border, the founder of the giant book chain Borders, who believed that new distribution methods and the Internet could allow him to leverage operating margins of 12 per cent rather than

<127>

the 4 per cent typical of normal supermarkets.[33] Webvan hired George Shaheen, previously CEO at Andersen Consulting, as its CEO. This duo looked impressive to Wall Street: Borders had past success in book retail and Shaheen had enormous credibility in the investment community. Neither, it should be noted, had any experience whatsoever in groceries.

Together they attempted to rebuild groceries from the bottom up. The strategy was simple: 'get big fast' (GBF) to secure the market before competitors could stake their claim. If 'the Net changes everything' had been the first misleading maxim of the dot-com boom, 'get big fast' was the second. In July 1999 Webvan ordered the construction of 26 massive distribution and delivery centres at a gargantuan cost of $1 billion. Webvan already had vast distribution centres in operation. The new centres would allow it to open into new regions across the US. As dot-com successes like Amazon had proved, staking an early claim on virgin territory could yield spectacular results. They did so by investing vast amounts of investors' capital and operated at a colossal loss. Amazon continuously lost money from 1995 until, finally, it made its first profit in the last quarter of 2001. It was a sign of the unusual times that, despite losing money for four consecutive years, its founder, Jeff Bezos, was named *Time* magazine's Person of the Year in 1999. While Amazon would eventually become profitable, the rush to stake a claim was a race to nowhere for many dot-coms. GBF strategies prompted massive, unsustainable growth. Netscape, for example, expanded its workforce from five programmers to two thousand in a single year. Such rapid expansion made corporate culture impossible to inculcate across the organization and made mistakes almost impossible to learn from.[34]

In the case of Webvan, the GBF strategy was particularly risky. As a *New York Times* journalist wrote:

> Grocery stores already operate on razor-thin profit margins without the added expense of delivery, and the perishable nature of many foods does not make operating from a central location feasible. By some estimates, an on-line grocer must do 10 times the volume of a typical store to be successful.[35]

Foremost among Webvan's difficulties was that it had to absorb an estimated $10 to $15 for each delivery.[36] One assessment even estimated that its losses on every order were over $130 when depreciation, marketing and other overheads were taken into account.[37] Webvan's collapse was spectacular. From a huge market value of $7.9 billion following its IPO in November 1999, the company was forced to file for bankruptcy and lay off two thousand employees by July 2001.

Yet while Webvan's managers attempted to rebuild the grocery business from scratch with the get big fast mantra and a $1 billion infrastructure, an established high-street grocer was building a viable online service. In 2001, the same year that Webvan folded, the established UK retailer Tesco reported that its online grocery service, Tesco.com, now reached 94 per cent of the UK population and had made sales of £146 million that year, a 76 per cent rise on the previous year. A small loss of £3 million was discounted as the cost of new facilities.[38] In contrast with the get big fast from scratch approach that had utterly failed with Webvan, Tesco had been making incremental changes and tests to develop Internet retail since 1996.[39] The Net, Tesco proved, did not change everything, or at least did not do so overnight.

A number of high-profile collapses were typified by brash, frivolous spending of investors' funds. Boo.com, a European fashion retailer, overspent on everything from executive luxuries to basic costs of operation. That it collapsed said nothing about the new economy that was not already known in conventional business. Other firms had simply miscalculated the fundamentals of profit and loss. One oft cited dot com failure was the company Pets.com. It launched in November 1998 and was quickly followed by a number of high-profile competitors: Petstore.com in May 1999, Petopia.com in July 1999, Petsmart.com in July 1999 and PetPlanet.com in September 1999.[40] Internet users in dire need of pet food would not be in want. None of these sites had a proven business model. A core problem was that the item in which most prospective customers might have an interest was pet food, which is commonly available at physical outlets. There simply was no compelling need for customers to shop on Pets.com or any other online pet store. Delivering the product not only imposed additional costs on the company but imposed a time delay on the customer's receipt of the goods. Yet despite the overcrowded market and the shaky logic of its business model, Pets.com raised $82.5 million in its IPO in February 2000, only to cease trading nine months later. Pets.com, as with all the get big fast dot-coms, spent massive amounts on advertising. As the post mortems established, many of the companies that failed were the best known. They had successfully built brands, but not businesses.[41]

<129>

Even when a start-up had a sound idea and a viable business plan, the adjustment, as businesses tried to calibrate their model to benefit from the Internet, led to many wrong turns. For a start, the consumer network was in its infancy. An October 1996 survey by AT&T showed that 67 per cent of sites were effectively off the Net for at least one hour per day because of overload.[42] Some faced technical problems that reflected nothing about the Internet so much as the short-term teething problems of the new and rapidly developed systems to deliver services and conduct commerce upon it. In 2000 Toys'R'Us was fined $1.5 million for failing to live up to its promise to deliver orders made through its site before Christmas.[43] It subsequently abandoned its own system of extensive servers and signed a ten-year deal with Amazon through which Amazon would handle the Internet technicalities.

A canny investor recalling the early decades of the automobile industry might have been better prepared for the bubble. Of the three thousand automobile businesses established between 1900 and 1925, only three survived into the modern era.[44] The dot-com boom had provoked such a burst of entrepreneurial activity that in 1999 one in twelve adult Americans surveyed apparently said they were developing a new business.[45] The candid assessment of one dot-com entrepreneur, the founder of GovWorks.com, encapsulated many of the faults of the failed start-ups. GovWorks moved too quickly with too little planning.[46] It had promoted 'unattainable financial expectations which disappointed our investors and board members'. Pursuing GBF, it had marketed to 'create brand instead of revenue' and 'marketed to investors, Wall St and the press instead of the customer'. Believing that the Net had changed everything, it 'didn't bring in experienced personnel and advisors early enough, did not create sustainable organizational structures'.[47] As Andrew Groove, Chairman of Intel, argued:

> The Internet doesn't change everything. It doesn't change supply and demand. It doesn't magically allow you to build businesses by turning investors' money into operating expenses indefinitely. The money always runs out eventually – the Internet doesn't change that.[48]

The Internet had not changed everything, but it had changed much. As the dust settled in the aftermath of the dot-com crash, it would become clear what the Net's true business potential was.

Fredrick Taylor and post/pre industrial artisans

Despite the carnage of 2000 and 2001, many dot-com start-ups survived. More in fact than might have been supposed: the number of companies folding in five years or less was no greater during the dot-com period than it had been during speculative bubbles driven by the advent of canals and railways.[49] Hasty investors had borne the financial brunt of change and the dot-com hype had laid solid foundations for real growth. Among the public, understanding of e-commerce began to permeate. Whereas in 1995 few had ever heard of e-commerce, by 1997 Amazon had a customer database of over one million names, addresses and credit cards.[50] With experience came trust: credit cards, the lifeblood of online sales, were more readily submitted to websites by customers who previously might have been reticent to entrust their details to companies with which they had never physically interacted. In the years after the dot-com bust the proportion of us retail conducted over the Internet continued to grow steadily, from just over half a per cent in 2000 to 3.4 per cent in 2008.[51] As the dust cleared, fundamental lessons were revealed about the Internet and the nature of enterprises that would prosper on it. Some market conditions had indeed changed, and changed dramatically. Geography and people were behaving differently in the emerging digital environment. So were smart organizations.

The tailored suit has a long history. The coat, waistcoat and breeches gradually became the gentleman's mainstay from the English Restoration in the 1660s, when elaborate dress fell out of favour at European courts. Embroidery and silk died out from the middle of the eighteenth century. Wool became the norm, particularly in circles with a democratic axe to grind. Benjamin Franklin made a splash at the French court by turning up in the sombre suit of a Quaker and, more rustic still, he wore his own hair rather than a wig.[52] In the wake of the French Revolution, even the nobility lost its enthusiasm for aristocratic dress. By this time the plain linen three-piece suit already marked the height of gentlemen's fashion in England. The gentleman's suit proved remarkably enduring and remained the mainstay of leading gentlemen from Charles II's reign in the seventeenth century to James Bond and Gordon Gekko in the late twentieth. Then, in 1996, Marc Andreessen, founder of Netscape, the company that had made the biggest IPO in

<131>

history the year before, appeared on the cover of *Time* magazine sitting on a throne. He wore a polo shirt and jeans and wore no socks or shoes. With the arrival of these strange, young leaders of the new digital industry, three centuries of the suit were forgotten. Google went as far as to include the maxim 'You can be serious without a suit' in their corporate philosophy.[53] Alan Levenson, the photographer who shot Andreessen for the cover of *Business Week* in 1998, recalled that the dot-com executives were not quite like artists or musicians, but they were 'more loose than other business people'.[54] Business culture, as Andreessen's bare feet told *Time* readers in 1996, was about to change.

The Internet had changed the nature of companies within as much as it had changed marketplace conditions without. Traditional hierarchical organizations, the logic went, were in deep trouble. At the heart of the new thinking lay a fundamental irony: the new model of management was in some respects a return to the pre-industrial artisan system, a return to the days before Frederick Taylor. Taylor, the father of management consulting, created a new, scientific approach to management in the early 1900s. In his book, *The Principles of Scientific Management*, he argued that apprenticeships and the irregular word-of-mouth process by which workmen in the pre-industrial age learned their trades created an unmanageable workforce of artisans. Managers, incapable of understanding the full breadth of individual skills within their workforce, were forced to rely on the initiative and experience of the workers.[55] Managers were forced to use special incentives such as improved conditions to gain their workers' goodwill. The answer, Taylor suggested, was the standardization and centralization of the accumulated lore that had been passed down from generations of apprentice workmen. Best practice studies could codify all workers' knowledge into standardized procedures. Personal initiative would then become immaterial and the artisan workforce would simply become directed labour. White-collar managers, now fully versed in the procedures for every task, would instruct and supervise the workforce in every specific task.[56] Taylor's model, though it set the stage for management and specialization, had become outmoded by the 1970s as lower levels of management and units within organizations were given increasing levels of responsibility. Only during the 'new economy' did initiative within organizations revert back to the level of the individual. Workers at the beginning of the new century would be artisans again, as they had been at the beginning of the last one, albeit digital ones.

The dot-coms like Amazon, where the old hierarchies were less pronounced, were widely thought to represent a new paradigm suited to the new, fast economy. The disjointed, varied wisdom of employees was no longer a threat to management. The lowest atomic unit of effective creativity within an organization became the individual employee, not the unit, or the division. Companies would prosper or fail on the strength of their employees' initiative and how well superiors could leverage the wisdom of their workforce.[57] The system of incentives that Taylor had railed against was back too. During the dot-com boom workers were offered stock options as incentives at levels so unprecedented that the Federal Reserve could not account for them in its tax intake.[58]

The empowerment of digital artisans owed much to the collaborative, irreverent hacker ethos that had evolved at MIT's RLE laboratory in the 1960s and '70s in which people at the bottom of the hierarchy could contribute at the highest level. The MIT hackers were driven by the compulsion to better understand and optimize software and computers. In the service of their compulsion, conventions of property, privacy and hierarchy were immaterial. The hackers violently reacted against any hint of bureaucratic intervention or central control. The idea that such a hacker workforce could be managed in any rigid sense was untenable. Some of this approach transferred to the private sector by way of the Digital Equipment Corporation, which spun off from the MIT Lincoln Laboratory in 1957. Employees at DEC were given leeway to 'do the right thing' and pursue approaches as they saw fit, even if their managers disagreed.[59]

This bottom-up approach to management was codified at Google where the '70–20–10' rule encouraged workers to expand their roles and liberated them from the narrow constraints of specific duties. Employees would spend 70 per cent of their time working on the task at hand, 20 per cent on exploring new related ideas, and 10 per cent on ideas bordering on the crazy.

Like the hackers, the businesses of the 'new economy' embraced an open approach to inputs and organization. This new approach was what management gurus Tapscott and Caston had called 'open networked organization' in the early 1990s, and what one Harvard Business School professor more vaguely called 'permeability' almost a decade later.[60] The example of the open-source movement in the 1990s and of Wikipedia in the 2000s had provided working proof that useful ideas and collaboration could come from virtually any source.

Perhaps the most dramatic example of the dramatic shift towards the open, collaborative approach within organizations that had previously been bastions of closed hierarchies is that which occurred within the US intelligence community from 2005 onwards. The 9/11 Commission reported that insufficient information sharing had contributed to national vulnerability. In 2005 the chief technology officer for the Central Intelligence Agency's Centre for Mission Innovation, D. Calvin Andrus, wrote an influential paper titled 'The Wiki and the Blog: Toward a Complex Adaptive Intelligence Community' in which he made the case that a Wiki system shared between the various intelligence agencies would solve the problems facing the intelligence community:

> Once the Intelligence Community has a robust and mature Wiki and Blog knowledge sharing web space, the nature of Intelligence will change forever. This is precisely the prescription we are looking for.[61]

By 2009, when *Time* magazine covered 'Intellipedia', the product of Andrus's concept, it had 'grown to a 900,000-page magnum opus of espionage, handling some 100,000 user accounts and 5,000 page edits a day'.[62]

<PHASE III>
THE EMERGING ENVIRONMENT

<10>
Web 2.0 and the Return
to the Oral Tradition

In keeping with much of the Internet's most popular terminology, the term Web 2.0 gives a nod to technical nerd-speak. The '2.0' evokes the programmer's convention of appending version numbers after the title of a piece of software to distinguish it from previous releases of the same package. Coined by Dale Dougherty in 2004, it signalled that the Web had entered a new phase. Release 1.0 had been revolutionary but limited. Most web-browsing software only allowed users to view what others had put on the Web. In many cases the early sites themselves were simply another way to broadcast information to an audience rather than a revolutionary mechanism through which audience members could talk back to the content producer and to each other. Ted Nelson, the creator of hypertext, had criticized www as just 'another imitation of paper'.[1] The developers of the first browsers were totally oblivious to the benefits of extending their browser software into editors, programs that could let any person create their own www documents. Robert Cailliau, who worked with Berners-Lee on the www at CERN, recalls that 'it was impossible to convince the programmers that the Web as a medium needed a different tool for creation of content, with different paradigms and different handles'.[2] The two-way potential of the www was not clear to individuals whose thinking had been shaped by explicitly one-way communications such as television and radio. Web 2.0 would correct this. The Web would become more than an imitation of paper. Yet in the aftermath of the dot-com collapse, a degree of suspicion, even cynicism, was understandable and probably necessary. Web 2.0, however, was the real deal. Release '2.0' would be revolutionary.

<137>

Saint Jerome and the perpetual beta

The dramatic growth of sites such as Wikipedia shows the increasing dominance that users rather than professional content producers have over the medium. From just under twenty thousand articles in January 2002, the English language version of Wikipedia grew to over 2.5 million by January 2009.[3] Virtually every single entry was created, edited, shortened or lengthened by people on the Internet who were not Wikipedia staff. Users, random and anonymous, are in control of the text. The result is that information is becoming increasingly plastic and malleable. In 1994, anticipating Web 2.0 by ten years, John Perry Barlow wrote 'information is an activity, not a noun'. 'As in an oral tradition', Barlow wrote, 'digitized information has no "final cut"'.[4] The interplay of ideas among people on Internet forums, the constant re-editing of Wikipedia entries and comments by visitors responding to blog postings all show the new plasticity of information. This is particularly so in controversial matters. Wikipedia proves the point. The Wikipedia article on George W. Bush has been edited 40,723 times as of 15 June 2009.[5] Heated editorial battles have centred around his idiosyncratic pronunciation of the word nuclear, his National Guard service and whether it is appropriate to categorize him under the heading 'alcoholic'.[6] The Wikipedia entry on George W. Bush may in fact be one of the most edited pieces of text ever distributed in human history.

The dawning era of plastic information has a surprising historical precedent. In AD 382 Pope Damascus commissioned Jerome to compile a bible that came to be known as the 'Vulgate' edition.[7] For centuries the Vulgate was the mainstay of the Roman Church. In 1546, almost 1,200 years after Jerome was commissioned to write it, his Vulgate was acknowledged as the only true bible of the Church. The Council of Trent decreed 'that no one is to dare, or presume to reject [Jerome's Vulgate edition] under any pretext whatever'.[8] In other words, the full weight of Rome was behind this particular version of text, and none but the bravest should consider deviating from it. Yet in the absence of the right technology it was impossible to relay accurate information across Christendom for a millennium by relying on manual transcription. Even a text of the Bible's importance, whose content underpinned the faith of a continent and was maintained by a centralized church and a cohort of highly disciplined monks, suffered the toll of generations of human error. Before the invention of the printing press the reproduc-

< 138 >

tion of information was unreliable and embellishments standard. Thus, even as the Council of Trent made its decree, the scholar Erasmus complained that there were as many different versions of Jerome's Vulgate as there were copies of the Bible.[9] Only the arrival of the printing press with movable type and printer's ink from the 1440s could allow faithful reproduction of the text. Gutenberg's press introduced a period of immutable information that extended into the twentieth century. Technologies such as commercial broadcast radio from the 1920s and television from the 1930s onwards merely continued the status quo of immutable information that Gutenberg had established.

The Internet, however, is different to the printing press, and to radio and television. At its very essence, the technology driving the Internet was designed to be open to further adaptation by users. Even the protocols that govern the communications of machines and networks were designed to be plastic and malleable. According to Steve Crocker:

> The architecture is open. We very deliberately viewed the protocols as a beginning, not an end, and we designed them fully expecting that others would create additional protocols, and that they could do so without having to go through an approval process.[10]

Web 2.0 takes this approach to its logical conclusion: information and content on the Internet are plastic and mutable, open-ended and infinitely adaptable by users. Perhaps plastic information is in fact a return to normality. The era of immutable information from Gutenberg's press to the TV set may have been the anomaly in the broad span of human existence. Elaborating on the concept of Web 2.0 in 2004, Tim O'Reilly outlined a new approach to software development that exemplified the plasticity of information.[11] The audience he was speaking to was familiar with the conventional software development cycle of progressive versions, from the earliest pre-alpha to the penultimate beta version that is released for testing before the final release candidate. Yet now, O'Reilly said, software should never progress beyond the penultimate beta stage. Instead it should constantly incorporate ideas and refinements from the global community of Internet users. Thanks to Web 2.0 there could be no final cut, no definitive version. The input of the empowered online audience of users would enrich those products that remained flexible. Software, and much else besides, would remain

<139>

in 'perpetual beta', like Jerome's Vulgate before it. Software, media and information would all be to some degree under the sway of the audience.

There had been false dawns of audience empowerment in the past. In the late 1960s and during the 1970s, cable TV appeared to promise a new era of media less fixed to the mainstream and in which there would be more outlets for expression from different voices. J.C.R. Licklider coined the term 'narrowcasting' in 1967[12] to define a future type of broadcast that appeals not to mass audiences but to individual viewers. In 1968, two major reports – a study commissioned by the Mayor of New York and one undertaken by Under Secretary of State Eugene Rostow for the President – both reported myriad opportunities and benefits from the extension of cable. The FCC in 1968 was infected with the same enthusiasm. It believed that the deployment of co-axial TV cable could allow many, many things, including 'special communications . . . to reach particular neighborhoods or ethnic groups . . . the provision of a low cost outlet for political candidates, advertising, amateur expression'.[13] In short, cable appeared to offer a more centrifugal form of television.

It delivered only partially. From the 1940s onwards a plurality of local television had sprung up in rural parts of America where community antenna television connected to cable allowed entrepreneurs to start up small broadcasters. Yet from the late 1960s a handful of larger television companies began to buy up the small fry and dominate the medium. Perhaps, unsurprisingly, jaded observers in the mid-1990s greeted the hype surrounding the www with a degree of cynicism.[14] Yet the Web revolution was real. Media was now changing. There was tangible proof.

The online audience is less content than the TV audience was simply to be a passive spectator of entertainment created by media professionals, or information delivered from hierarchical structures such as governments or newspapers. Throughout 2006 the number of people in the US who visited websites that relied on users to upload the bulk of their content, such as YouTube, Wikipedia or Facebook, had grown by 100 per cent.[15] At the same time the number of new Internet subscribers had grown by only 2 per cent. A Pew survey reported at the end of 2007 that 64 per cent of online teens in the US had created and uploaded photos, artwork or videos to the Internet.[16] Of the fifty most popular websites in the world at the beginning of 2009, 24 were user

< 140 >

driven.[17] Of the remaining 26, sixteen were merely portal or search sites
that link to other sites, and only ten are what could be considered one-
to-many, non-user-driven sites such as CNN.com or Microsoft.com.
The viewing public, who had been passive recipients of television and
radio broadcast for most of the twentieth century, were transforming
themselves into the masters of content. On the Web the user was
now king.

User-driven nerd norms

Among the first popular user-driven websites was the classified adver-
tisements site Craigslist.com, established in 1995. It evolved from an
e-mail newsletter that Craig Newmark regularly circulated among
friends with notices of events in San Francisco. The e-mail then became
a website where anyone could post items of interest such as upcoming
events, personals ads or items for sale. The website grew and grew. It
attracts more than 20 billion page views per month[18] and is among the
top fifty most viewed websites in the world. According to one reckoning, it attracts more visits than either eBay or Amazon.com, which have
sixteen thousand and twenty thousand employees respectively.[19] Its
users self-publish more than 50 million new local classified ads in 550
cities in more than fifty countries for everything from events to second-
hand cars to dating each month.[20] Yet for all its scale, the site required
no venture capital, has no advertising budget and has a staff of only
thirty. What is the secret of Craigslist's success?

Underlying its success are two characteristics that perfectly fit the
digital culture. First, it is user driven at a deep level. Users of Craigslist
do more than simply contribute ads. To some extent they have control
of the site on matters both small and large. Small matters include
policing the site's content. If, for example, enough users flag a notice
they believe should be removed, it is automatically dropped. Users
also have a say in issues of strategic importance. Whether Craigslist
expands into a new city, for example, depends on how many requests
it receives to do so. Moreover, with no advertising, the rate of growth
in activity in the new city is as fast as the users in that city want it to be.

The second characteristic is the site's adherence to what its founder
calls 'nerd values'. The site is wary of commercialization. Its sole revenue
stream is that it charges fees for job ads in ten cities, for brokered apartment listings in New York City, and, where legally required, for listings

<141>

related to prostitution. Newmark is cautious about commercialization and expansion:

> People are really good at telling whether you're doing so through an honest intent of connecting with the community, of trying to connect with other people, or whether you're just trying to make a lot of money right away.[21]

As Jim Buckmaster, Craigslist CEO, said in an interview:

> Companies looking to maximize revenue need to throw as many revenue-generating opportunities at users as they will tolerate. We have absolutely no interest in doing that, which I think has been instrumental to the success of craigslist.[22]

This is the lesson that Carter & Siegel, the first commercial spammers, learned in 1994.[23] They had broken elementary rules of Internet conduct. Within days the couple were receiving death threats.[24] They remained oblivious, as they later wrote:

> Those who buy into the myth that Cyberspace is a real place also believe that this illusory locale houses a community, with a set of laws, rules, and ethics all its own. Unfortunately, the perceived behavior codes of Cyberspace are often in conflict with [real world] laws.[25]

(As it turned out, real world rules had been broken somewhere. Carter was disbarred by the Supreme Court of Tennessee in 1997 for the spamming and other misconduct.)

'Nerd Values' are immune to a rigid definition. Trust is the key. As Kevin Kelly, the founding editor of *Wired*, observed, the value of physical goods inevitably diminished as industrialization had made them ever easier to reproduce. In the digital economy it would be things other than the physical that would be of value:

> Those things that cannot be copied will become the true currency, the true sources of wealth. What cannot be copied? Trust. Authenticity. Immediacy. Presence. Experience. Relationships.[26]

< 142 >

Newmark's nerd values and the degree of user control on Craigslist enabled it to become a community of users who trust the service. Larry Brilliant, one of the founders of The Well, remarked on Craigslist's 'authentic' feel.[27] This may be because Newmark views the site as a public service, as 'a commons in the sense that we're providing a public service'.[28] As more users start to use the site regularly, they begin to benefit from network effects or what might better be called community benefits: more users put up ads and notices, more users check ads and notices, more people maintain the relevance of the site by removing spam, which generates more expectation of finding useful results, and thereby attracts new users and more regularity among existing users, which in turn produces more varied, more granular and competitive options among the listings, which attracts more users. Nerd values give Craigslist, which has no advertising budget, what the GBF dot-coms could not buy: a community of regular users built around the site.

Central to this are the community benefits accrued within Craigslist from the input of individual users and the community of their peers.

The peer-driven Internet

When he established *Philosophical Transactions* in 1665, Henry Oldenburg not only founded the world's first academic journal but also created the process of peer-review to maintain the standard of its articles. Authors who wanted to publish in his journal would have to run the gauntlet of a review by other academics at the Royal Society. According to a more recent formulation, peer-review is 'a critical, judicious evaluation performed by one's equals'.[29] In practice, peer-review gives academics the power to approve or reject new developments in their respective areas[30] and, it seems fair to say, belongs to the world of academic nitpicking. Yet peer-review also describes the open, democratic process by which information on the Internet is filtered by its readers. Our peers influence the review and reception of information and media content on the Internet, whether feedback on an eBay seller or a positive comment on the blog of a presidential candidate.

If commerce had become a conversation, it had become a busy one. As of 31 March 2008 eBay members worldwide have left more than 7 billion feedback comments for one another regarding their eBay transactions.[31] On an Internet where the Internet user is increasingly the creator or critic of content, word-of-mouth peer recommendation has a greater authority than normal one-to-many advertising. For YouTube, peer-review was an important contributor to its growth. Only after its introduction of comments and peer rating of videos did the site begin to attract large numbers of visitors. Yet peer-review presented a challenge to other enterprises. Amazon took a significant risk when it decided to allow users to write negative reviews under books on its site. Conventional practice would have been to put an indiscriminately positive spin on all items. As Jeff Bezos told *Business Week*, allowing peer-review seemed counter-intuitive to some:

> When we first did it, we got letters from publishers saying, 'Maybe you don't understand your business. You make money when you sell things.' Our point of view is . . . negative reviews are helpful in making purchase decisions. So it's a very customer-centric point of view. Negative reviews will be helpful for customers, and that will ultimately sell more products than if you tried to cherry-pick the reviews.[32]

By allowing users to write negative reviews, Amazon effectively put the fortunes of each retail item in its customers' hands. To at least a small extent, this was handing over the profitability of the company. The leap of faith paid off. Amazon became not just a place to buy things but to find them reviewed by impartial critics as well.

Across the Internet, word of mouth among users became the force that began to sift the good from the dross from the early 2000s, much as peer-review had done in academic circles since the mid-1660s. Kevin Kelly lamented that:

> As the Web expands in scope to include everything, the best gets overwhelmed . . . I want someone I trust to say to me: 'I've seen all the stuff, and I've used most of it, and this is the one you want.' I don't usually find that on the Web. First, trust is in short supply, and second, comparative evaluation is in short supply.[33]

Word of mouth became a collaborative sifting and categorization, a 'folksonomy' in other words.[34] As Nicholas Negroponte and Pattie Maes wrote in 1996, 'the noise of the Net is its beauty, and navigating this noise will become easier and easier because of electronic word of mouth'.[35] In 2003 Joshua Schracter founded 'Del.icio.us', a directory of bits and pieces of Web content that users had tagged with reference phrases to denote that it was of interest for one reason or another. Essentially, tagging became not only a way of categorizing content on the Internet, but also a way of maintaining a personal library of book-marked content and of finding like-minded people's tagged content. Del.icio.us displayed details of users who created each tag, and allowed other users to look at collections of tagged content in their libraries. All Web content could thus be rated by 'social bookmarking', according to how many users thought it was worth tagging, and could be categorized according to what tags were used. The user, therefore, is not only a creator of content but also an arbiter of what content is viewed by their peers.

Some advertisers, acknowledging the pivotal role of peer-review and user commendation, have begun to court influential bloggers to draw attention to their products. This is peer-to-peer, 'conversational' marketing. In 2007 the television series *Battlestar Galactica* sought to promote itself among its target market of science fiction enthusiasts and ran a press tour unlike any other, inviting prominent bloggers rather than print journalists to the studio for a tour of the sets and interviews with the cast. Similarly, Panasonic paid the expenses of a handful of bloggers to attend the annual Computer Electronics Show in Las Vegas in 2009 at which is was demonstrating new products in [36] Panasonic, while unable to moderate or influence what the bloggers would write about its products, was nonetheless assured of online coverage. According to one conversational marketing firm, this is called a 'sponsored conversation':

A sponsored conversation is a social media marketing technique in which brands provide financial or material compensation to bloggers in exchange for posting social media content about a product, service or website on their blog.[37]

It is interesting to consider that when combined with Google Ad-Words, a service that allows any individual to sell advertising space on their site through Google, the Internet now allows any individual in theory to make money based purely on how much other Internet users enjoy their content.

<145>

Collaboration, social networking and media

The elements of Web 2.0 (the perpetual beta, the increasing dominance of user-generated content, peer-review by other users) had empowered the individual computer user in a way that even the 1970s hippy groups could not have imagined as they railed against the IBM style of centralized, bureaucratic computing. The individual Internet user had become the atomic unit of creativity on the Internet. Yet something further was in prospect from 2001 onwards. The user had been empowered and now that empowerment would be built into something broader: mass-collaboration between users.

In 2004 an entrepreneur named Jimmy Wales wrote, 'Imagine a world in which every single person on the planet is given free access to the sum of all human knowledge. That's what we're doing.'[38] Half a century earlier, in 1945, the economist Friedrich Hayek had mulled over the problem of relying on imperfect knowledge to perform economic planning for a society. The conundrum was that the breadth of a society's knowledge was so vast and so fragmented among its disparate holders that no single mind could consider it.[39] A society was incapable of marshalling all the knowledge of its citizens by conventional means:

> We cannot expect that this problem will be solved by first communicating all this knowledge to a central board which, after integrating *all* knowledge, issues its orders. We must solve it by some form of decentralisation.[40]

Hayek was writing in defence of market capitalism as the best available solution since its pricing mechanism was effective in gathering information about scarcity from diverse sources across a society. Any more sophisticated method was not possible. In 1999, inspired by Hayek's article, Jimmy Wales decided to start a free, collaborative encyclopaedia. He had gleaned from Eric Raymond's study of Linux in 'the cathedral and the bazaar' that mass collaboration could work.[41] Within the Linux community, Linus's Law stipulated that more eyeballs produce fewer bugs. This could also apply, Wales believed, to an encyclopaedia of human knowledge:

< 146 >

The fact that it [Wikipedia] *is* open to everyone that makes a lot of these articles pretty good, and ever-improving, as we review and build on each other's work.[42]

Here was a price mechanism along the lines Hayek had discussed that worked not only for market information but for all kinds of information.

Yet before establishing Wikipedia, Wales had made a first attempt called 'Nupedia' in 2000 that failed. Rather than relying on the efforts of the community of unknown Internet users, Nupedia had an off-putting twelve-step procedure through which articles had to pass before appearing to the public, which included being vetted by a panel of experts.[43] This process was too arduous to attract widespread participation and Nupedia had few contributors and fewer articles. However, in January 2001, its editor, Larry Sanger, learned about a system called WikiWikiWeb that allowed Internet users to discuss documents and edit them collaboratively. Eight days later, on 10 January 2001, Wikipedia went online. It was intended only to feed draft articles to Nupedia, which would then process them according to its twelve-step procedure. Yet Wikipedia quickly overshadowed its parent encyclopaedia. Within fifteen days of its establishment it had 270 articles, and by the end of its first month it had 617.[44] By 1 January 2002, just under a year after its establishment, Wikipedia contained 19,700 articles.

This new site embodied the centrifugal imperative that had driven the hacker and GNU movement. As its policy and guidelines page announced:

Wikipedia lacks an editor-in-chief or a central, top-down mechanism whereby progress on the encyclopedia is monitored and approved. Instead, active participants monitor the recent changes page and make copyedits and corrections to the content and format problems they see. So the participants are both writers and editors.[45]

The WikiWikiWeb on which Wikipedia was built was developed in 1994 by Ward Cunningham, who had been inspired by the early 1980s Apple 'hypercard' program, a system of hypertext/hypermedia that predated the Web. Larry Sanger observed that the Wiki system promoted an open, decentralized approach to information:

<147>

wiki *software* does encourage . . . extreme openness and de-centralization: openness, since . . . page changes are logged and publicly viewable, and . . . pages may be further changed by any-one; de-centralization, because in order for work to be done, there is no need for a person or body to assign work, but rather, work can proceed as and when people want to do it. Wiki software also *dis*courages (or at least does not facilitate) the exercise of author-ity, since work proceeds at will on any page, and on any large, active wiki it would be too much work for any single overseer or limited group of overseers to keep up. These all became features of Wikipedia.[46]

Previous instances of collaboration such as the development of the ARPANET and Internet protocols and the development of the GNU and Linux software had required specialist knowledge. Wikipedia allows any individual within society to contribute to a common repository of knowledge. Their peers would then judge whether to alter and refine the entry.

There was some degree of governance in the Wiki system. Echoing the tone of the RFCs, Wikipedia initially featured a page called 'Rules To Consider' that proposed loose guidelines. These were enforced to the extent that users added their names behind them in support.[47] The first rule listed was 'Ignore all the rules', which underlined that the rules were flexible guidelines. Yet an increased degree of governance was required as Wikipedia became more popular. From October 2001, administra-tors were appointed from among the user community to act against abuse of the system. In 2004 the '3R' rule was introduced under which three reversions of the same material by the same user in one day would automatically block the user from accessing the site for a day. Articles that promoted a particularly large flood of edits could also be temporarily locked to allow heated arguments about their content to cool down before editing resumed. This feather-touch regulation of the site, however, kept control in the hands of its users. Peer-power rather than Nupedia's panel of experts would be the arbiter of quality, for better or worse. The results, uneven and spectacular, began to make Hayek's big idea more feasible.

In the early 2000s social networks emerged as the most popular pro-ducts of Web 2.0. This had been foreseen. At the beginning of the Web

< 148 >

1.0 years, and despite the hype then gathering around Mosaic, the first commercially successful web browser, its creator, Marc Andreessen, knew that web browsing alone was not the main event of the www. He predicted a decade before the social networking boom that 'the applications that are going to be successful over the next five to ten years are the ones that link people'.[48] A remarkable statement perhaps, from the man who brought Web 1.0 to the masses, but it should have come as no surprise. The long-term trend in the development of networking had been that it facilitated the establishment of communities. In the 1970s ARPANET administrators had been shocked by the popularity of e-mail and discussion lists. In the 1980s much of home-computer networking had revolved around online communities such as The Well and the BBSS. With the invention of the www it was perhaps only a matter of time before a new wave of online communities evolved to exploit it.

Thus in January 1997 a young entrepreneur named Andrew Weinreich established the first social network. It was called sixdegrees.com, and it allowed users to build a personal network of their friends by entering the e-mail addresses of people they knew. Each person's network would grow as new users added the e-mail addresses of yet more users. Yet though this was the model on which social networks would continue to be based years later, something was missing. Sixdegrees was virtually text only and lacked the streams of photographs that users uploaded of their friends, and which would drive later social networks.[49] Social networking came into its own half a decade later when cheap digital cameras and faster Internet connections became available to consumers. In contrast the early sixdegrees.com was virtually text only. This was a problem so acute that the board members of sixdegrees.com considered hiring a hundred interns to manually digitize photographs submitted in hard copy to display on users' accounts.[50] This, among other problems, was fatal. Yet though six - degrees ceased operations at the end of 2001, it was a sign of things to come.

In March 2003 Friendster went online, heralding a new wave of social networks. It featured photos and attracted a large following. It was founded by Jonathan Abrams, who had previously founded Hotlinks, one of the first social bookmarking sites. By June, Friendster had 835,000 members, rising to two million only two months later.[51] Despite its initial popularity, Friendster was hampered by boardroom difficulties and intractable engineering problems. Friendster was quickly

<149>

surpassed by MySpace, a competitor that was set up later in 2003 to follow Friendster's example. MySpace's growth was yet more dramatic: its millionth user profile was created in 2006, and attracted in the region of sixty million visitors per month by September 2008.[52]

As Andreessen predicted, linking people was the new focus of the Web. In late 2003, venture capital investment in social networking sites including Friendster signalled a resurgence of confidence in the Web in the wake of the dot-com collapse. Rupert Murdoch, who had been chastened when News Corp's New Media Division folded in 2001, nonetheless bought MySpace in 2005 for $580 million. Social networks, the money believed, were the way of the future.

From 2004 onwards, refined web technologies allowed users to produce and distribute not only text and photos but video too. Underlying the more complex Web 2.0 websites was an array of technologies known as AJAX (AJAX stands for 'Asynchronous JavaScript and XML').[53] AJAX allowed users to do far more than simply read websites. In effect, it extended websites into usable programs, turning the Web into a computing platform and transforming website readers into producers of content ranging from text to video. Social networking sites using AJAX were able to evolve into platforms where friends could play games against each other online. Also from the same period, faster 'broadband' Internet connections were replacing the far slower telephone line 'dial-up' connections. In tandem, digital cameras, experimental since the early 1970s, had become widespread consumer items. Internet users began to create and watch amateur videos with gusto, and broadband connections to the Internet allowed them to upload them. Foremost among the new venues for user-created videos was the site 'YouTube', which launched its beta version to the public in May 2005. By mid-2007, YouTube users were uploading six hours of video every minute.[54] By mid-2009 they were uploading twenty hours of video every minute. Every video could be copied, rated and tagged by their peers. On the Internet, the user was king, and the selection and promotion of content was peer-driven. The impact that this would have as culture and news moved beyond TV and print media and gravitated towards the Internet would be profound. It would in fact change the landscape of human media and culture.

< 150 >

<11>
New Audiences, the Fourth Wall and Extruded Media

Disruptive distribution

Since Edison's first recording of 'Mary had a little lamb' on a tinfoil cylinder phonograph in 1877, the recording industry has undergone successive crises of technical transition: first from cylinder to disc, then from acoustic to electric recording, to magnetic tape, to cassette, to 5-inch compact disc in 1982, and to MP3 in 1992. The expansion of Internet access among PC users from the mid-1990s may have produced the most seismic shifts yet.

In 1996 the song 'Until it sleeps' by Metallica became the first track to be illegally copied from CD and made available on the Internet as a compressed MP3 file. A pirate nicknamed 'NetFrack' was responsible.[1] He announced the MP3 revolution in music piracy to *Affinity*, an underground electronic magazine:

I've thought of the idea of somehow pirating, music . . . The problem in the past . . . was [hard disk] space . . . We eliminated the size constraints. We use a new format to compress our music. The MP3 format.[2]

MP3 music compression, NetFrack announced, could turn a 50MB copy of song from a +CD into a 3 or 4MB file, and turn hours per download into minutes. By 2008, according to the International Federation of the Phonographic Industry, 95 per cent of all music downloaded on the Internet would be illegal.[3]

Before sound compression was invented, sound waves generated by human speech were generally relayed along telephone cable as analogue waves and degraded in quality the further they travelled. Recorded

<151>

sound could be digitized using pulse-code modulation (PCM), which records a digital copy of the analogue signal by taking samples of it at regular intervals that can then be reproduced indefinitely and perfectly. However, the problem was that digitization requires the transfer of so much data that standard telephone lines could not carry it. In the 1970s a researcher at Erlangen–Nuremberg University in Germany named Dieter Seitzer had begun researching the problem of relaying digitized speech across standard phone lines. Yet even as he and his students worked a new generation of ISDN lines and fibre-optic cabling was introduced that was sufficient to carry digitized speech. Seitzer turned his attention to the transmission of high-quality music, which remained beyond the new system's capacity to transmit.

One of his students, Karlheinz Brandenburg, approached the problem using psychoacoustics, the same discipline that had first introduced Licklider and BBN to computer networking. Modern microphones are capable of picking up a range of frequencies far beyond the human ear's threshold of audibility. Humans hear sound between 20 Hz and 20,000 Hz and are incapable of deciphering sounds masked by other sounds occurring at the same time, or, depending on the sound, immediately after.[4] Brandenburg realized surplus sound beyond the threshold of audibility could be excluded from recordings to produce high-quality recording using less data. In 1987 Eureka, an intergovernmental European research fund, supported further development of digital sound encoding at Erlangen–Nuremberg University, now partnered and lead by the Fraunhofer Institute for Integrated Circuits. In 1989 Brandenburg submitted his PHD thesis on 'optimum coding in the frequency (OCF) domain', which contributed to an encoding system that could allow the transmission of music in real time at reasonable quality over telephone lines. The Moving Picture Experts Group (MPEG), a part of the International Standards Organization (ISO), adopted a refined version of the OCF system under the none-too-catchy name 'ISO MPEG Layer 3' in December 1991. MPEG 3 was initially used to relay sound footage between TV and radio facilities. By 1995, however, PCs were becoming fast enough to decode MPEG 3 files. An internal staff poll at Fraunhofer decided on a new type of file for the PC that would use MPEG 3. They called it 'MP3'.[5] To demonstrate MP3 to PC users, Fraunhofer released a demonstration program called 'WinPlay3' which, as a sign of things to come, was promptly illegally copied by a student in Australia.[6] The doors to Internet music piracy were cast open.

Within two years the combination of more powerful PCs, free MP3 software and faster Internet speeds made music piracy a widespread phenomenon. By May 1997 a *USA Today* headline announced that 'sound advances open doors to bootleggers'.[7] In March 1998 a Korean firm released the first portable MP3 player, the 'MPMan F10', which had a capacity of 32MB, sufficient for only eight or nine tracks. Then in September 1998 Diamond Multimedia released the first popular MP3 device, 'The Rio'. Diamond sweetened the deal for consumers by working with a new website called MP3.com which agreed to provide music to Rio owners. Immediately, the Recording Industry Association of America (RIAA) launched an injunction against the manufacture of the Rio on the grounds that the device violated the US Home Recordings Act. After extensive legal action it was determined at the US Court of Appeals in 1999 that the Rio was legal.[8] Now MP3 would become a consumer format.

As the RIAA v Diamond case was drawing to a close an undergraduate at Northeastern University named Shawn Fanning was busy developing software to simplify the process of acquiring illegal MP3s. Fanning, whose online nickname 'Napster' later became famous, was perfecting a new type of 'peer-to-peer' (P2P) software.[9] It was also called Napster, and it allowed Internet users to find and copy music easily. Napster was a decentralized system by which Napster users could search and download from each other's collections. Not only would Napster allow one to find music far more easily than illegal music sites that were constantly being shut down, it also included discussion tools to let users participate in online communities based on shared music tastes.[10] Napster quickly gained popularity on US university campuses where high-speed connections fuelled an explosion in music piracy. By the end of 1999 the RIAA had sued Napster and on 13 April 2000 the band Metallica, whose track had been the first ever MP3 pirated by NetFrack in 1996, also sued Napster, along with several universities whose networks had been used for downloading. In February 2001 the Napster service was forced to shut down after a year of legal battles. By this time the genie was out of the bottle.

MP3 was proliferating across the Internet and former Napster users had a choice of new services to choose from. In October 2001, the year Napster was shut down, Apple computer launched its first 'iPod' MP3 player. The 5GB iPod had well over a thousand times the capacity of the first MP3 player three years before, allowing listeners to carry '1,000

< 153 >

songs in your pocket'.[11] Former users of Napster drifted off to a range of successor services. Many adopted a new technology called 'BitTorrent', a refined peer-to-peer system used among the Linux community from 2001 to transfer large programs.[12] By simultaneously downloading different parts of the file from many users, BitTorrent dramatically sped up the rate of transfer while lowering the load on individual users' connections. Like the segmented data packets invented by Paul Baran and Donald Davies at the dawn of digital networking in the 1960s, the BitTorrent method of segmenting large downloads into chunks from different users was very efficient. The more popular a given file became the more people could 'seed' parts of it and the faster it could be downloaded by a 'leecher'.

As more Internet users began to connect using 'broadband' speeds, television programmes and popular films became standard fodder for pirates using BitTorrent. Now not only the music industry but film and TV were grievously threatened by the Internet. NetFrack, who had hailed the advent of 4MB music file in 1996, could now pirate an entire movie, a thousand times larger, less than a decade later. The film and music industry watched aghast as entire movies began to circulate around the Internet in advance of their commercial release.

Choice and availability, assertive audiences and extruded content

Digital distribution, legal or illegal, gave audiences two revolutionary things that broadcast and physical retail distribution had not: choice and availability. Since audio content is far less data-intensive than video it was the music industry that first experienced the consequences of the Internet. The difference is sales figures for the top ten albums in the US in 1999 and 2008 show the emerging media trends. Between 1999 and 2008 sales of the top ten albums fell from over $54.6 million to $18.7 million.[13]

2008 marked a peak of four consecutive years of growth in US digital music sales: $1.5 billion in 2008, up from $1.4 billion in 2007, $1.2 billion in 2006 and $1 billion in 2005.[14] In 2008 the international digital music business grew by roughly a quarter, to a value of $3.7 billion.[15] By 2008 the proportion of music purchased through digital channels had reached 20 per cent of total sales.[16] In April 2008 Apple announced that the 'iTunes Store', its online digital music outlet, had become the largest music retailer in the US, surpassing Walmart, the dominant physical retail chain.[17] As album sales declined, music labels began to sell to niche markets and musicians started licensing their music in advertising, film and computer games.[18] Yet aside from diversification in distribution, music's move to digital had a deeper impact.

While album sales have contracted, consumer choice has expanded. In 2008 the US consumer purchased 1.1 billion individual digital tracks but only 66 million albums.[19] Online sales of individual music tracks grew by 27 per cent over the previous year.[20] The move to more music but fewer albums is due to the new choice and availability afforded by digital distribution. Before the Internet and the MP3 the distribution of music on physical media made albums far more economic to sell since an album of twelve tracks on a compact disc costs the same to distribute as only one track on the same disc. It was in the recording industry's interest to sell albums irrespective of whether every song on the album was of interest to the consumer. In much the same vein, consumers had to develop all 24 photos on a role of film in order to get a few good shots, and encyclopaedia publishers sold multiple volumes to a readership that in many cases wanted only specific items of trivia on demand.[21] In physical retail one often had to buy the dross to get the gem.

Aside from allowing the consumer to select the gem in isolation, digital consumption has broader, more profound cultural consequences. In the past TV and radio pushed content to the audience according to a best guess of what would appeal to the most people in order to generate the best advertising revenues. Physical retailers sought to satisfy the most possible mainstream consumers with the limited quantity of stock that they could physically store. In effect the pre-Internet constraints of push-broadcast and physical retail have reinforced the mainstream, the common cultural and commercial denominator. Because these constraints are far weaker on the Internet the mainstream will become far less important in the coming decades.

In 1968 Paul Baran, the inventor of the distributed packet-switch communications on which the Internet is based, foresaw a new era of consumers in the year 2000. He wrote of a new system of 'pull' advertising replacing the old model of 'push' advertising that had been 'designed for mass media, selling a few mass produced products'.[22] Indeed only ten years after 2000 the choice available to digital consumers is far greater than Baran could have envisaged. Digital audiences

<155>

with BitTorrent, iTunes, YouTube and many other channels at their disposal can pull whatever content they wish from wherever they choose and access it according to their own schedules. The move from push broadcast to pull download signals the end of conventional 'prime time' scheduling. If viewers can download and watch a given episode of a given TV series at will on their PC there is little prospect that they will wait until an appointed hour determined by a TV channel scheduler to do so on their TV. Nor will they necessarily have to sit through advertisement breaks to do so. They may also be less inclined to queue at a cinema box office to watch a film that they can download at home. In short, the audience member is becoming master of their own schedule.

Dramatic though this seems, this change has been building momentum for at least a decade and a half. Writing in the first ever edition of *Wired* in 1993, Nicholas Negroponte predicted a future when 'prime time is my time':

> The six-o'clock news can be not only delivered when you want it, but it also can be edited for you and randomly accessed by you. If the viewer wants an old Humphrey Bogart movie at 8:17 p.m., the telephone company will provide . . .[23]

Indeed, as early as 1983 Home Box Office executives considered, but did not pursue, providing stripped-down PCs to customers as set-top boxes to revolutionize pay-per-view TV.[24] The idea was that the home audience could choose what to watch from a wide selection, and could control when they would watch it. Earlier yet, in 1970, a former FCC commissioner, Nicolas Johnson, argued in his book *How To Talk Back to Your Television* that cable TV was the best hope of ending 'the tyranny of banal mass-audience programming'.[25] The cable revolution, for reasons that Johnson well understood, never happened and the mainstream stayed mainstream. Yet the choice and availability imagined by the visionaries of the abortive cable revolution may now, it seems, finally be realized. Niche tastes could be digitally served in a way they had never been physically. The first sign came from Amazon, and it had a rather surprising title.

In July 1995 the book *Fluid Concepts & Creative Analogies: Computer Models of the Fundamental Mechanisms of Thought* became the first item ever sold on Amazon.com.[26] Neither a catchy title nor a book aimed at a mainstream market, it reflected Amazon's focus on a 'the hard middle'.

This is the term coined by Jeff Bezos, Amazon's founder, for the market of low-cost, low-margin items that appeal only to a small niche. Much as retail stores stock mainstream, popular items due to the physical constraint of shelf capacity and rental cost, cinemas show only films for which there was a guaranteed local audience.[27] According to the 20:80 rule, 20 per cent of products make up 80 per cent of sales. This is yet another application of the 'Pareto principle', a vague but universal rule of thumb among economists that 20 per cent of factors produce 80 per cent of results. Yet on the Internet these physical constraints do not apply. In the sale of digital music on public jukeboxes, where distribution costs are very low, the 20:80 ratio flips to 98:2, with only 2 per cent of tracks not being played at least once a quarter.[28] As Chris Anderson recognized when he coined the phrase 'the long tail', unlimited choice is expanding demand.[29] While the most popular tracks remain popular, the 'long tail' of less popular tracks also appeals to certain niche audiences. With physical storage no longer a constraint, the long tail can be extended by stocking more and more unpopular tracks to appeal to yet more niche tastes. When iTunes launched in 2003 it had a target of selling one million songs in the first six months. By January 2005 it was selling a million songs every day.[30]

As Bezos told an interviewer, it would be uneconomic to find 'the right 15,000 people' to buy an archaic title if Amazon were a physical bookshop. Yet such titles now constitute the bulk of Amazon's sales.[31] The Internet had created a new and previously inaccessible market on the margins of the mainstream. Much as communities could, since the days of SF-Lovers on the ARPANET, draw together by common interest rather than proximity, consumers of common taste, no matter how niche, can now cluster around a preferred product. Producers of niche content can at last find viable markets.

User-driven content, and adaptation or criticism of professional media, is shattering the theatrical fourth wall. Yet not only are Internet users using Web 2.0 tools to filter professional media into personalized packages, they are also beginning to interact with professional media producers and articulate their preferences. Niche audiences with an interest in specific types of content are likely by virtue of their pronounced tastes to be sophisticated viewers. The more fractured an audience is, presumably the more informed a given audience segment is about a particular genre or topic. A TV viewer with a taste for black

<157>

and white cowboy TV series from the 1950s, for example, presumably has a deeper knowledge of this particular kind of content than the average viewer has of mainstream content. The more niche a type of content is the more specialized its audience. Moreover, the more niche an item of content is, the narrower its audience base and thus the more sensitive its producers may be to its audience's preferences. Where audiences are particularly fragmented, an increasingly assertive and discriminating niche audience will exert such force on media that it becomes malleable in the same manner as information in the era of the 'perpetual beta'. Assertive audiences will not only pull content, they will shape it. Niche content will be extruded through the die of audience preferences.

As with the SF-Lovers discussion list on ARPANET decades before, it was science fiction that showed how networks could be used in 2005: in this year one of the producers of the science fiction series *Battlestar Galactica* (2003–9) began a dialogue with his audience. The producer, Ron D. Moore, began to produce online commentaries on each episode in which he candidly explained narrative choices and production difficulties. This was part of an effort to court the online community, and interaction between the series creators and audience became regular and practical. By delving into the detail of plot and production issues Moore was educating his audience to become more sophisticated viewers. In return, fans regularly engaged with the producers through websites and blogs, suggesting directions in plot or ideas to develop. This two-way dynamic, where the content producer courts an audience and the audience contributes to the content, may result in increasingly sophisticated and finely tuned extruded content in the future.

The coming global media boom

The conditions for an unprecedented global media boom in the next decade are coming into alignment. First, devices and media that had previously been separate are now part of the great technological convergence of formats and platforms. The mobile phone is an immediate example. The first hand-held mobile phones were released in the US in 1983. These devices, such as the Motorola DynaTAC 8000x, were limited to making and receiving phone calls. Though mobile telephones capable of displaying video and images were prototyped by various companies in the 1990s, none could connect to the Internet until the

< 158 >

Sharp J-SH04 was released in Japan in 2001. Now standard mobile phones can handle e-mail, display satellite maps, play music and create and display video. Moreover, a second trend is creating the conditions for a global digital media boom. The global population of Internet users is growing, as is the bandwidth to deliver converged content to them. The global explosion of high bandwidth connections will create a truly global and massive market for digital media content, whether niche or mainstream.

Which media best prospers in this boom will be determined by adherence to one or more of two cardinal characteristics that have defined much of the Internet's development since the early 1970s: the empowerment of users with a high degree of control or authority; and the enabling of users to develop human relationships with other users and participate in communities. A prime example of the second is a computer game called *World of Warcraft*. Since its release in 2005 this game has built a steadily increasing following of loyal subscribers. 11.5 million people across the globe were paid subscribers as of December 2008. The subscription cost is not negligible: subscribers in the EU pay approximately €131.88 per year[32] and incur additional charges for services within the game such as the transfer of their personalized avatar from one continent in the game to another and for altering the character's appearance. All these costs are additional to the price of the soft ware and update packages required to run and expand the game, the latest of which sold 2.8 million copies worldwide on the very first day of its release in November 2008.[33] These are colossal figures for a new market that simply did not exist before the Internet. The secret of the game's enormous success is that players make a personal investment to small communities of other players whom they meet through the game. Players form guilds to go on combat raids or quests together. Strong communal bonds develop between guild members. They also become attached to their own virtual avatar, which they groom and upgrade as the game proceeds. The secret of *World of Warcraft*'s success capitalizes on the characteristics of the Internet – subscription, personalization and shared experience. Players build up their reputations slowly over many months, upgrading their characters and developing extensive social networks. In addition, a limited degree of customization is permitted by players of the game itself.

If *World of Warcraft* is an exemplar of the new era, the media of the coming boom may appear alien to those familiar with conventional media. Assertive audiences will use and extrude media rather than watch it. To understand the nature of the coming global media boom, reflect on the birth of break beat hip-hop music. In the early 1970s a high-rise apartment building on 1520 Sedgwick Avenue in New York's Bronx became the birthplace of a new culture, and a new style of editing and adapting music. Clive Campbell, aka 'Kool DJ Herc', a Jamaican-born resident, began playing records at events in and around the building. DJ Herc began to edit music on the go. He used a dual turntable system common to disco music, switching between two records of the same track to isolate and loop the instrumental percussive sections of funk music records to emphasize and repeat rhythmic beats. He and other Bronx DJs further developed the Jamaican practice of toasting, or speaking over the record. This new way of remixing records at all-night parties in the basketball and tennis courts of Bronx neighbourhoods in the early 1970s marked the birth of hip-hop. It was also an early example of popular user-driven innovation. The funk music that hip-hop re-edited was itself a fusion of rhythm and blues, soul and jazz. The hip-hop DJs who adapted this into something new, though performers themselves, were at a remove from the original creation of the music. Rather than musicians in the traditional sense, they were a new type of empowered user. The turntables of the Bronx, like the hackers, the homebrew clubs and the perpetual beta of Web 2.0, are an instance of an enabling technology and the human impulse to adapt and hack. The media that prospers in the digital age will be highly participatory. If, for example, the old quiz show format of the 1950s features in the coming years it will do so invigorated by the user-empowered culture born of the hip-hop scene that emerged in the Bronx in the early 1970s, and by the technology of Web 2.0 and the perpetual beta. In short, popular culture may become a game in which all listeners become participants and all viewers become designers.

The record industry can leverage the value in its back catalogue to transition to the digital era. Even though individual consumers no longer need to pay for music, which they can illegally download, the digital revolution has done nothing to negate the enormous cultural and monetary value that the recording industry holds in its back catalogues. The maturing computer game industry, for example, is still required to pay for the right to use the record industry's content. It also happens to be perfectly placed to sell music to the very people

< 160 >

that the recording industry is now unable to sell to directly, though in the form of a participatory experience. For example, the computer games *Guitar Hero* and *Rock Band*, in which the users participate to a limited degree in the performance, generated $1.6 billion in 2008 alone.[34] Computer games increasingly use a subscription based model that is immune to piracy, providing access to online communities and experiences. High street retail may be dead, but what can now be sold is the right to use, re-edit and perform popular music online. To enter the digital era the record industry should position itself for mergers or acquisitions with the computer game industry.

The daily me and the fourth estate

At the end of 2000 Amazon began to show a personalized welcome page that recommended books to each visitor based on that person's previous purchases. The technology to do this had been in development even before the commercialization of the Internet. In the early and mid-1990s, Pattie Maes's team at MIT developed 'agent' programs that could predict from a user's habits and preferences what actions the user was likely to take based on records of similar users' preferences.[35] This collaborative filtering, which could for example give a user suggestions about music they might like based on the tastes of other users with similar tastes, was rightly hailed as one of the most promising technologies of the mid-1990s.[36] This and other web technologies such as 'really simple syndication' (RSS), bookmarking of websites, and e-mail updates etc., all allow individuals to feast on a tailored media menu that Negroponte called 'the Daily me'.

Thus not only can audiences pull news and entertainment media from various sources according to their whim; individual audience members can specify the kind of content that most interests them and wait for the content to come to them. With such technologies available to help a user explore their own tastes, audience members with niche tastes are no longer slaves to the tastes of the masses. This, it might be expected, could have wider social consequences.

Not least among them was the decline of the mainstream print newspapers and magazines. Much as sales of the top ten albums had suffered over the same period and niche individual tracks had found a new market online, so articles rather than entire newspapers were being digested in titbits from diverse sources. For those who bought the newspaper only for the sports report, the sports section could now be had without the expense of the full paper. Newspaper and magazine circulation dwindled as news and opinion became freely available on the Internet. In May 2009 the Newspaper Association of America issued figures revealing a 29.7 per cent decline in newspapers' print advertising revenues in the first four months of the year.[37] This, presumably, was partly due to an economic crisis affecting the economy at large, and newspapers' online advertising revenue also declined, though by only 13.4 per cent. Yet figures for the first quarter of the previous year point to a trend: print advertising declined 14.38 per cent in 2008 even as newspapers' online advertising rose by 7.20 per cent. Longer-term data from 1940 to 2008 highlights a rise and fall in newspaper circulation that correlates with Internet expansion.[38] Newspaper circulation had grown steadily from the 1940s, reaching over 62 million readers per year in 1989 and remaining in this bracket until 1995. Thereafter, a gradual decline began that coincided with the commercialization of the Internet and dramatic growth in the number of connected computers, from only 3.4 million in late 1994 to 12.8 million by mid-1996.[39] Between 1995 and 2003, US newspaper circulation fell from 62 million to 58.5 million. The decline gathered pace from 2004 onwards, reaching a low of 49 million in 2008 – a return to the circulation figures of 1966.

Yet there was more to the decline of the newspaper than the ascent of the Internet. As David Simon, a veteran of the *Baltimore Sun* and writer of *The Wire*, writes, many newspapers had failed to maintain high-quality depth of coverage.

At the moment when the Internet was about to arrive, most big-city newspapers, having survived the arrival of television and confident in their advertising base, were neither hungry, nor worried, nor ambitious. They were merely assets to their newspaper chains. In place of comprehensive, complex and idiosyncratic coverage, readers of even the most serious newspapers were offered celebrity and scandal, humour and light provocation – the very currency of the Internet itself.[40]

Perhaps in this perfect storm it is little wonder that by 2005 the majority of US home broadband users relied on Internet sources as their primary news source.[41]

In April 2005, Rupert Murdoch told the American Society of Newspaper Editors:

I'm a digital immigrant. I wasn't weaned on the web . . . Instead,
I grew up in a highly centralized world where news and information were tightly controlled by a few editors, who deemed to tell
us what we could and should know. My two young daughters, on
the other hand, will be digital natives.[42]

Thus, as Yochai Benkler writes, a nine-year-old girl doing a Google
search for Barbie will find not only the product itself but also a range
of anti-Barbie websites. Thus 'the contested nature of the doll becomes
publicly and everywhere apparent, liberated from the confines of
feminist-criticism symposia and undergraduate courses'.[43] Yet according to an alternative view, the future of the 'digital natives' will be a
poorer one, because the decline of common news sources and liberation from mainstream media is itself a threat to the shared culture and
information that binds a democratic society together. Cass Sunstein
warns that the 'daily me' phenomenon could produce a public ignorant
of politics, ghettoized by ethnicity and moving towards political
extremism.[44] The decline of the newspaper may result in a dearth of
in-depth reporting and legislative scrutiny and its replacement by a 'new
media world will be one of tunnel vision and self-selected expertise'.[45]
Instead of the lowest common denominator media of the pre-Internet
era, future generations could glut on content that caters to the lowest
particularist denominator within specific and increasingly polarized
groups. Essentially, what Sunstein argues is that the centrifugal trend
that empowers the individual may at the same time be harmful to
society at large.

This may be mitigated to some degree by the rise of citizen journalism online, which is beginning to create a useful but uneven system
of informal news reporting straight from the blogger's own camera.[46]
At the same time, the serious investigative newspapers may find that
they may have to adopt the model of a non-profit trust, seeking endow-
ments for providing a necessary public good in a similar manner to
Britain's *Guardian* newspaper, or a university.[47] The trust model, provided it is combined with high-quality coverage that is worth paying for,
could be the salvation of the Fourth Estate. The Internet, far from being
the killer of the newspaper, could be its redemption. There may be space
for both the in-depth newspaper and the blogger-citizen journalist.

<12>
Two-way Politics

In 1998 Jesse Ventura, a Navy SEAL-turned-wrestler-turned-actor-turned-politician, defied every calculable set of odds to become Governor of Minnesota. He was an independent. He had a single staff member and no organized network of volunteers. As his campaign manager recalls, 'when Ventura announced his intention to run, there was not a single precinct worker in place'.[1] Moreover, his budget was puny, at just over half a million dollars. Yet Ventura beat established candidates from the Democratic and Republican parties who had spent millions on their campaigns. The secret of his success was the Internet.

Digital soap box

The Ventura campaign relied on a loose community of supporters to take the initiative and organize local rallies across the state. The candidate's website, JesseNet, provided a campaign plan and supporters took it upon themselves to act on their own initiative. Ventura's three-day 'Drive to Victory' tour of Minnesota just before voters went to the polls was coordinated online. The campaign 'distribute[d] the local rally plans to people we never met before but counted on to carry them out'.[2] The centre was weak, but the periphery strong. Connecting the two was the Internet, the campaign's 'nervous system'.[3] Not only were the volunteers organizing, but they were spending too. Between 30 and 40 per cent of Ventura's funding was generated through the campaign's website in small donations.[4] At a more superficial level, people who had attended rallies could visit Ventura's site and see pictures of themselves with the candidate when they got home. As *The Minnesota Star Tribune* put it, 'in effect, the Web site became a $600 alternative to a tradi-

<164>

tional party apparatus'.[5] This was new, and profoundly different to mainstream campaigning.

Even at this early stage in the Web's development it had a discernable impact on Ventura's electoral fortunes. He was supported by a pronounced youth vote. Almost half (46 per cent) of voters aged between eighteen and 29 cast ballots for him.[6] This may have been in part due to the candidate's colourful persona. Ventura was, after all, the only former pro-wrestler running for governor that year. Yet the youth vote also reflected a segment of the constituency who were early adopters of the Internet. 'Could Jesse have won four years ago?' Phil Madsen, Ventura's campaign manager, wondered. 'No ... We would not have had the online constituency we do now.'[7] Ventura's victory stunned the Democratic and Republican Parties, alerting them to the prospect that loosely organized grassroots movements connected to each other and to a candidate online could challenge and beat long-established party electoral machines. As more voters went online, the Ventura victory indicated, US politics could become less predictable.

As Ventura told *The New York Times*, e-mail would help him once elected: 'If I need to put any word out – boom! We can put the word out to 5,000 people in minutes.'[8] This, however, was only half the picture. The value of his extensive e-mail list was, as Sarnoff the radio tycoon would have realized, as a broadcast mechanism. Yet Phil Madsen had a deeper intuition about the potential of the Internet. It was 'not about technology. It's about relationships'.[9] Madsen emphasized the importance of conversational rather than one-to-many conversation over Jesse Net:

> We give people real information there. We're not giving them a line of crap. We're not giving them scripts ... We use our e-mail list back and forth with our supporters to maintain a very real relationship with the governor'.[10]

The Ventura website was a crude mechanism for what this book calls 'two-way politics'. Two-way politics refers to a dynamic in which the political representative or candidate is informed and responds to the electorate, and the voter has a high degree of participation in the representative's decision making or the candidate's campaign.

Ventura had successfully used e-mail and a web page to win the governorship of a comparatively small state. Five years later, in 2003, a campaign to elect another unusual candidate would test more advanced tools for online participation and push the Internet firmly into the mainstream of American political life.

'Open-source' campaigns

In 2003 Howard Dean, the Governor of Vermont, a small and politically insignificant state in the us, began his campaign for the presidency of America. His campaign would transform American politics. An audit of Dean's political assets in January 2003 would not have been promising: his campaign funds were just over a tenth of a million dollars; his supporters numbered fewer than five hundred people; and he had only seven people working on his campaign. Moreover, he had entered the race very late, and was politically to the left of his party's centre at a time when this was a high-risk position. Sensible pundits rated his chances of winning his party's nomination to run for the presidency as nil.

With odds so slim, Dean's team decided 'that we were an insurgent. We had to run a totally different, decentralized campaign to get any oxygen'.[11] By virtue of its conventional weakness, like the Ventura campaign, the Dean campaign was suited to the Net. For Ventura and Dean the Net was not simply another medium in a well-oiled public-relations strategy but a lifeline to distant pockets of supporters. The key to this strategy was to embrace the centrifugal power of the Internet.

Dean himself was uncomfortable with new technology. He preferred not to use mobile phones, had only recently converted to e-mail and was one of the few candidates who travelled without a computer.[12] His office stored records of his supporters on scraps of paper stored in shoeboxes. In short, Dean was a Luddite.[13] Yet he was also politically outspoken in a manner that garnered an early Internet following. Dean's strong position against the Iraq War had begun to attract attention from pockets of the public curious about his alternative approach to politics. Self-organizing supporters of Dean began spontaneously to gather through the site MeetUp.com for meetings in support of him. Dean's campaign manager, Joe Trippi, had been an advisor to Progeny Linux Systems in 2001 and understood the principles of the free software movement and open-source development. He recognized an opportunity in the growing support base on MeetUp. com. MeetUp.com enabled the Dean campaign to draw together a community of individuals and groups using their own initiative to

< 166 >

further his campaign. It also provided an infrastructure with which a large number of supporters could make very small financial donations. The Dean campaign relied on online supporters to 'use the online community, to organize in their offline community'.[14]

Before the MeetUp.com revelation, the campaign had made an initial foray on to the Internet with a hurriedly constructed blog called 'Call to Action'. It was a simple one-to-many website that broadcast the candidates' message rather than listening to users' responses, much as every modern presidential campaign had ever done. Trippi believed that the campaign needed a blog 'where people could comment, where there was interaction, and where we were building a community'.[15] Once the campaign had established a new blog, 'Blog for America', on which users could freely comment, ideas and comments began to stream in from Internet users across the country. Lawrence Lessig, observing the Dean campaign gathering pace, noted that a successful blog 'is a tool for building community. The trick is to turn the audience into the speaker'. The secret is that 'by getting the audience to type, candidates get the audience committed'.[16]

Trippi observed a parallel between orthodox politics, which he saw as a flawed system 'closed to everyone except the few that aim to keep control', and closed software design.[17] Working on Linux gave him 'insight as to what open-source politics would be like and how the same principles could be applied'. He began to apply the centripetal logic of the Linux community to political campaigning. Rather than rigorously controlling the campaign message from the campaign headquarters, as campaigns customarily do in order to enforce a consistent political message, the Dean campaign would invite input from outside the formal structures of the campaign. Trippi told his team to stop policing Dean's blogs for negative comments, much as Amazon had made the leap to allow users to write negative reviews of products advertised on the site. He believed that 'we need the blogger community regardless of a blog's support, opposition, or neutrality'.[18] He believed that the most successful blogs 'have about them the unruly whiff of rebellion'.[19]

Indeed, so unruly was the atmosphere surrounding the campaign that David 'Doc' Searls, recalling his visit to the Dean campaign's headquarters, wrote that 'what I saw was the equivalent for politics of the Tech Model Railroad Club [the early Hackers' stomping ground at MIT] or the Home Brew Computer Club'.[20] The Dean campaign had learned – to the candidate's extraordinary benefit – that the trend of the

times would favour whomever opted for mass-participation in political dialogue, even going to the lengths of allowing opponents to post
critical comments to one's own website. As Trippi told Lawrence Lessig
during the election:

> In terms of the control thing: that's one of the reasons I don't
> think the other campaigns are having any success on the Internet.
> This is my 7th presidential campaign. In all of them, everything I
> ever learned was that you're supposed to have strong community
> control military command over everything in the organization.
> You give commands to your state directors who give it to the
> county directors who order the precinct captains around. I've
> worked with enough tech involving the Net to know that you
> will absolutely suffocate anything that you're trying to do on the
> Internet by trying to command and control it. It's hard to let go,
> but you know, we've decided that's what we were going to do.[21]

The resulting dynamo of online involvement in the campaign made
a previously penniless contender the major spender in the contest.

This centrifugal approach broke every rule of presidential campaigning. The Dean campaign was not only open to comment but
invited the online world into its private counsels. It shared intimate
decisions with supporters that would usually be reserved for backroom
meetings. The controversial matter of whether Dean would break with
the standard Democratic Party practice of limiting himself to federal
matching funds or would for the first time compete with a Republican
candidate on an equal footing was opened to a decision by online supporters rather than being taken in private by the campaign itself.

Previous attempts to harness a large constituency of small donors
had failed. Governor Jerry Brown, who made a bid for the presidency
in 1992, had attempted to win the election without taking large donations that could indebt him to lobbyists seeking undue influence. He
announced that he would only accept donations from individuals, and
none over $100. His campaign set up a toll-free phone number through
which people could contribute. His focus was to distribute power
among a broad base of citizens rather than a select few large donors.
Though he raised $5 million in small donations and rose from being an
also-ran to become Bill Clinton's main competitor in the last stages of
the Democratic primary, Brown's initiative was hampered by the

< 168 >

absence of the Internet, without which his campaign did not have an infrastructure capable of harnessing the level of broad participation and fund-raising across society required to credibly challenge conventional candidates supported by large donations.[22]

The Dean campaign sought to revitalize the Jerry Brown approach. Instead of toll-free phone lines it now had the Web at its disposal. Dean courted the grass-roots small contributor and criticized the status quo of lobbying and large donations. Trippi viewed the Internet as the means to

> get people to participate in their democracy again. If people did that, and if thousands of them take small actions a few hours of their time, a few dollars out of their wallet there's a real chance that when a candidacy like ours wins the White House, the people will actually own their government again.[23]

Conventionally, political campaigns revolve around a candidate's ability to secure large donations from a select group of people, which are then spent on short TV ads to propagate the candidate's sound bites and criticize other candidates. The Internet, however, enables the sourcing of larger numbers of small donations from the general public, and facilitates deeper political debate than could fit in a thirtysecond TV ad. The Net could, it was hoped, make politics more responsive and less superficial.

As the campaign built momentum, Dean's team broke with convention by announcing their funding targets from late June 2003 onwards. Campaigns are generally loath to release their funding targets for fear of pundits making noise over a failure to achieve them. As a totem of the funding target, the campaign posted a baseball bat in the corner of the 'Dean for America' website with an initial target of $4.5 million before the end of June. The bat became a meme, reproduced on sites across the Internet as Dean supporters took up the fund-raising cause. Not only was the target surpassed, but in one single day – 30 June – Dean contributors donated $828,000 online. This enormous sum was roughly a sixth of what John Kerry and John Edwards, the Democratic Party frontrunners, had raised in three months.[24] Howard Dean, thanks to the Internet, was a political asterisk no more.

In late July 2003 the media reported that Dick Cheney, the Vice President and a prime target of the Dean supporters' vitriol, was planning

<169>

to host a $2,000-a-plate lunch for a select group of rich supporters to raise $250,000. Beating this became a challenge on the Dean blog, and in the weekend before Cheney's lunch, 9,601 donors contributed $508,540.31 in small donations.[25] Their average contribution was $52.97 versus the $2,000 Cheney donors. The message was that the average American could beat the elite by acting together on the Internet.

As its focus on the Internet continued to pay dividends, the Dean campaign became increasingly centrifugal, relying ever less on directives from headquarters and more on the initiative of supporters at the periphery. When Dean went on a speaking tour in August 2003, a suggestion was received through the campaign's blog that if he were successful in meeting the fund-raising target set for August, he should hold aloft a red baseball bat at the last speech of his tour as a sign to the online community. Trippi knew the gesture 'would mean very little to the reporters and pundits, but those thousands of our [online] supporters would know the significance'.[26] The baseball bat was Dean's fund-raising meme and by walking on stage and holding it aloft he proved that a crude but powerful two-way dynamic was in operation. As Trippi put it, 'someone could . . . suggest it on the internet and then, forty-five minutes later, see us do it'.[27] Crude the two-way dynamic may have been but it was real in a way that could not have been possible in the TV age.

Ultimately the Dean campaign failed to win the nomination, and he came in third place behind Kerry and Edwards. Yet this was remarkable for a candidate initially dismissed by sensible pundits as 'a candidate without money, campaign staff, or national following'.[28] Another political journalist recalled that when Dean started, 'his most wildly optimistic fantasies' were to raise $10 million in campaign finances.[29] This he had surpassed in six months. By the end of the first year of his campaign, he had raised more money than any Democrat in history, beating the record that Bill Clinton had set while still president.[30] His impact was so profound that the Democratic Party moved from its cautious stance on the Iraq War and other issues toward Dean's assertive position, and he was made Chairman of the Democratic Party.

Yet the Internet was not the panacea for all weak political campaigns. As with the dot-com bubble, there were false dawns for those who ventured recklessly. For those who believed in wake of the Ventura campaign in 1998 and the Dean campaign in 2004 that the Internet was changing politics irrevocably, the case of Andrew Rasiej was instructive.

< 170 >

Following his failed campaign for the Public Advocate Office of New York, his campaign manager Micah Sifry wrote a post mortem note in late 2005.[31] The crux of the campaign plan had been to develop the campaign's blog as the hub for interesting community conversations. This would require daily posting, and 'constant attention to the feedback rolling in'. It would be important to 'show the network that it exists' for much the same reason as Dean had appeared on stage with the red baseball bat. Yet, in the wake of the Dean success, Rasiej's campaign 'overestimated how much the Internet could compensate for our weaknesses'.[32] From the beginning, the campaign faced a number of difficulties. It had started late and the candidate was unknown. Most importantly, New York City did not yet have a political blogging culture. The campaign results were sobering. Although 90 per cent of the campaign's funds were raised online, more than half may have been a result of someone involved in the campaign having made personal contact with the donor by phone in the first place.[33] Yet despite the limitations of online politics, it was clear that something had indeed changed. Writing in 2004, Joe Trippi predicted that 'the 2008 election will be the first national contest waged and won primarily over the Internet'.[34]

In early 2007, Marc Andreessen, the founder of Netscape, was visited by a young senator named Barack Obama for an hour and a half. The senator was about to begin his campaign for the Democratic Party's nomination for the presidential election. The World Wide Web had existed for less than sixteen years and the senator believed that now was the time when it would play an important role in his race for the White House. Andreessen recalls the meeting:

In particular, the Senator was personally interested in the rise of social networking, Facebook, YouTube, and user-generated content, and casually but persistently grilled us on what we thought the next generation of social media would be and how social networking might affect politics – with no staff present, no prepared materials, no notes. He already knew a fair amount about the topic but was very curious to actually learn more.[35]

Not only was this candidate personally web-savvy, he also had at his disposal veterans of the Dean campaign. Former Dean campaign staff

<171>

members founded Blue State Digital, the consultancy that created my.BarackObama.com. This site not only announced campaign events, but it provided a platform for supporters to advertise events that they had organized themselves in their local neighbourhoods. According it the site's designer, 'the first priority was to make it easy for somebody coming onto the website to host a house party'.[36] This was centrifugal force in action taken to the next level.

The strategy paid off. In late 2007 Barack Obama began to raise more funds than his competitor, Hillary Clinton. Figures for March 2008, for example, show that his campaign raised over $40 million from over 442,000 donors (compared to Hillary Clinton's $20 million).[37] 218,000 of Obama's donors in March were first-time donors in a presidential campaign, and they donated less than $100 each on average.[38] In April 2008 it was announced that 40 per cent of the funds donated to the Obama campaign for the Democratic nomination were contributed in sums of $200 or less. Judging by disclosed figures the total contributions to Obama's nomination and presidential campaign amounted to $336,314,554 from 313,585 donors.[39] This means the average aggregate donation, including multiple small donations at different times during the campaign from the same individuals, was $1,072.48. The small donor had played a very significant role in the election of Barack Obama. Indeed, after his election his transition team received a further $4.5 million in donations at an average of $75 per donation.[40] These figures represent a paradigm shift in dollar terms. Four years earlier, during the 2004 Democratic nomination, Zephyr Teachout, a senior figure in Dean's online campaign, had talked of a process of 'redemo-cratization'.[41] The Internet was making the financing of elections 'the province of the many, not of the few'.[42]

Reflecting on Barack Obama's victory in 2008, Joe Trippi wrote an article titled 'From Linux to Obama' in which he reflected that

> bottom-up transformation has completely changed the way elections operate – from recruiting new supporters, to raising money, to pushing new ideas (and rejecting bad ones). And it changed how communities form and ordinary citizens communicate across the board – from political organizing to parenting advice.[43]

Dollar by dollar, electoral power is shifting from large donors to individual voters.

<172>

'Network governance': a new way for humans to organize their affairs

The world is not short of utopians at moments of technological change. Some years after their defeat in New York, Sifry and Rasiej wrote an article entitled 'Politics 2.0' in which they set out the potential of the Internet for political change. Their tone, though leavened by the experience of Rasiej's 2005 defeat, remained optimistic:

> Over time, online strategies that shift power to networks of ordinary citizens may well lead to a new generation of voters more engaged in the political process. That, in turn, could make politicians more accountable, creating a virtuous circle where elected officials who are more open and supportive of lateral constituent interaction, and less top-down, are rewarded with greater voter trust and support.[44]

This is a utopian future of mass participation, with more transparency, more political accountability, in which every person an activist and every activist at least partially informed. Yet a similar political transformation had been promised four decades before. In the late 1960s and through the 1970s, many within the US media and policy community believed that cable could not only bring more television channels to American homes but that a newly wired nation would enable Americans to participate in political life in a new way. History, however, passed differently.[45] Yet, while the utopians of the 1960s and '70s were disappointed, the utopians of the digital era might not be. Ralph Lee Smith, who wrote 'The Wired Nation', the seminal article predicting the transformative impact of cable in 1970,[46] recently reflected that the Internet was transformative in a way that cable had not been:

> There is no doubt that the Internet delivered on two of the promises that cable ultimately could not deliver, namely, full two-way communications and on-demand access to information.[47]

As the campaigns of Ventura, Dean, Obama and others have proven, the Internet is transforming elections. It may also become an organizing force in society and mark a new chapter in the history of humanity's search for a better means of organizing its affairs. For

<173>

context, consider the long-term development of human political organization. Up to about ten thousand years ago, small groups of hunter-gatherers organized themselves in 'band' societies in most parts of the world.[48] These were groups of a few dozen individuals who hunted together, owned common lands and made decisions collectively. According to anthropological convention, there were no formal leaders.[49] In the early Neolithic period from about 9500 BC, cultivation and then animal husbandry began to enable larger groups to settle at permanent sites.[50] Tribal communities emerged, and with them more complicated social structures based on kinship.[51] Decision-making became a centralized activity and society was organized in a stratified manner. Eventually, tribal communities grew to the order of thousands of individuals. Chiefdoms and bureaucracy emerged. The organization of society moved from an equalitarian, collective model to a top-down model of hierarchy and centralization. As tribes grew and coalesced to the order of tens of thousands of citizens, the city-state and systems of civilization emerged. Social stratification became less dependent on kinship and there was an increase in the specialization of labour. Taxation provided for public architecture, bureaucracy, and law.

By the end of the twentieth century, when the Web was invented, the democratic states had developed a system of 'representative democracy' in which citizens enjoy the right to elect governments but for the most part play only a minor role in law making. Now, a decade into the twenty-first century, two-way communications appear to offer 'network governance'. While the Obama election showed the power of the Internet as a form of new soapbox, the Internet is changing more than electoral politics. It has begun to change how societies organize themselves and make policy. Whereas representative democracy puts the citizen at a remove from decision-making, new tools emerging on the Internet promise to allow more direct, participatory democracy. After a ten-thousand-year hiatus, some of the consensus decision-making features of the early band societies may be about to make a comeback in democratic states. The Internet may enable a new approach to consensus decision-making.

George Gallup, one of the pioneers of public-opinion polling from the mid-1930s, believed that polling gave the average citizen 'a chance to be heard'.[52]

<174>

Through nearly five decades of polling, we have found the people to be extraordinarily sound, especially on issues that come within the scope of the typical person's experience. Often the people are actually ahead of their elected leaders in accepting innovations and radical changes.[53]

Or, as Kevin Kelly wrote in 1998, 'The surest way to smartness is through massive dumbness.'[54] This can be applied in two areas: public opinion and scrutiny of law-making. In the broadest, crudest sense, the Google zeitgeist and other data on popular web searches gives an insight into the climate of opinion. The Web 2.0 folksonomy of highly rated blog posts and sites also gives a sense of which ideas resonate most with Internet users. Yet more advanced forms of networked opinion polling may be in prospect. Already, as of June 2009, 52 million homes across the world are equipped with a sophisticated polling system of which Gallup, who died in 1984, could only have dreamed.[55] This is a computer game console called the Nintendo Wii. On Valentine's Day 2007, Nintendo released a new application called 'Everybody Votes' for the Wii that allows six users per machine to participate in local, regional and worldwide polls over the Internet.[56] The first poll was held in Japan and asked, 'Which do you like, udon or soba?'[57] When the results were displayed on the screen, there were clear divides between different parts of Japan. Owners of another popular computer games console, the Xbox 360, took part in an early poll in advance of the 2008 US presidential election. The results, though perhaps skewed by the prevalence of younger respondents, predicted the actual outcome of the election.[58] Although most polls on entertainment consoles are of a trivial nature, the presence of so many of these consumer items attached to family television sets around the world suggests a future in which regular, granular polling will be commonplace.

Polling, however, is a necessarily limited pursuit. A deeper change in how society runs its affairs could be possible with the advent of collective policy scrutiny. Frederick Hayek's 1945 article 'The Use of Knowledge in Society' reasoned that it was impossible to harness the knowledge of all a society's participants to inform perfect decision-making by government. Yet both Wikipedia and Linux prove that it is possible for large collaborative projects to harness the knowledge of many individuals to produce complex results. Even as early as the 1980s the Usenet newsgroups had begun to fulfil the functions of a

<175>

'worldwide, multimillion member, collective thinktank ... to answer any question from the trivial to the scholarly'.[59] The combination of increasingly sophisticated mass-collaborative projects and easy-to-use polling tools that an owner of a computer game console can use at home suggests that a new model of political participation is in view. Some proactive citizens may, for example, scrutinize or comment on draft legislation, while others may vote on amendments online.

In 1980 J.C.R. Licklider, one of the pivotal figures behind the ARPA's networking and interactive computing work from the 1960s, foresaw a new form of 'interactive politics' in which the citizens would be better informed and would have access to candidates' voting records and other data.[60] Citizens poring over legislation online are increasingly capable of providing oversight of the motives of their political representatives. A number of new web services enable citizens to sift through data on donations to determine where undue influence may have corrupted the law-making process. In the US a new group of citizen watchdogs have begun using new web tools to examine policy making.[61] A body called the Centre for Responsive Politics operates the site OpenSecrets.org on which data is available on political representatives' voting records and on the sources of the donations they have received. Earmarkwatch.org invites visitors to create an account and use its database of 'earmarked' funds allocated by members of Congress for specific projects that are 'to meet pressing needs or pass out political favors'.[62]

Another site called GovTrack.us provides a tool where bills of pending legislation can be studied and easily compared with new drafts as the legislation proceeds through the law-making process. Visitors can track the progress of legislation in which they have an interest. There are limits to this approach, as the founder of GovTrack readily admits:

> The goal has changed a lot over the years. Certainly when it began the idea was direct accountability. Citizens could see the bills being voted on, see if they agree with the votes, and then go to the polls better informed. But I now think that was short sighted. Or wishful thinking. It sounds cynical, but it's really just practical – the world is complicated and for good reason we elect representatives to make decisions so we don't have to read 500 page bills.[63]

However, when one reflects on the level of complexity in the millions of lines of code in the Linux operating system, the prospect of sophisticated collaborative analysis of new legislation seems at least possible. As Eric Raymond terms it in the world of Linux development, 'many eyeballs tame complexity'.[64]

‹13›
Promise and Peril

To the reader of the Internet's history much must appear obvious that was opaque to its participants. The young graduate students working on the protocols through which networked computers would communicate could not have known that they were writing the constitution of a new world. Nor could Ray Tomlinson, who invented e-mail without his superiors' approval in the early 1970s, have realized that he was building a tool through which political outsiders could become governors. Indeed Ventura himself, that inimitable bodybuilderaction-hero-politician, could not have known that his Internet campaign for the governorship of Minnesota was the first step toward the first African American's entry to the White House on a tide of small donations contributed by newly enfranchised Internet activists. The centrifugal trend tying these events together is evident only in hindsight. The future of the Internet and its impact on business, government and society remains oblique. Peering through the veil with an ear cocked to history one may offer a few predictions, and what is certain is that seismic shifts await as the Internet enters its second decade of popular existence.

Globalization, grids and platforms

As the new century approached in the late 1990s, the reach and influence of large multinational corporations aroused suspicions that choice was being choked out of markets, that undue political influence was being bought and that produce was being sourced from corners of the globe where working standards and prices were low. This at least is what the shattered remains of various Starbucks and GAP outlets indicated after a succession of huge protests at international meetings of the WTO in Seattle in 1999, the G8 in Genoa in 2001, and at various other meetings since. A diverse array of left-leaning groups regarded globalization, or perhaps more accurately the preponderance of capitalism in the aftermath of the Soviet collapse and the evolving and uneven framework of international trade, with growing suspicion. The collapse of the Berlin Wall had not suddenly salved the woes of the world's poor. Anti-globalist protestors tended to view Western corporate icons such as Starbucks and GAP as the sole benefactors of globalization. Yet true globalization matured in parallel with the Internet. Even as the anti-globalization protestors planned the routes of their marches and communicated their manifestos in the late 1990s, they did so over the newly popular Internet. With the passing of a decade, what it meant to be globalized was different by the late 2000s to ten years before. In the new mould, the individual, not the multinational, is the primary agent.

As the 2000s draw to a close, the age of the micro-entrepreneurs is dawning. As Steve Jobs observed in 1996, the Web is 'an incredible democratizer':

A small company can look as large as a big company and be as accessible . . . on the Web. Big companies spend hundreds of millions of dollars building their distribution channels. And the Web is going to completely neutralize that advantage [1]

By connecting prospective providers and customers directly, it neutralizes the advantage of large companies who have built expensive distribution channels. The Web gives any individual at any location direct access to remote niche markets. The small trader in low-cost economies can now reach buyers in high-cost markets. In 2009, for example, I ordered a memory card for a camera on eBay from a small trader in China. Some weeks later the item and this accompanying note arrived in my postbox at Cambridge, having travelled over 9,500 kilometres:

Greeting!!
    Wish you be happy when opening the parcel.
    China is far away; many thanks to allow us more considerable shipping time.
    We check and test it very well before shipping. If any damage during the transport which is out of our control, pls tell us and we will help you to solve it. Thanks.

Please value our services five stars by Detailed Seller Ratings. Our hard work needs your encouragement. We also value you a nice feedback!

Do not hesitate to contact us if any question or problem, give us a chance to help you solve any problem! Thanks :)[2]

The conditions are set for a new era of entrepreneurial activity in which tiny creative operations can produce innovations and sell services and products. Globalization in the digital age will feature Starbucks and GAP, but it will also feature a multitude of tiny, niche operations such as the cottage industry producer of Ireland's traditional Aran woollen sweater sold through eBay, or debut albums of a music band recorded in a Californian garage and sold over iTunes.

The dice were further loaded in favour of micro-entrepreneurs with the rise of 'cloud computing'. Sun Microsystems' marketing mantra, 'The network is the computer', may have struck many as odd when it was coined in 1994. Eric Schmidt, now Google's CEO and then Sun's chief technologist, told *Fortune* magazine in 1995: 'We always knew that microcomputers made the most sense not in isolation but when they were linked in networks'.[3] This is the technical irony of the Internet: PCs liberated users from the old bureaucratic approach of mainframe industrial-style computing, yet increased connectivity allowed mainframes, now reborn as data centres, to reassume their old roles as hubs of processing power and data storage. However, though the mainframe has a key role in the new grid computing platforms, the old bureaucratic, centralized model of mainframe computing is gone. In its stead arose a communal grid of computing power.

In 2000 Leo Beranek, one of the founders of the firm that built the IMPs for the initial ARPANET, predicted:

In the next stage of progress, operating systems, word processing, and the like will be centralized on large servers. Homes and offices will have little hardware being a printer and a flat screen . . .[4]

The change Beranek described had in fact already begun. In the late 1990s an entrepreneur called Marc Benioff began to investigate a new form of software that would be delivered over the Internet. He was

<180>

interested in the market for software that companies used to keep track of their customers and products. His idea was simple, but revolutionary:

> If we hosted it ourselves and used the Internet as a delivery platform, customers wouldn't have to shut down their operations as their programs were installed. The software would be on a Web site that they could access from any device anywhere in the world, 24/7. This model made software similar to a utility, akin to paying a monthly electric bill.[5]

In 1999 he founded a company called Salesforce.com that began to offer services delivered directly to subscribers' computers from the Salesforce.com's own servers rather than selling the software physically and requiring clients to implement it on their own servers. This 'software as a service' model and the subsequent rise of cloud computing, in which remote data centres deliver computing power and services across the network, had a historical parallel from the 1910 to 1930s during which Samuel Insull's 'power pool', a growing utility network of electrical grids, allowed businesses in the US to abandon their own private generators and plug into the emerging national grid.[6]

Cloud computing has expanded to include simple applications such as document editing and e-mail and complex applications such as video editing. Remote data centre capacity, ready-made platforms for distribution, cheap tools of production, all reduce the expense of starting from scratch. An example is the popular social network site Facebook, on which users can now create and sell simple services. Provided the educational and infrastructural requirements are in place, more and more micro-entrepreneurs, relying on fewer resources and acting at a younger age, will introduce commercially viable innovations and content to the global market. A new generation of what might be called 'micropreneurs' can establish cottage industries that engage in a global market of niche demands. Moreover, from 2008 a new generation of very cheap PCs, costing as little as $300 or less, flooded the market.

This is an opportunity not just for individuals, but for governments too. This is not to accept that the world, with all its divisions and varied levels of prosperity, is 'flat',[7] to use Thomas Friedman's phrase, or to reject that it is irreparably spiky, to use Richard Florida's.[8] Rather,

<181>

those smart nations who seize on the opportunity to take advantage of the new dispensation can position themselves to create a national commercial renaissance in which every citizen can be engaged through a laptop. This would be 'Total Commerce', a phrase intentionally evocative of the total wars of the last century in which industrial states harnessed their entire citizenry in the war effort. To achieve this, governments must inculcate digital instincts through far-sighted educational reform, promoting revolutionary talent early in life and producing a generation capable of competing with their global peers. Digital instincts are a foundation of basic digital skills in young children that allow them to adapt easily to new technologies as they emerge. This is no longer the preserve of rich countries. Countries slow to benefit from the industrial age may have better fortunes in the digital era. First-generation computer users in the BRIC countries (Brazil, Russia, India, China), for example, will be able to compete on an equal footing with their peers in the US, Canada, the EU, Australia and Japan.

Control in a centrifugal world

In the twenty-seventh century BC, according to legend, the princess Xi Ling-Shi of the Chou Dynasty discovered the secret of the silkworm. From the day that a worm fell into the princess's tea and revealed the secret of its thread, China enjoyed a three-thousand-year monopoly on sericulture, the cultivation of the worm, until the third century BC. Persian industrial espionage eventually facilitated the smuggling of silkworms to Persia in AD 410. A century later the Emperor Justinian in Rome took action against Persia's stranglehold on silk production. In the AD 530s he dispatched two Nestorian monks with his blessing who smuggled silkworm eggs from China.[9] Not that Rome herself was beyond monopoly: the traders of the Empire ventured far beyond her borders, penetrating barbarian lands and selling all manner of goods to strange peoples far and wide. One of the items they carried was wine. The precious vine, however, remained at home. Indeed, in the first century BC, five centuries before Justinian's action against Persia's sericulture monopoly, the Roman senate had prohibited viticulture in the Empire's provinces[10] and a further decree in AD 91 by Domition prohibited viticulture to non-Romans. By retaining her monopoly on wine production at home, Rome guaranteed a market for Roman produce abroad. Only in the late second century did Emperor Probus lift

< 182 >

the prohibition on viticulture in the provinces.[11] China, content to trade silk but not the worm, and Rome, happy to sell wine but not the vine, knew as empires do the value of control over the platform of a valuable commodity's production and consumption. What is new in the digital age is the centrifugal and open imperatives of the Internet. How these two forces act on each other is the question on which the future of digital business hinges.

Balance the desire and benefit of maintaining control over their platforms and the countervailing pressure of the Internet's centrifugal push toward openness will determine which digital companies prosper and which will fail in the coming decade. Perhaps the closest parallel in history is the choice of the British parliament in the 1840s to embrace something approaching free trade, casting off protective tariffs in the hope of furthering domestic prosperity through more trade. Google's Android platform, only recently appearing on mobile phones and small computers, embraces an entirely open platform in the Linux mould. Google anticipates that profits will come not from any one device or application but from wider use of the Internet at large. Platform owners such as Facebook, Apple, Nokia, Microsoft and Nintendo, however, all face the difficult question of how to establish the most vibrant platform while maintaining sufficient control to profit by it. A guiding principle is that computers and devices with the best selection of software applications available to them are most attractive to consumers, and therefore attract yet more developers to create further software applications for them.

Apple's iPhone, with which mobile phones operating Google Android compete, provides a useful example of the difficult question of control. Apple Inc.'s corporate history makes it acutely aware of the importance of its devices not just as products in themselves but as platforms for software. In the mid- to late 1990s, following the release of Windows 95, PC sales rose to almost 100 million units per annum, while Apple sales fell from 4.5 million in 1995 to 2.7 million in 1998.[12] Even though Apple could avail of economies of scale to produce high-quality machines in production, the number of Apple computer users was dwindling to the point where it became less economic for software developers to continue writing applications for Apple computers. Instead, software developers could simply migrate to the more popular platform of PCs running Microsoft Windows.[13] The release of the iPhone in 2007, and the subsequent introduction of a program to attract software developers to write applications (called 'apps') for it in early 2008, gave Apple an opportunity to build a more sustainable platform. In July 2009 Apple announced that users had downloaded 1.5 billion pieces of software for their iPhones from its App Store, and over 65,000 pieces of software created by over 100,000 software developers are available to download as of mid-2009.[14] These apps, for example, enable an iPhone to check the weather, find local radio stations, reserve a place at the golf course and show where the bad traffic is on the way. The more devices that are sold, the more widely purchased and used apps are likely to be, which attracts more developers to write apps for the device, which makes the device more useful, which finally results in more devices being sold. The platform functions like an ecology in which the platform owner, software developer and user all play a part.

However, a teething problem in the App Store's early days illustrates the delicacy of the control issue. When Apple first distributed the software development kit (SDK) to allow programmers to write apps for the iPhone in 2008, a controversy emerged over the legal conditions that Apple attached. Programmers who used the SDK had first to agree to a non-disclosure agreement (NDA) preventing them from discussing the SDK with anyone else. On the one hand, this prevented them from revealing the features of the iPhone to competitors, yet on the other it prevented software developers from tapping into the knowledge and expertise of their peers. As one iPhone programmer blogged, 'Anything that I've been able to do on computer has been because somebody else has laid the foundation . . . none of us is as smart as all of us.'[15] The alternative, without peer collaboration, is that each developer is unable to exploit the knowledge of the community, and must operate in isolation. The community of iPhone developers rebelled. One developer, Justin Williams, created the website 'www.fuckingnda.com' to provide a clearinghouse for the battery of complaints that programmers were making about the NDA on twitter and other forums. The site got over fifteen thousand unique hits in the first day.[16]

> There was no way to share best practices, discuss bugs and other issues that developers run into during the daily workflow. It was a frustrating experience that I think hindered the quality of iPhone software.[17]

Realizing the threat to its platform, Apple changed its position in October 2008.

The Craigslist approach of democratizing the platform and allowing users to vote on strategic decisions may prevent a business from enjoying a massive burst of growth, but it also forestalls user rebellions. Other platforms, perhaps most particularly those that depend on user-driven content for their success, face difficulties as they consider how to monetize their service. Facebook, for example, has encountered repeated user revolts in its efforts to leverage users' personal data in new advertising ventures. As Paul Baran warned in 1965, 'there is a widespread belief that somehow the communications network used will possess a God-given sanctuary to privacy, but "it ain't necessarily so . . ."[18] Social networks like Facebook and its competitors face the grievous prospect that users might begin en masse to demand the ability, for example, to transfer all their photographs, messages and contacts to a competitor social network. If a social network were to attempt to assert control or ownership over these data, the trust and community components of their platform would be mortally wounded. Yet without doing so, the prospect of massive monetization that would justify the enormous valuations of such businesses will be difficult to realize. Even when the stakes are high, control is an elusive element on the Internet.

The ultimate platform, if it could be controlled, would be the network itself. The telephone operators had already made abortive attempts to develop centrally controlled networks from the mid-1970s (using x.25). The contest between the Vailian imperative to control from the centre and the centrifugal trend of Internet development is not yet concluded. A new debate on 'network neutrality' began in the us in the late 1990s. The prospect of vertical integration of cable companies and isps hinted at a future in which the Internet would go the way of the cable network in the 1970s. In December 1999, law professors Lemley and Lessig made the case to the Federal Communications Commission that a merger between AT&T and cable company providing local access in various us regions, MediaOne, should be prevented:

> The architecture thus represents a significant change from the existing End-to-End design for a crucial segment of the residential Internet market. Further, there is in principle no limit to what

<185>

AT&T could bundle into its control of the network. As ISPs expand beyond the functions they have traditionally performed, AT&T may be in a position to foreclose all competition in an increasing range of services provided over broadband lines.[19]

The complaint of network-neutrality advocates was that a company in control of the 'last mile' connection between a subscriber's modem and the network switch that connects that modem to the Internet should be prevented from using this control to force the subscriber to use other services such as an online video rental service. Similarly in 2005 Internet service providers proposed tiered access whereby they would provide preferential access to services from their partners, and reduce speeds of access to services and content from their competitors.[20] As Tim Wu said in testimony before a US congressional committee on the matter in 2006, Americans would be shocked 'if the electric company one day announced that refrigerators made by General Electric would henceforth not work quite as well as those made by Samsung'.[21] The result, the net neutrality advocates argue, would be an injury to competition, and to what Jonathan Zittrain calls the Internet's 'generative'[22] character that enables its users to innovate spontaneously.

The emerging debate on network neutrality is focused on the new, mobile battleground, and on users' ability to use voice over Internet protocol (VOIP) on mobile devices. VOIP allows users to make telephone calls either freely or at very cheap rates by sending telephone audio data as standard Internet data packets. This, understandably, threatens mobile telephone companies whose revenues depend on tariffs on standard mobile phone calls. However, since mobile phone networks typically bundle devices with access, they can restrict which devices can be used on their networks, and how. Thus in 2009 the voice over Internet protocol company Skype was forced to remove its ability to transmit VOIP over telephone from its app before Apple would permit it to appear in the iPhone App Store in the US. Skype on the iPhone could only be accessed over wireless LAN networks where it does not compete with the 3G-telephone tariff service provided by AT&T in the US. A similar pattern had emerged in the early history of radio, the most dramatic example being the Nazi 'peoples' radio' the *Volksempfänger*, which was designed as a discriminating technology that made it difficult to receive broadcasts not transmitted by German stations.[23] If they are to respect the model of the 'common carrier', in which ports, postal services and wired Internet networks handle goods from all comers without discrimination, mobile Internet devices, like radios before them, should not discriminate between particular types of sources of content or equipment.

On mobile networks, network neutrality remains a burning question.[24] This is not the only prospect of a change to the network: even if ISPs should not threaten the neutrality of the network, other parties may. For security and society, the state may stake a claim.

Digital subversion and the ink state

In 1933 Hitler announced to the German people that the government 'will embark on a systematic campaign to restore the nation's moral and material health'.[25] Germany was to undergo what Hitler called 'political decontamination'. This was a project suited for the age of ink and industry when an all-powerful dictator could control film, print and radio. Thus, on 10 May 1933, standing before the German State Opera House on Berlin's Opernplatz, Joseph Goebbels proclaimed the end of the Jewish intellectual tradition, a consigning of everything unGerman to the fire. Thousands of books by Jewish writers burned on the square before him as he spoke. Across Germany, the pyres lit the night.

The Nazi pyres represented the supremacy of the state over the printed word at its most robust, most draconian. Yet no pyre, nor flames across an entire state could burn away digital text hosted on multiple Internet servers. In the digital era, materials proscribed by one state can find refuge in another. However, states can attempt to prevent their citizens from accessing proscribed content even if they are powerless to destroy it at the source. Yet though the state at its most draconian was master of ink, online text now trumps the state. As Paul Baran noted in 1964, packet networks with distributed communications would avoid the administrative censorship found in previous military communications systems by virtue of focusing on 'user-to-user rather than emphasis on centre-to-centre operation'.[26] Distributed packet-switched networks have a propensity against control, against hierarchy. Thus, for example, a Cambridge University researcher revealed vulnerabilities in the Chinese Internet censorship system, the so-called great firewall of China.[27] Moreover, the economic bounties of the Net force governments to step softly. Where once a Chinese Internet user

<187>

had to fill a customs declaration to send an e-mail,[28] the risk that inadvertent blocking of content could hinder commercial life is now considered too great for almost any state to accept. Draconian censorship, where one proposes to benefit economically from the Internet, is virtually impossible.[29]

Perhaps first to learn this was the government of Mexico following the armed uprising by the Zapatista National Liberation Army (EZLN) in January 1994. The EZLN took over a number of towns and a city in Chiapas, southern Mexico. The government responded with force. The rebels withdrew into the jungle, where they were pursued by tanks and attacked with air strikes until 12 January, when the government declared a ceasefire and called for negotiation.[30] A year later, in February 1995, the government again ceased a new military operation in which it had again had the upper hand. Both the army and EZLN were surprised by the government's restraint.[31] The answer to the puzzle was that while the EZLN was losing the physical war, it was winning a media war against the Mexican government, largely fought online.

The Mexican government was increasingly concerned about the involvement of activists, NGOs and media, and the resulting attention that the EZLN was gaining Latin America and beyond. The rebels and NGOs sympathetic to them were able to bypass the unsympathetic mainstream Mexican media and feed information directly to foreign media outlets by fax and e-mail. Foreign coverage eventually forced the reluctant Mexican media to cover the EZLN. Thus in April 1995 the Foreign Minister of Mexico, Jose Angel Gurría, said:

There has not been a shot fired in the last fifteen months . . . The shots lasted ten days, and ever since the war has been a war of ink, of written word, a war on the Internet.[32]

The spokesman for the rebels, Subcomandante Marcos, responded:

one space . . . so new that no one thought a guerrilla could turn to it, is the information superhighway, the Internet. It was territory not occupied by anybody.[33]

The Mexican state had not yet adjusted to the emerging media environment. The EZLN had.

< 188 >

In May 2007 three men appeared at Woolwich Crown Court in London accused of inciting terrorism using Internet chatrooms, videos and forums. On day two of the trial the proceedings were interrupted by the presiding judge, Mr Justice Peter Openshaw. He paused the trial to note, 'The trouble is I don't understand the language. I don't really understand what a website is.'[34] Among the suspects was Younis Tsouli, a nineteen-year-old hacker who lived in his parents' basement and had the look of one who rarely exposed himself to sunlight. His Internet name was '*Irhabi* 007' (terrorist 007) and he was a media baron of militant Islamism.

Tsouli was not recruited, nor was he connected by family or friends to militant circles. He took the initiative and announced his talents on militant web forums from where his abilities were recognized and he gained credibility and an increasing degree of responsibility. Following the London bombings in 2005, police and security agencies became increasingly concerned about the prospect of isolated, curious teens like Tsouli 'self radicalizing' in support of militant Islamism and under-taking terrorist operations against their peers in European cities. Self-radicalization of isolated individuals into amorphous, underground communities is, however, nothing new.

Over a decade previously, in November 1994, *Wired* published a feature on a phenomenon almost exactly the same occurring within another, very different, community:

> Just 10 years ago, most queer teens hid behind a self-imposed don't-ask-don't-tell policy until they shipped out to Oberlin or San Francisco, but the Net has given even closeted kids a place to conspire . . . AOL's [America Online] gay and lesbian forum enables him to follow dispatches from queer activists worldwide, hone his writing, flirt, try on disposable identities, and battle bigots – all from his home screen.[35]

But for its dramatically different subject group *Wired*'s feature could easily be rewritten to describe al-Qaeda sympathizers in post-11 September western Europe. In both cases the Internet allows a con-nection to an amorphous community to discuss matters regarded in wider society as subversive, to find mentors, seek out justification and learn methods and mores relevant to their chosen lifestyles.

An underground digital culture gave Tsouli his status, nickname and identity, the norms he observed online, a willingness to use his

<189>

initiative, to think differently and practically like a hacker, and a meritocracy in which to operate. Like the phone phreakers from the 1950s onwards, Irhabi 007 found online a community of common interest in which he could invest himself, and through which he could gain respect for his talents. In the words of 'The Mentor', a young network hacker writing in 1986 following his arrest, the floating world of the bulletin board and the hacker fraternity was irresistible:

> then it happened . . . a door opened to a world . . . rushing through the phone line like heroin through an addict's veins, an electronic pulse is sent out, a refuge from the day-to-day incompetencies is sought . . . a board is found.[36]

'The Mentor' was the handle of 21-year-old Loyd Blankenship, who also went by the name of 'the Neuromancer', and who was a member of hacking groups including 'the Legion of Doom', 'the PhoneLine Phantoms', 'the Racketeers' and 'Extasyy Elite'. The Mentor was part of 'the Scene', the loose culture of software and phone pirates directly descended from the phone phreaks and elements of the hacker culture. Like the young, blind phone phreaks and homosexuals who connected with their respective amorphous communities of interest, The Mentor found through the BBSs a community where he could fit in. In his Manifesto, he described his feeling when he encountered the online world:

> This is where I belong. I know everyone here . . . even if I've never met them, never talked to them, may never hear from them again . . . I know you all.[37]

Within the Scene, different groups competed for prestige by racing to release new 'warez' (Scene slang for pirated software).[38]

To be part of an elite network, particularly a conspiratorial one, might be a large part of a person's social existence. For Joe Engressia, the blind phreaker who had discovered how to control the phone network as a young boy, this was so central to his being that he adopted his hacker nickname, 'Joybubbles', as his legal name by deed poll in 1991. Engressia's obituary in *The New York Times* described how 'every night he sits like a sightless spider in his little apartment receiving messages from every tendril of its web'.[39] The image of Engressia as a spider at the

< 190 >

centre of a web linking the various isolated individuals within a broad, amorphous community is uncannily like Irhabi 007 who was jailed in the UK in July 2007 for disseminating violent radical material and acting as an online matchmaker, connecting prospective militants with missions in al-Qaeda theatres.

Since the days of the MIT hackers and the Homebrew scene there had been something implicitly subversive about the emerging digital culture. Part of the hackers' cultural inheritance from the Tech Model Railroad Club at MIT was the mentality behind the club's 'midnight requisitions committee'. The hackers, some of whom became certified locksmiths for the purpose, made keys for every repository of equipment they might need in MIT. They then stole as required. At the Homebrew Club in the 1970s, the hacker ethos of openness and sharing was mixed with a disregard for property on the part of many attendees. Thus in 1976 a young Bill Gates wrote to the Homebrew community urging it to crack down on illegal copying of his software.[40] In Engressia, the phone phreaker who called himself Joybubbles, in Loyd Blankenship, the hacker who called himself The Mentor, and in Younis Tsouli, the militant media baron who called himself 'Irhabi 007', are common characteristics of the new subversive medium: amenability to amorphous communities of interest, resilience and inbuilt resistance to censorship, and the 'perpetual beta' proclivity of digital natives to question authority.

In a momentous announcement on 12 January 2010 David Drummond, Google's Chief Legal Officer, disclosed the search company's 'new approach' to China:

> We have decided we are no longer willing to continue censoring our results on Google.cn, and so over the next few weeks we will be discussing with the Chinese government the basis on which we could operate an unfiltered search engine within the law, if at all. We recognize that this may well mean having to shut down Google.cn, and potentially our offices in China.[41]

Ostensibly the reason for Google's change of posture was a battery of hacking attacks on Google's infrastructure to steal information from it and from human rights activists, and also attacks on the infrastructure of at least twenty other companies. Yet beyond this specific incident something deeper and more profound is in play. A clash of two new and distinct models of capitalism is underway between China's authoritarian capitalism driven by that country's need to maintain political stability while sustaining economic growth, and Google's principled capitalism grounded in the oddball values and nerd norms of engineers and programmers.[42]

China is resource hungry, cash rich, and rights oblivious. Its model of 'authoritarian capitalism' relies on the government's ability to deliver 8 per cent growth in GDP per year, thereby providing employment and rising living standards, and staving off wide-scale unrest.[43] Herein lies the irony of Google's clash with the Chinese government: while Google and China represent two opposed models of capitalism, each is the product of a culture entirely at odds with capitalism in the first place: authoritarian capitalism on the one hand, and nerd norms on the other.

Number six among Google's ten corporate principles is 'You can make money without doing evil'.[44] Consider the potentially massive scale of Google's sacrifice to uphold this principle. In the short term, Google already faces significant competition within China from the search engine Baidu, which holds over half of the market. Should Google quit China then Baidu will almost certainly profit, and could pose a strategic threat to Google's business beyond China in the coming decades. The market agreed with this assessment, boosting Baidu's share price by almost 14 per cent on the day after Google made its announcement.

In the medium and longer term China represents a market of strategic opportunity. Between 2008 and 2009 alone, according to the Chinese Academy of Sciences, 90 million additional Chinese connected to the Internet. From 30 June 2008 the reported number of Chinese Internet users finally eclipsed the number of users in the United States.[45] Yet even fewer than a third of the total Chinese population is online and the potential for growth is immense. China is now and will remain for the foreseeable future the home to the largest population of Internet users on the planet. It will become a truly massive market for Internet business of all hues in the coming decade. Neglecting such a market of which it currently has at least a quarter share could be massively damaging for Google.

While Western nations with high Internet penetration currently dominate Google's revenues this may not be the case in the future. Though Google's share of the Chinese search engine market (conservatively estimated as at least a 25 per cent share) apparently represented less than 5 per cent of the company's current global revenue, the spread in Internet use from the late 2009 figure of 29 per cent of the population[46] to the entire Chinese population could increase the value of the Chinese Internet search market threefold. Had Google maintained – or expanded on – its quarter share as the market grew overall then China could represent 15 per cent or more of its current global revenues. This figure might have been considerably higher as if profits from advertising services in China rose in line with China's target 8 per cent annual growth in GDP. For Google's shareholders the prospect of a withdrawal from a potential market of 1.3 billion users might seem a terrible cost to uphold the company's principles.

Yet Google is acting as a principled capitalist. Its 'do the right thing' mantra has roots as deep as the Internet. When Google entered the Chinese search market in January 2006 it courted widespread controversy by adhering to the Chinese Government's legal requirement to censor its search results. It did so; according to the company this was in effect breaching its core principles, but it did so 'in the belief that the benefits of increased access to information for people in China and a more open Internet outweighed our discomfort in agreeing to censor some results'.[47] The reason for Google's discomfort then and for its decision to face down the Chinese Government now is that it espouses corporate principles that are more than just window dressing. Rather, they are deeply rooted in the foundations from which the Internet, and Google, sprang. It remains to be seen whether this nerd norm capitalism extends beyond Google, and examples such as Craigslist, to a wider section of corporate life.

In the coming years the world may be divided between those who Google and those who do not. On 22 January 2010, just ten days after Google's announcement, the US Secretary of State, Hillary Clinton, made a major speech on Internet freedom. Channeling President Kennedy's ghost she dipped into the rhetoric of the Cold War, evoking the Berlin Wall and announcing that the United States stands for 'a single Internet where all of humanity has equal access to knowledge and ideas'.[48] Yet those portions of the globe that adhere to an authoritarian capitalism, presumably including China and a number of commodity rich African trading partners, may direct their growing population of Internet users toward Baidu and other services willing to adhere to the conditions of state control. At the same time the free Google of the rest of the world may become what American blue jeans and rock and roll

<193>

were to generations of Communist Bloc teens during the Cold War: an icon of liberty.

As governments adjust to the new balance of power between the state and subversives, tough measures such as attempts at Internet censorship or user registration schemes threaten to alter the nature of the medium. It would be as well to recognize that the Internet is a new global commons with an uncertain future.

iWar and the new privateers

On 27 April 2007 a blizzard of distributed denial of service attacks hit important websites in Estonia and continued until at least as late as mid-June. Targets included the website of the president, parliament, ministries, political parties, major news outlets and Estonia's two dominant banks, which were rendered incapable of interacting with customers.

For Estonia, the Web represented independence and opportunity. In the aftermath of the Soviet collapse, forward-looking Estonians started to ponder how they could rapidly modernize their economy. 'We had nothing,' recalls Toomas Ilves, now the President of the Republic of Estonia.[49] Estonia's telephone interchanges dated from the 1930s. Its steel and concrete infrastructure would lack for years. To Ilves and the cohort of Internet revolutionaries in the early 1990s, the Internet promised the young nation an opportunity to make the leap of fifty years. He had been influenced by Jeremy Rifkins's 1995 book, *The End of Work*, which lamented that computers would put Americans out of work. For Estonia, however, the lesson was the reverse: a small country with a comparatively tiny workforce could use technology to liberate people from unnecessary jobs. The Estonian government provided matching funding for schools that established Internet connections, established online tax returns, and banks adopted online banking to reduce costs. By 2000, the Internet was part of Estonia's national image, and Internet access was made a constitutional right of citizens. As well as disrupting state, bank and media services over a prolonged period, the attacks on prominent websites and services were emotionally sensitive.

Denial of service (DOS) attacks have existed in various forms since at least as early as the 'Morris Worm' in 1988. A DOS attempts to overwhelm a computer or networking system by bombarding it with a high volume of information requests. If successful, the attack renders the targeted system unable to respond to legitimate requests, which could

<194>

include providing access to a particular website. A distributed denial of service (DDOS) attack operates on the same principle, but multiplies its impact by directing a 'botnet' of networked computers that have been remotely hijacked to bombard the target system with many requests at the same time. Botnets can be controlled by a single individual.

This form of conflict is different to what militaries refer to as 'cyber-war'. The attacks on Estonia targeted the consumer rather than military or critical infrastructures such as water, power or air traffic control systems. Moreover, the attacks were undertaken by individual 'hacktivists' united by their shared umbrage at a specific political event. 'iWar' is a useful shorthand for what would otherwise be confused with cyberwar. iWar can be waged by nations, corporations, communities, or by any reasonably tech-savvy individual. This is a fundamental shift in the balance of offensive capability, empowering individuals with the power to threaten the activities of governments and large corporations. Yet as a corollary, almost anybody can be harmed as a result of an iWar attack. For example, this could include migratory workers who use online services to remit money to their families in poverty-stricken regions as much as transnational corporations that migrate their daily operations to virtualized Internet services reliant on data centres.

A number of factors make a conflagration of iWar a grave concern in the near future. Early gunpowder weaponry enabled the levying of armies of unprecedented size. Matchlock troops could be trained in a matter of weeks, compared to the lifetime of training required to produce effective longbow men. Like the matchlock musketeer, the iWar attacker is equipped with cheap, powerful technology that requires little training. Offensive action can be conducted by an unprecedented number of amateurs whose sole qualification is their connection to the Internet.

iWar, perhaps for the first time, is liberated from the expense and effort that traditionally inhibits offensive action against geographically distant targets. Conventional destruction of targets by kinetic means is enormously expensive and comparatively slow. A single B-2 'Spirit' stealth bomber, which costs US$2.1 billion to develop and build, must fly from Whiteman Air Force base in Missouri in order to drop ordinance on a target in Afghanistan. iWar, though it delivers far less offensive impact, can inflict damage from any point on the globe at a target anywhere on the globe at virtually no cost.

For the same reason, iWar will proliferate quickly across the globe. It is not limited by the geographical constraints that impeded the

<195>

spread of earlier military innovations. The proliferation of gunpowder in Europe puts this in perspective: appearing in China in the seventh or eighth century, gunpowder finally made its European debut as late as 1314, first in Flanders, then in England seven years later, and in France five years after that. In contrast, new tools and know-how necessary to wage iWar proliferate easily across the Internet. During the Estonian attacks, 'dummies' guides' to DDOS attacks were distributed through Internet forums to allow more people to participate in the attacks.

More alarmingly still, the dearth of arrests or formal accusations by the Estonian government illustrate that iWar can be waged anonymously and is difficult to punish. iWar is deniable. It remains unclear whether Estonia was the victim of a 'cyber riot' in which like-minded 'hacktivists' orchestrated the attacks without authorization from the Kremlin, or whether the attacks were orchestrated with official sanction. Even if official culpability could be proven, it is unclear how one state should respond to an iWar attack by another. A criminal investigation would be no less problematic. If digital forensic investigation could trace a malicious botnet to a single computer controlling a DDOS attack, it is unlikely that effective action could be taken to prosecute. The culpable computer might be in another jurisdiction from which cooperation would not be forthcoming. If cooperation were forthcoming, the culpable computer might have been operated from an Internet cafe or at another anonymous public connectivity site, making it impossible to determine who among the many transient users was involved in a DDOS attack that typically lasts only a short period of time.

The potency of this form of warfare will grow as the economies, governments and communities of the world embrace the Internet to interact and deliver services. In Estonia, for example, there are almost 800,000 Internet bank clients in a population of almost 1.3 million people, and 95 per cent of banking operations are conducted electronically.

This should not be seen as a technical problem for IT security experts alone but as a broad challenge of what is known as 'the commons'. The Internet is a common resource of humanity, much like the atmosphere that surrounds Earth. Successive technological developments, from animal husbandry, which enabled the use of common grazing lands, to maritime navigation, which opened new trade and communications routes on the high seas, have forced human society to consider how it governs shared common resources. Unilateral initiatives will not be effective against iWar because iWar, like piracy before it, is a global phenomenon, and the Internet is a common recourse like the high seas. The Internet, like the high seas before it, transcends national boundaries and comes under the jurisdiction of no particular state. Pompeii's campaign to eradicate piracy in 67 BC was effective because the writ of Roman law was enforceable throughout the Mediterranean waters. Today, no single state has such power over the Internet. The question is not how a particular type of DDOS attack can be averted on a particular network, but how humanity will choose to govern the Internet.

J.C.R. Licklider foresaw that 'if networks are going to be to the future what the high seas were to the past, then their control is going to be the focus of international competition'.[50] Two examples of approaches to global commons should provide faint solace salted with caution. The example of the Law of the Sea might illuminate the path ahead for policymakers. Here is an example of an international body of law established on the foundations of informal customary laws, which evolved to protect universal access to the high seas. Since the opportunities for trade and communications provided by the high seas were commonly accepted as invaluable by all nations, informal customary laws gradually evolved to protect access to the sea for these purposes. The unlawfulness of piracy, which injures trade and maritime communications, became a universally accepted norm. The question remains whether a similar legal framework will evolve to protect access to the Internet in the long term.

Yet, even if an international framework does eventually arise to protect the Internet, the history of piracy suggests that this could take some time. State-sanctioned privateering was only finally outlawed in 1856 under the 'Paris Declaration in respect of maritime law', many decades after an international consensus against piracy had emerged. Painful progress on climate change should give pause for thought. If governments are only now reaching a fragile consensus on this, the most visible challenge of the commons, the development of robust new international norms of behaviour on the Internet could be decades away. Humanity faces the risk of ruining the Internet even before it becomes a mature technology, before its benefit as a global commons can be fully realized. Humanity needs to consider how it will deal with the new commons. It must weigh the prospect of failure.

Glossary

AJAX	Asynchronous JavaScript and XML
AOL	America OnLine
ARPA	Advance Research Projects Agency
ARPANET	ARPA's land packet network
AUTODIN	DCA's automatic digital network
BBN	Bolt, Bernaek and Newman
BBS	Computer Bulletin Board System
BITNET	'Because its there' network
BRICS	Brazil, Russia, India, China
CCIRN	Coordinating Committee for Intercontinental Research Networks
CCITT	Consultative Committee on International Telegraphy and Telephony
CERN	Conseil Européen pour la Recherche Nucléaire
CREN	Corporation for Research and Educational Networking
CSNET	Computer Science Network
DCA	Defense Communications Agency
DDN	Defense Data Network
DDOS	distributed denial of service
DEC	Digital Equipment Corporation
DECNET	Digital Equipment Corporation's proprietary network system
DNS	Domain Name System
DOS	Denial of service
EARN	European Research Network
EZLN	Zapatista National Liberation Army
FCC	Federal Communications Commission
FTP	file transfer protocol
GBF	'get big fast', one of the mantras of the dot-com boom
GNU	'GNU's not Unix', free software movement acronym
GPL	GNU General Public License
GUI	graphical user interface
HEPNET	High Energy Physics Network
HTML	Hypertext Markup Language
IAB	Internet Activities Board
IAHC	International Ad Hoc Committee
IANA	Internet Assigned Numbers Authority

< 198 >

IANW	International Academic Networkshop
IATA	International Air Transport Association
ICANN	Internet Corporation for Assigned Names and Numbers
ICB	International Cooperation Board
ICBM	intercontinental ballistic missile
ICCB	Internet Configuration Control Board
IEFT	Internet Engineering Task Force
IEPG	Intercontinental Engineering Planning Group
IMPS	Interface Message Processors
INWG	International Network Working Group
IP	Internet Protocol
IPO	initial public offering
IPTO	Information Processing Techniques Office
IRTF	Internet Research Task force
ISDN	Integrated Services Digital Network
ISO	International Standards Organization
ITU	International Telecommunications Union
LAN	Local Area Networking
MAD	mutually assured destruction
MERIT	Michigan Educated Research Information Triad
MIT	Massachusetts Institute of Technology
MP3	International Standards Organization Moving Picture Experts Group Layer 3
MPEG	Moving Picture Experts Group
NASA	National Aeronautics and Space Administration
NCSA	National Centre for Supercomputing Applications
NLS	Douglas Englebart's 'oN-Line System'
NPL	UK National Physics Laboratory
NSF	National Science Foundation
NSFNET	National Science Foundation Network
NSI	NASA Science Internet
OCF	'optimum coding in the frequency'
OSTP	US President's Office of Science and Technology Policy
P2P	peer-to-peer
PCM	pulse-code modulation
PCS	personal computers
PPTS	governmental ministries of posts, telegraph, and telephone
PRNET	ARPA's radio packet network
PUP	PARC Universal Packet
RAM	Random Access Memory
RAND	The RAND Corporation, a think tank whose acronym stands for research and development
RARE	Réseaux Associés pour la Recherche Européenne
RFCS	Request for Comments
RIAA	Recording Industry Association of America
RIPE	Réseaux IP Européens
RLE	MIT Research Laboratory of Electronics

<199>

RSCS	remote spooling communications system that IBM machines used to communicate
RSS	really simple syndication
SAGE	the United States' Semi-Automatic Ground Environment defense anti air system
SATNET	ARPA's satellite packet network
SDK	software development kit
SGML	Standard Generalized Markup Language
SITA	Société Internationale de Télécommunications Aéronautiques
SLAC	Stanford National Accelerator Laboratory
SRI	Stanford Research Institute
TCP	Transmission Control Protocol
TCP/IP	The Internet suite built around the TCP and IP protocols
TMRC	MIT's Tech Model Railroad Club
UCL	University College London
URI	Universal Resource Identifier
VOIP	voice over Internet protocol
WAIS	Wide Area Information Servers
WGIG	Working Group on Internet Governance
WIPO	World Intellectual Property Organization
WWW	World Wide Web
X.25	an International Telecommunications Union networking standard

< 200 >

References

1 A CONCEPT BORN IN THE SHADOW OF THE NUKE

1 'A Report to the President pursuant to the President's directive of January 31, 1950', NSC 68 (7 April 1950), p. 54.
2 Gregg Herken, *Counsels of War* (New York, 1985), pp. 96–7.
3 NSC 162/2.
4 'A study on the management and termination of war with the Soviet Union', NET Evaluation Subcommittee of the National Security Council (15 November 1963) (URL: www.gwu.edu/~nsarchiv/NSAEBB/NSAEBB31/05-01.htm, last accessed 9 December 2008), pp. 4–13.
5 'Report of the NET Evaluation Subcommittee of the National Security Council', transcript of oral briefing to the President, date of transcript 27 August 1963 (URL: www.gwu.edu/~nsarchiv/nukevault/special/doc08.pdf, last accessed 9 December 2008), p. 19.
6 'A Report to the President', p. 54.
7 'The Unknown History of the Internet', *Stanford Unknown History of the Internet* series (September 2003) (URL: www.org/entrevista_ej.pdf, last accessed 13 January 2009).
8 Paul Baran, interviewed by David Hochfelder (24 October 1999), IEEE History Centre (URL: www.ieee.org/portal/cms_docs_iportals/iportals/aboutus/history_center/oral_history/pdfs/Baran378.pdf, last accessed 16 January 2009), pp. 7–8; see also Paul Baran speaking in Keenan Mayo and Peter Newcomb, 'How the Web was Won: An Oral History of the Internet', *Vanity Fair* (July 2008).
9 Paul Baran, 'On a Distributed Command and Control System Configuration' (Santa Monica, 1960) (URL: www.rand.org/pubs/research_memoranda/RM2632/).
10 Interview with Paul Baran in Stewart Brand, 'Founding Father', *Wired* (March 2001) (URL: www.wired.com/wired/archive/9.03/baran.html?pg=2, last accessed 15 October 2008).
11 Paul Baran, 'On Distributed Communication Networks' (Santa Monica, CA, 1962).
12 Ibid., p. 33.
13 Paul Baran, 'Summary Overview: On Distributed Communications' (Santa Monica, CA, 1964) (URL: rand.org/pubs/research_memoranda/RM3767/), p. 18.
14 Interview with Baran in Brand, 'Founding Father'.
15 Baran, interviewed by Hochfelder, p. 13.
16 Recommendation to the air staff on the development of the distributed adaptive

message-block network, 30 August 1965 (URL: www.archive.org/details/RecommendationToTheAirStaff, last accessed 29 January 2009).

17 Ibid., p. 4.

18 Paul Baran, 'Reliable Digital Communications Systems Using Unreliable Network Repeater Nodes' (Santa Monica, 1960).

19 Baran, interviewed by Hochfelder, p. 12.

20 Ibid., p. 14.

21 Leonard Kleinrock, 'Information Flow in Large Communication Nets', Proposal for a PhD thesis, MIT (31 May 1961) (URL: www.cs.ucla.edu/~lk/LK/Bib/REPORT/PhD/, last accessed 10 July 2009).

22 Thomas Marill and Lawrence Roberts, 'Toward a cooperative network of time-shared computers', Proceedings of the November 7–10, 1966, Fall Joint Computer Conference, American Federation of Information Processing Societies, New York (November 1966).

23 Baran, interviewed by Hochfelder, p. 12.

24 Paul Baran, interviewed by Mike Cassidy, 'Internet Pioneer Paul Baran Sees Net's Peaceful Purpose', Mike Cassidy's loose ends blog (25 September 2008) (URL: blogs.mercurynews.com/cassidy/2008/09/25/INTERNET-pioneer-paul-baran-sees-nets-peaceful-purpose/, last accessed 13 January 2009).

25 Paul Baran, interviewed by Judy E. O'Neill (5 March 1990), Charles Babbage Institute, University of Minnesota (URL: special.lib.umn.edu/cbi/oh/pdf.phtml?id=295, last accessed 3 July 2009), p. 34.

26 Timothy Moy, War Machines: Transforming Technologies in the US Military, 1920–1940 (College Station, TX, 2001), p. 96.

27 Karl T. Compton, 'Organisation of American Scientists for the War' (20 May 1943), reprinted in Science, XCVIII/2535 (30 July 1943), p. 94.

28 Watson Davis, 'Science is Decisive', Science News Letter, XLI/18 (2 May 1942).

29 Otto Eisenschil, 'The Chemist in Three Wars', Science, XCVI/2495 (23 October 1942), p. 371.

30 Vannevar Bush to Franklin Delano Roosevelt (16 July 1941) (URL: www.fdrlibrary.marist.edu/psf/box2/a13e01.html, last accessed 22 November 2008).

31 Vannevar Bush, Pieces of the Action (New York, 1970), pp. 121–8, 135.

32 'National Inventors Council to serve as clearing house', Science News Letter (17 August 1940), p. 100.

33 Bush, Pieces of the Action, p. 137.

34 'This Month in Physics History, October 22, 1938: Invention of Xerography', American Physical Society (URL: www.aps.org/publications/apsnews/200310/history.cfm, last accessed 3 December 2008).

35 'Scientific Events: National Inventors Council', Science, XCV/2453 (2 January 1942), p. 12.

36 'Ideas From Talent Search Winners Given to Government', Science News Letter, XLII/3 (18 July 1942), p. 38.

37 Compton, 'Organisation of American Scientists', p. 97.

38 President Roosevelt to Bush, 17 November 1944 (URL: www.nsf.gov/about/history/nsf50/vbush1945_roosevelt_letter.jsp, last accessed 28 November 2008).

39 Vannevar Bush, 'Science: The Endless Frontier' (July 1945), United States Government Printing Office, Washington (URL: www.nsf.gov/od/lpa/nsf50/vbush1945.htm, last accessed 25 November 2008).

< 202 >

40 Bush, *Pieces of the Action*, pp. 63–4.
41 General Arnold to Von Karman, 7 November 1944, quoted in Fred Kaplan, *Wizards of Armageddon* (New York, 1991), p. 56.
42 H. H. Arnold and J. W. Huston, *American Airpower Comes of Age: General Henry H. 'Hap' Arnold's World War II Diaries* (Darby, PA, 2001), p. 28.
43 Address of Brig. Gen. H. H. Arnold, assistant chief of the Air Corps, at the Western Aviation Planning Conference, 23 September 1937, quoted in Dik Daso, 'Origins of Airpower: Hap Arnold's Command Years and Aviation Technology, 1936–1945', *Air Power Journal* (Fall 1997) (URL: www.airpower.maxwell.af.mil/airchronicles/apj/apj97/fal97/daso.html, last accessed 1 January 2009).
44 Bruce Smith, *The RAND Corporation: Case Study of a Non-profit Advisory Corporation* (Cambridge, MA, 1966), pp. 42, 74–6.
45 'Preliminary Design of an Experimental World-Circling Spaceship', report SM-11827, Project RAND, Douglas Aircraft Company, 2 May 1946; see also David Hounshell, 'The Cold War, RAND, and the Generation of Knowledge, 1946–1962', *Historical Studies in the Physical and Biological Sciences*, pp. 244–8.
46 Smith, *The RAND Corporation*, pp. 45–8.
47 Burton Klein, 'A Radical Proposal for R. and D.', *Fortune*, 57 (May 1958), pp. 112–13.
48 Ibid.
49 R. D. Specht, 'RAND: A Personal View of its History' (23 October 1958) (URL: www.rand.org/pubs/papers/P1601/, last accessed 7 January 2009), p.19.
50 Baran, interviewed by Hochfelder, p. 7.
51 David Novick, internal memorandum, 19 June 1961, quoted in Smith, *The RAND Corporation*, p. 157.
52 Specht, 'RAND: A Personal View of its History', p. 25.
53 Herken, *Counsels of War*, p. 75.
54 Specht, 'RAND: A Personal View of its History', p. 4.
55 'The Unknown History of the Internet'.
56 Smith, *The RAND Corporation*, pp. 60–65.
57 Baran, 'On Distributed Communication Networks', p. 40.

2 THE MILITARY EXPERIMENT

1 'Soviet Fires Earth Satellite Into Space; It Is Circling the Globe at 18,000 MPH; Sphere Tracked in 4 Crossings Over US' and 'Soviet Claiming Lead In Science', *New York Times* (5 October 1957).
2 'Red Moon Over the US', *Time* (14 October 1957).
3 'Scientists Wonder if Shot Nears Moon', *New York Times* (5 November 1957).
4 'Deterrence and Survival in the Nuclear Age', Security Resources Panel of the Science Advisory Committee (7 November 1957), p. 22.
5 John F. Kennedy, 'Speech to the Senate, 14 August 1958', *The Strategy of Peace* (London, 1960), p. 3.
6 'Vanguard's Aftermath: Jeers and Tears', *Time* (16 December 1957).
7 'US Delay Draws Scientists Fire', *New York Times* (5 October 1957).
8 'The Organisation Man', *Time* (13 January 1958).
9 Katie Hafner and Matthew Lyon, *Where Wizards Stay Up Late: The Origins of the Internet* (London, 2003), p. 13.
10 Lawrence G. Roberts, interviewed by Arthur L. Norberg (4 April 1989), San

<203>

Francisco, Charles Babbage Institute (URL: http://special.lib.umn.edu/cbi/oh/pdf.
phtml?id=233, last accessed 4 September 2009), p. 41.

11 Jack P. Ruina, interviewed by William Aspray (20 April 1989), Charles Babbage
Institute (URL: www.cbi.umn.edu/oh/pdf.phtml?id=238, last accessed 18 January
2009), pp. 3, 9.

12 Arthur L. Norberg, 'Changing Computing: The Computing Community and
ARPA', *IEEE Annals of the History of Computing*, XVIII/2 (1996), pp. 42, 44.

13 J.C.R. Licklider, 'Memorandum for members and affiliates of the intergalactic computer network' (23 April 1963) (URL: www.packet.cc/files/memo.html, last accessed
12 January 2009).

14 Lawrence Roberts, 'The ARPANET and Computer Networks', Proceedings of the
Association for Computing Machinery Conference on the History of Personal
Workstations (9–10 January 1986), p. 51.

15 Roberts, interviewed by Norberg, p. 47.

16 Hafner and Lyon, *Where Wizards Stay Up Late*, pp. 41–2.

17 Ibid., p. 41.

18 Charles Herzfeld, interviewed by Arthur L. Norberg (6 August 1990), Charles
Babbage Institute, University of Minnesota (URL: www.cbi.umn.edu/oh/pdf.
phtml?id=149, last accessed 18 January 2009), p. 16.

19 Roberts, interviewed by Norberg, p. 10.

20 Lawrence Roberts, 'Internet Chronology: 1960–2001' (15 December 2007) (URL:
http://packet.cc/INTERNET.html, last accessed 1 July 2009).

21 Roberts, interviewed by Norberg, p. 17.

22 Ibid., p. 18.

23 Robert Taylor to David Farber et al., '[IP] more on 35th Anniversary of the Internet (well the start of the Arpanet anyway djf)' (6 October 2004) (URL: http:// mail.
computerhistory.org/pipermail/inforoots/2004-October/001415.html, 2 July 2009).

24 D. W. Davies, K. A. Bartlett, R. A. Scantlebury and P. T. Wilkinson, 'A Digital
Communication Network for Computers Giving Rapid Response at Remote
Terminals', presented at the October 1967 ACM Symposium on Operating System
Principles, Gatlinburg, TN.

25 Leonard Kleinrock to Lawrence Roberts, November 1967 (URL: ia360930. us.
archive.org//load_djvu_applet.cgi?file=1/items/SummaryOfTheRandMeeting/
SummaryOfTheRandMeeting.djvu, last accessed 1 February 2009)

26 Roberts, 'The ARPANET and Computer Networks', p. 52.

27 Roberts, 'Internet Chronology'.

28 'Interactive Computer Network Communication System', Lawrence Roberts to
E. Rechtin, Memorandum (21 June 1968), (URL: www.archive.org/details/Inter
activeComputerNetworkCommunicationSystem, last accessed 19 April 2009), p. 1.

29 Paul Baran, interviewed by Judy E. O'Neill (5 March 1990), Charles Babbage Institute, University of Minnesota (URL: special.lib.umn.edu/cbi/oh/pdf.phtml?
id=295, last accessed 3 July 2009), p. 37.

30 Leonard Kleinrock, 'Information Flow in Large Communication Nets', Proposal for
a PhD thesis' MIT (31 May 1961), p. 1 (URL: www.cs.ucla.edu/~lk/LK/Bib/REPORT/
PhD/part1.pdf).

31 Roberts, interviewed by Norberg, p. 47.

32 Richard J. Barber, *The Advanced Research Projects Agency, 1958–1974* (Washington,
DC, 1975), pp. 23–7.

< 204 >

33 Herzfeld, interviewed by Norberg, p. 26.
34 Leonard Kleinrock, e-mail to author (18 April 2009).
35 Roberts, interviewed by Norberg, p. 22.
36 'Interactive Computer Network Communication System', Roberts to Rechtin, p. 1.
37 'Resource Sharing Computer Networks', ARPA request for quotation (3 June 1968), p. 4.
38 Frank Heart, interviewed by Judy E. O'Neill (13 March 1990), Charles Babbage Institute, University of Minnesota (URL: www.cbi.umn.edu/oh/pdf.phtml?id=144, last accessed 18 January 2009), p.10.
39 Hafner and Lyon, *Where Wizards Stay Up Late*, pp. 94–6.
40 Heart, interviewed by O'Neill, p. 17.
41 Hafner and Lyon, *Where Wizards Stay Up Late*, p. 80.
42 Frank Heart and Robert Kahn, 'The Interface Message Processor for the ARPA Computer Network', BBN tender for request for quotation no. DAHC15 69 D 0002, p.II-2 [1968] (URL: www.archive.org/details/TheInterfaceMessageProcessorFor TheArpaComputerNetwork, last accessed 23 April 2009).
43 Leo Beranek, 'Roots of the Internet: A Personal History', *Massachusetts Historical Society*, II (2000) (URL: www.historycooperative.org/journals/mhr/2/beranek.html, last accessed 13 January 2009); Leonark Kleinrock, 'The Day the Infant Internet Uttered its First Words' (URL: www.cs.ucla.edu/~lk/LK/Inet/1stmesg.html)
44 Robert Kahn, interviewed by Judy O'Neill (24 April 1990), Charles Babbage Institute, pp. 21–2.
45 Vint Cerf, interviewed by Judy O'Neill (24 April 1990), Charles Babbage Institute.
46 David Walden, 'Experiences in Building, Operating, and Using the ARPA Network', Second USA-Japan Computer Conference, Tokyo (August 1975), p. 5.

3 THE ESSENCE OF THE INTERNET

1 Steve Crocker, 'How the Internet Got Its Rules', *New York Times* (6 April 2009); Steve Crocker, Request for Comments (7 April 1963) (URL: www.ietf.org/rfc/rfc0001.txt, last accessed 21 October 2008).
2 John Naughton, *A Brief History of the Future: From Radio Days to Internet Years in a Life Time* (New York, 2000), pp 134–5.
3 Crocker, 'How the Internet Got Its Rules'.
4 Ibid.
5 Steve Crocker, e-mail to author (19 April 2009).
6 Vint Cerf, e-mail to author (April 2009).
7 Steve Crocker, RFC 3 (April 1969) (URL: www.faqs.org/rfcs/rfc3.html, last accessed 23 April 2009).
8 Historic American Buildings Survey, HABS No. CA-2139 (February 1983).
9 Editorial, *Stanford Sequoia* (February 1908), quoted in Orrin Leslie Elliott, *Stanford University: The First Twenty-five Years* (New York, 1939), p. 387.
10 Quoted in Elliott, *Stanford University*, p. 388.
11 Steve Staiger, 'Echoes of Alpine Inn's Early Days', Palo Alto Online.com (24 January 2001) (URL: www.paloaltoonline.com/weekly/morgue/spectrum/2001_Jan_24. HISTRY24.html, last accessed 22 April 2009).
12 Don Nielson, 'The SRI Van and Computer Internetworking', *Core*, 3.1 (February 2002), p. 2.

<205>

13 Vint Cerf, 'Packet Satellite Technology Reference Sources', RFC 829 (November 1982), p. 1.

14 Joseph Paul Martino, *Science Funding: Politics and Porkbarrel* (New Brunswick, NJ, 1992), p. 143.

15 Cerf, interviewed by O'Neil.

16 'Intelsat IV: Fifth Generation Commercial Communications Satellite', Boeing (URL: www.boeing.com/defense-space/space/bss/factsheets/376/intelsat_iv/intelsat_iv.html, last accessed 24 April 2009); 'Explorer 1 and Jupiter-C Data Sheet', Department of Astronautics, National Air and Space Museum, Smithsonian Institution (URL: history.nasa.gov/sputnik/expinfo.html, last accessed 24 April 2009).

17 Seth Stein and Michael Wysession, *An Introduction to Seismology, Earthquakes, and Earth Structure* (Hoboken, NJ, 2003), p. 26.

18 'NORSAR and the Internet', NORSAR website (URL: www.norsar.no/pc-5-30-NORSAR-and-the-Internet.aspx, last accessed 14 August 2009); Peter Kirstein, 'Early experiences with ARPANET and INTERNET in the UK' (28 July 1998) (URL: nrg.cs.ucl.ac.uk/mjh/kirstein-arpanet.pdf, last accessed 21 April 2009), pp. 2, 5.

19 Vint Cerf, e-mail to author (15 August 2009).

20 Kirstein, 'Early Experiences with ARPANET and INTERNET', p. 1; Vint Cerf, e-mail to author (15 August 2009).

21 Peter Kirstein, 'UK Experiences With the ARPA Computer Network' in *Exploitation of Seismograph Networks*, ed. K. G. Beauchamp (Leiden, 1975), pp. 72–4.

22 Robert Kahn, 'The Introduction of Packet Satellite Communications', National Telecommunications Conference, Washington, DC (27–9 November 1979), p. 2.

23 Vint Cerf, 'How the Internet Came to Be' in *The Online User's Encyclopedia*, ed. Bernard Aboba (1993) (URL:www.netvalley.com/archives/mirrors/cerf-how-inet.html, last accessed 9 June 2009).

24 Louis Pouzin, 'Presentation and Major Design Aspects of the CYCLADES Computer Network', Proceedings of the Third ACM Symposium on Data Communications and Data Networks: Analysis and Design (1973); Vinton Cerf and Robert E. Kahn, 'A Protocol for Packet Network Intercommunication', *IEEE Transactions on Communications*, XXII/5 (May 1974).

25 Douglas K. Smith and Robert C. Alexander, *Fumbling the Future* (New York, 1988).

26 Janet Abbate, *Inventing the Internet* (Cambridge, MA, 2000), p. 126.

27 Ed Taft and Bob Metcalfe, 'Pup Specifications', inter-office memorandum (30 June 1978), p. 1. (URL: www.bitsavers.org/pdf/xerox/alto/pupSpec.pdf, last accessed 1 December 2009).

28 Cerf and Kahn, 'A Protocol for Packet Network Intercommunication', p. 11.

29 Steve Crocker, e-mail to author (15 April) 2009.

30 Abbate, *Inventing the Internet*, p. 127, n. 13.

31 David Clark, 'The Design Philosophy of the DARPA INTERNET Protocols', *ACM SIG-COMM Computer Communication Review*, XVIII/4 (August 1988), p. 2.

32 Nielson, 'The SRI Van and Computer Internetworking', p. 4.

33 Cerf, 'How the Internet Came to Be'.

34 Cerf, interviewed by O'Neill.

35 'A Brief History: Origins', AT&T (URL: www.corp.att.com/history/history1.html, last accessed 15 May 2008).

36 'Annual Report of the Directors of the American Telephone & Telegraph Company

< 206 >

to the Stockholders for the Year Ending December 31, 1908', p. 21 (URL: www.porticus.org/bell/pdf/1908ATTar_Complete.pdf, last accessed 15 June 2008).
37 Bell advertising slogan, 1908 (URL: https://www.corp.att.com/history/milestone_1908.html, last accessed 15 May 2008).
38 'Interactive Computer Network Communication System', Lawrence Roberts to E. Rechtin, Memorandum (21 June 1968), p. 2.
39 J. R. Halsey, L. E. Hardy and L. F. Powning, 'Public Data Networks: Their Evolution, Interfaces, and Status', IBM System Journal, XVIII/2 (1979), p. 224.
40 J.C.R. Licklider, 'Computers and Government' in Michael Dertouzos and Joel Moses, The Computer Age: A Twenty-year View (London, 1980), p. 109.
41 Described in detail in Abbate, Inventing the Internet, pp. 150–76.
42 Ibid., pp. 160–61.
43 'Resource Sharing Computer Networks', ARPA request for quotation (3 June 1968), p. 1.
44 Abbate, Inventing the Internet, p. 161.
45 Vint Cerf, e-mail to author, 18 April 2009.
46 See for example the exponential growth of connections during the Merit project, which allowed campus and other networks to connect in the early 1990s: Merit's History: The NSFNET Backbone Project, 1987–1995 (URL: www.livinginternet.com/doc/merit.edu/phenom.html, last accessed 5 May 2009); and MERIT statistical data, 1 September 1997 (URL: www.ccwhois.org/ccwhois/cctld/merit.history.hosts.txt, last accessed 3 May 2009).
47 Vint Cerf, e-mail to author (April 2009).

4 COMPUTERS BECOME CHEAP, FAST AND COMMON

1 William P. Delaney and William W. Ward, 'Radar Development at Lincoln Laboratory: An Overview of the First Fifty Years', Lincoln Laboratory Journal, XII/2 (2002) p. 152.
2 David F. Winkler, Searching the Skies: The Legacy of the United States Cold War Radar Defense Program (Champaign, IL, 1997), p. 24.
3 Frank Heart, interviewed by Judy E. O'Neill (13 March 1990), Charles Babbage Institute, University of Minnesota (URL: www.cbi.umn.edu/oh/pdf.phtml?id=144, last accessed 18 January 2009), p. 6.
4 'Art of Compiling Statistics', US Patent Office, Patent No. 395,782 (8 January 1889).
5 'The Whirlwind I Computer Description' (April 1955), MIT memo (URL: www.bitsavers.org/pdf/mit/whirlwind/Whirlwind_I_descr_Apr1955.pdf, last accessed 10 June 2009).
6 Chigusa Ishikawa Kita, 'J.C.R. Licklider's Vision for the IPTO', IEEE Annals of the History of Computing, XXV/3 (July–September 2003), p. 63.
7 Wesley Clark, 'The Lincoln TX-2 Computer Development', Papers Presented at the Western Joint Computer Conference: Techniques For Reliability, Los Angeles (26–8 February 1957), p. 142.
8 Alan R. Earls, Digital Equipment Corporation (Mount Pleasant, SC, 2004), p. 9.
9 J.C.R. Licklider, 'Man-Computer Symbiosis' IRE Transactions on Human Factors in Electronics (March 1960), p. 5.
10 Leo Beranek, 'BBN's Earliest Days: Founding a Culture of Engineering Creativity', IEEE Annals of the History of Computing, XXVII/2 (April–June 2005), p. 10.

<207>

11 J.C.R. Licklider quoted in Richard J. Barber, *The Advanced Research Projects Agency, 1958–1974* (Washington, DC, 1975), p. 298.

12 J.C.R. Licklider, *Libraries of the Future* (Cambridge, MA, 1965), p. 9.

13 Thierry Bardini, *Bootstrapping: Douglas Engelbart, Coevolution, and the Origins of Personal Computing* (Palo Alto, CA, 2000), p. 11.

14 Douglas Engelbart, 'Augmenting Human Intellect: A Conceptual Framework', summary report prepared for the Director of Information Science, Air Force Office of Scientific Research (October 1962), p. 1.

15 Douglas Engelbart, 'A Research Centre for Augmenting Human Intellect', American Federation of Information Processing Societies Records Fall Joint Computer Conference, San Francisco (1968).

16 'System 3', Tech Model Railroad Club (URL: http://tmrc.mit.edu/sys3/, last accessed 10 May 2009).

17 Steven Levy, *Hackers: Heroes of the Computer Revolution* (New York, 2001), p. 40.

18 John A. McKenzie, 'TX-0 Computer History', RLE Technical Report No. 627 (1 October 1974) (URL: dspace.mit.edu/bitstream/handle/1721.1/4132/RLE-TR-627-42827671.pdf, last accessed 10 May 2009), p. 19.

19 Levy, *Hackers*, pp. 29, 89.

20 McKenzie, 'TX-0 Computer History', p. 19.

21 Levy, *Hackers*, p. 43.

22 Ibid., p. 31.

23 Ibid., p. 54.

24 J. M. Graetz, 'The Origin of Spacewar', *Creative Computing* (August 1981).

25 Ibid.

26 Ivan Edward Sutherland, 'Sketchpad: A Man-machine Graphical Communication System', PhD thesis, MIT (1963), p. 17.

27 Alan Blackwell and Kerry Rodden, introduction to Sutherland, 'Sketchpad', reprinted in 2003 edn (URL: www.cl.cam.ac.uk/techreports/UCAM-CL-TR-574.pdf, last accessed 1 May 2009), p. 3.

28 'Miniaturized Electronic Circuits', patent number: 3,138,743; filing date: 6 February 1959; issue date: June 1964; inventor: Jack S. Kilby; Assignee: Texas Instruments, p. 1.

29 'Semiconductor device-and-lead structure', patent number: 2981877; filing date: 30 July 1959; issue date: April 1961; inventor Robert N. Noyce, p. 1.

30 'Announcing a New Era of Integrated Electronics', Intel advertisement (15 November 1971), reproduced at Intel Museum site (URL: www.intel.com/museum/archives/4004.htm, last accessed 21 January 2009).

31 Martin Campbell-Kelly, *From Airline Reservations to Sonic the Hedgehog: A History of the Software Industry* (London, 2003), p. 201.

32 'Fun Facts: The Intel 4004 Microprocessor', Intel.com (URL: www.intel.com/museum/archives/4004facts.htm, last accessed 13 May 2009).

33 'Speed and Money', ENIAC Museum Online (URL: www.seas.upenn.edu/~museum/fastmoney.html, last accessed 13 May 2009).

34 Ed Roberts, quoted in Levy, *Hackers*, p. 182.

35 *Popular Electronics* (January 1975), p. 33.

36 Forrest M. Mims III, 'The Altair Story; Early Days at MITS', *Creative Computing*, x/11 (November 1984), p. 17.

37 'People's Computing Company newsletter', issue 1 (October 1972), cover.

38 Community Memory flyer, 1972.

< 208 >

39 *Guide To Using The Community Memory* (date unknown).
40 'Resource One newsletter', no. 2 (April 1974), p. 4.
41 'Homebrew newsletter', issue 1 (15 March 1975).
42 Steve Wozniak, 'Homebrew and How the Apple Came to Be' in *Digital Deli: The Comprehensive, User-Lovable Menu of Computer Lore, Culture, Lifestyles and Fancy*, ed. Steve Ditlea (New York, 1984).
43 Ibid.
44 'Apple II Reference Manual' (1978).
45 See Jonathan Zittrain, 'The Generative Internet', *Harvard Law Review*, CXIX (May 2006).
46 Dan Brinklin, 'Special Short Paper for the HBS Advertising Course' (1 December 1978), p. 3 (URL: http://www.bricklin.com/anonymous/bricklin-1978-visicalc-paper.pdf, last accessed 10 December 2009).
47 IBM 25-year anniversary feature (URL: www-03.ibm.com/ibm/history/exhibits/pc25/pc25_intro.html, last accessed 14 May 2008).
48 *New York Times* (11 June 1984).
49 Richard Nolan, *Dot Vertigo: Doing Business in a Permeable World* (New York, 2001), pp. 6, 8–9.
50 Ibid.
51 Gordon E. Moore, 'Cramming More Components onto Integrated Circuits', *Electronics*, XXXVIII/8 (19 April 1965), p. 2 of article.
52 Clayton M. Christensen, *The Innovator's Dilemma: When New Technologies Cause Great Firms to Fail* (Cambridge, MA, 1997), pp.7, 9.
53 William Gibson, *Neuromancer* (London, 1986), p. 12.
54 Ibid., p. 67.
55 'Multimedia PC Level 1 and Level 2 Specifications', Microsoft.com (URL: support.microsoft.com/kb/106055, last accessed 26 February 2009).
56 IBM 25-year anniversary feature.
57 IBM Information Systems Division press release, 'Personal Computer Announced By IBM' (12 August 1981).
58 IBM PC brochure, 1982.
59 *New York Times* (5 February 1984).
60 'Gartner Says More than 1 Billion PCs In Use Worldwide and Headed to 2 Billion Units by 2014', press release, Gartner, 23 June 2008.

5 THE HOI POLLOI CONNECT

1 John R. McNamara, *The Economics of Innovation in the Telecommunications Industry* (Westport, CT, 1991), p. 5.
2 Horace Coon, *American Tel & Tel: The Story of a Great Monopoly*, reprint of 1939 edn (Manchester, NH, 1971), p. 61.
3 Peter William Huber, Michael K. Kellogg and John Thorne, *Federal Telecommunications Law* (New York, 1999), p. 17.
4 Coon, *American Tel & Tel*, p. 2.
5 *Hush-a-Phone v. United States*, 238 F.2d 266 (DC. Cir. 1956)
6 John Steele Gordon, 'The Death of a Monopoly', *American Heritage* (April 1997).
7 Nicholas Johnson, 'Carterfone: My Story', *Santa Clara Computer & High Tech. Law Journal*, XXV (2009), p. 686.

8 FCC tariff no. 132 (1957)

9 13 FCC 2d 420 (1968), 'In the matter of use of the Carterfone device in message toll telephone service; in the matter of Thomas F. Carter and Carter Electronics Corp., Dallas, Tex. (complainants), v. American Telephone and Telegraph co., Associated Bell System companies, Southwestern Bell Telephone Co., and Genera Telephone Co. of the Southwest (defendants)' (URL: www.uiowa.edu/~cyberlaw/FCCops/1968/13F2-420.html, last accessed 1 July 2008).

10 Johnson, 'Carterfone: My Story', p. 686.

11 'Electronic code of Federal regulations' (URL: ecfr.gpoaccess.gov/cgi/t/text/text-idx?c=ecfr&tpl=/ecfrbrowse/Title47/47cfr68_main_02.tpl, last accessed 8 June 2009).

12 Ward Christensen, 'History: Me, Micros, Randy, Xmodem, CBBS (LONG)' (18 March 1989) (URL: timeline.textfiles.com/bbs/CBBS/history.cbbs, last accessed 2 April 2009).

13 Ibid.

14 Ibid.

15 Randy Suess, 'The Birth of BBS' (1989) (URL: chinet.com/html/cbbs.html, last accessed 2 April 2009).

16 Noel Thomas and Kim Thomas, 'So, You Want to be a SYSOP?', ANALOG Computing, no. 19 (June 1984), p. 74.

17 Paulina Borsook, 'The Anarchist', Wired (April 1996).

18 Tom Jennings, 'FidoNet history and operation' (8 February 1985) (URL: wps.com/FidoNet/fidohist1.txt, last accessed 8 June 2009).

19 John Souvestre, David Troendle, Bob Davis and George Peace, 'EchoMail Specification, Revision 2' (28 July 1993) (URL: www.ftsc.org/docs/fsc-0074.001, last accessed 8 June 2009).

20 Jack Rickard, 'Home-grown BB$', Wired (September/October 1993).

21 Vint Cerf, e-mail to author (18 April 2009).

22 S. E. Goodman, L. I. Press, S. R. Ruth and A. M. Rutkowski, 'The Global Diffusion of the Internet: Patterns and Problems', Communications of the ACM, XXXVII/8 (August 1994), p. 27.

23 'Commute By Jet', Popular Mechanics (April 1950), p. 149.

24 Gerald Milward-Oliver, SITA: Celebrating the Future, 50 Years of Vision (Middlesex, 1999), p. 18

25 Ibid., p. 24.

26 Ibid., p.2 5; 'SITA history' (URL: www.sita.com/content/sita-history, last accessed 22 March 2009).

27 R. Blair Smith, interviewed by Robina Mapstone (29 May 1980), Charles Babbage Institute (URL: www.cbi.umn.edu/oh/pdf.phtml?id=258, last accessed 22 March 2009), p. 40.

28 Martin Campbell-Kelly and Daniel D. Garcia-Swartz, 'The History of the Internet: The Missing Narratives' (2 December 2005) (URL: ssrn.com/abstract=867087, last accessed 3 April 2009), p.3.

29 Martin Campbell-Kelly, From Airline Reservations to Sonic the Hedgehog: A History of the Software Industry (London, 2003), p. 1.

30 Paul A. Strassmann, The Squandered Computer: Evaluating the Business Alignment of Information Technologies (New Canaan, CT, 1997), pp. 217–23.

31 Ibid., p. 220.

32 Campbell-Kelly, From Airline Reservations to Sonic the Hedgehog, p. 203.

< 210 >

33 Strassmann, *The Squandered Computer*, p. 224.
34 John Romkey, interviewed by Bernard Aboba (18 December 1993) (URL: http://madhaus.utcs.utoronto.ca/local/internaut/pc-ip.html, last accessed 3 May 2009).
35 MERIT statistical data, 3 February 1994 (URL:www.textfiles.com/INTERNET/hosts.hst, last accessed 2 May 2009).

6 COMMUNITIES BASED ON INTEREST, NOT PROXIMITY

1 J. Christopher Westland and Theodore H. K. Clark, *Global Electronic Commerce: Theory and Case Studies* (Cambridge, MA, 1999), p. 56.
2 Ron Rosenbaum, 'Secrets of the Little Blue Box', *Esquire* (October 1971) (URL: www.lospadres.info/thorg/lbb.html, last accessed 28 April 2009).
3 John T. Draper, 'The Story So Far' (URL: www.webcrunchers.com/crunch/story.html, last accessed 1 May 2009).
4 Taran King and Knight Lightning, 'Real Phreakers Guide Vol. 1' (6 October 1985) (URL: artofhacking.com/IET/RAGS/PHREAKS.REL, last accessed 28 April 2009).
5 Doctor Dissector, 'The Phreaker's Handbook #1' (3 July 1989) (URL: www.scribd.com/doc/11313841/The-Phreakers-Handbook1, last accessed 28 April 2009).
6 J.C.R. Licklider and Robert W. Taylor, 'The Computer as a Communication Device', reprinted from *Science and Technology* (April 1968) (URL: memex.org/licklider.pdf, last accessed 22 October 2008), p. 21.
7 John Naughton, *A Brief History of the Future: From Radio Days to Internet Years in a Life Time* (New York, 2000), p. 75.
8 Robert Taylor, speaking at 'The Path to Today' seminar at the University of California, 17 August 1989, transcript excerpted in Leo Beranek, 'Roots of the Internet: A Personal History', *Massachusetts Historical Society*, II (2000) (URL: www.historycooperative.org/journals/mhr/2/beranek.html, last accessed 13 January 2009).
9 Richard Watson, 'A Mailbox Protocol', RFC 196 (20 July 1971).
10 Ray Tomlinson, 'Frequently Made Mistakes' (URL: http://openmap.bbn.com/~tomlinso/ray/mistakes.html, last accessed 12 June 2009).
11 Leonard Kleinrock, e-mail to author (April 2009).
12 Ray Tomlinson, 'The First Network e-mail' (URL: http://openmap.bbn.com/~tomlinso/ray/firstemailframc.html, last accessed 12 June 2009).
13 'A History of ARPANET: The First Decade', Report 4799, BBN (April 1981), pp. III–110; see also pp. III–67.
14 Steven Walker to Message Group, 'MSGGROUP# 002 Message Group Status' (7 June 1975) (URL: www.dataswamp.net/computerhistory/archives/msggroup/001_jun75-jul75.txt, last accessed 12 June 2009).
15 Ronda Hauben, 'The Evolution of USENET News: The Poor Man's ARPANET', speech at the Michigan Association for Computer Users in Learning (MACUL) (3 December 1993) (URL: http://neil.franklin.ch/Netizen/ch.1_poorman_ARPA, last accessed 12 June 2009).
16 J.C.R. Licklider and Albert Vezza, 'Applications of Information Networks', *Proceedings of the IEEE*, LXVI/11 (November 1978), p. 1331.
17 Thread of discussion archived (URL: www-2.cs.cmu.edu/~sef/Orig-Smiley.htm, last accessed 12 July 2009).
18 Andy Tenenbaum to comp.os.minix, 'Linux is obsolete', (29 January 1992) (URL: http://groups.google.com/group/comp.os.minix/browse_thread/thread/c25870d7a

< 211 >

41696d2/ac1b04eb0e09c03e?lnk=gst&q=#ac1b04eb0e09c03e, last accessed 24 June 2009).

19 Linus Torvalds to comp.os.minix, 'Linux is obsolete' (30 January 1992) (URL: http://groups.google.com/group/comp.os.minix/browse_thread/thread/c25870d7a 41696d2/ac1b04eb0e09c03e?lnk=gst&q=#ac1b04eb0e09c03e, last accessed 24 June 2009).

20 Ruth Davis, 'Computing Networks: A Powerful National Force', excerpted in ARPANET News, issue 1 (March 1973), p. 8.

21 Lawrence G. Roberts, interviewed by Arthur L. Norberg (4 April 1989), Charles Babbage Institute, pp. 16–17.

22 'A History of ARPANET: The First Decade', pp. III–108.

23 Hauben, 'The Evolution of USENET News'.

24 Steven M. Bellovin, e-mail to author (12 July 2009).

25 Stephen Daniel quoted in Hauben, 'The Evolution of USENET News'.

26 Cluetrain manifesto (1999) (URL: www.cluetrain.com/book/95-theses.html, last accessed, 1 January 2009).

27 'ARPANET Study Final Report', RCA Services Company (24 November 1972), p. 2.

28 Frank Heart, interviewed by Judy E. O'Neill (13 March 1990), Charles Babbage Institute, University of Minnesota (URL:www.cbi.umn.edu/oh/pdf.phtml?id=144, last accessed 18 January 2009), pp. 25–6.

29 Licklider and Taylor, 'The Computer as a Communication Device', p. 40.

30 'Macintosh Shapes Up a Winner', Los Angeles Times (29 January 1984).

31 'Telecommunications Talk; Modem Speed: What Does it Mean to You?', Creative Computing, XI/2 (February 1985), p. 30; and 'Personal Computers; Modems: How Much Speed Makes Sense?', New York Times (30 April 1985).

32 Quoted in John Brockman, Digerati: Encounters with the Cyber Elite (1996) (URL: www.edge.org/documents/digerati/Brand.html, last accessed 20 May 2009).

33 'A Timeline of the First Ten Years of the WELL', The Well (1995) (URL: www.well.com/conf/welltales/timeline.html, last accessed 20 May 2009).

34 Katie Halfner, 'The World's Most Influential Online Community (And It's Not AOL)', Wired (May 1997).

35 John Markoff, 'Sausalito Journal; Whole Earth State-of-Art Rapping', New York Times (15 August 1989).

36 'Annual Report of the Directors of the American Telephone & Telegraph Company to the Stockholders for the Year Ending December 31, 1908', p. 21 (URL: www.porticus.org/bell/pdf/1908ATTar_Complete.pdf, last accessed 15 June 2008).

37 S. J. Liebowitz and S. E. Margolis, 'Network Externalities (Effects)', The New Palgrave's Dictionary of Economics and the Law (Basingstoke, 1998) (URL: www.utdallas.edu/~liebowit/palgrave/network.html, last accessed 15 June 2008).

38 George Gilder, 'Metcalfe's Law and its legacy, Forbes ASAP (13 September 1993) (URL: http://www.seas.upenn.edu/~gaj1/metgg.html, last accessed 22 April 2009).

39 Bob Metcalfe, 'Metcalfe's Law Recurses Down the Long tail of Social Networks', VC Mike's Blog (URL: vcmike.wordpress.com/2006/08/18/metcalfe-social-networks/, last accessed 13 January 2009).

40 Ibid.

41 David Reed, 'That Sneaky Exponential – Beyond Metcalfe's Law to the Power of Community Building', Context (Spring 1999) (URL: http://www.contextmag.com/archives/199903/digitalstrategyreedslaw.asp, last accessed 31 October 2009).

< 212 >

42 David Reed, 'Weapon of Math Destruction', *Context* (Spring 1999) (URL: http://www.contextmag.com/archives/199903/digitalstrategy.asp?process=print).

43 David Reed, interviewed in *Journal of the Hyperlinked Organization* (19 January 2001) (URL: http://www.hyperorg.com/backissues/joho-jan19-01.html, last accessed 31 October 2009).

44 Reed, 'That Sneaky Exponential'.

45 David Reed, 'The Law of the Pack', *Harvard Business Review*, LXXIX/2 (February 2001), p. 24.

46 Reed, interviewed in *Journal of the Hyperlinked Organization*.

47 Reed, 'That Sneaky Exponential'.

48 Douglas Engelbart, 'Augmenting Human Intellect: A Conceptual Framework', summary report prepared for the Director of Information Science, Air Force Office of Scientific Research (October 1962) (URL: bootstrap.org/augdocs/friede-waldo30402/augmentinghumanintellect/AHI62.pdf, last accessed 29 April 2009), p.106.

49 Ronda Hauben and Michael Hauben, 'Preface: What is a Netizen?', *Netizens*, net-book last updated 6 December 1996 (URL: www.columbia.edu/~hauben/book/, last accessed 20 January 2009).

50 Howard Rheingold, 'The Tragedy of the Electronic Commons', *San Francisco Examiner*, 19 December 1994.

51 David Clark, 'A Cloudy Crystal Ball: Visions of the Future', IETF (July 1992) (URL: xys.ccert.edu.cn/reference/future_ietf_92.pdf, last accessed 20 April 2009).

7 FROM MILITARY NETWORKS TO THE GLOBAL INTERNET

1 Quoted in William von Alven, 'Condensed History of Telecomunications', Communication Certification Laboratory (May 1998) (URL: http://www.cclab.com/billhist.htm, last accessed 11 December 2009).

2 Joseph Haughney, ARPANET newsletter, no. 1 (1 July 1980).

3 Glynn Parker, DOD *Network News*, no. 11 (2 March 1982).

4 H. H. Arnold and J. W. Huston, *American Airpower Comes of Age: General Henry H. 'Hap' Arnold's World War II Diaries* (Darby, PA, 2001), p. 28.

5 Glynn Parker, DOD *Network News*, no. 12 (11 June 1982).

6 Joseph Haughney, ARPANET *News*, no. 6 (30 March 1981).

7 'TCP/IP Digest', 1/10 (5 January 1981) (URL:ftp://ftp.rfc-editor.org/in-notes/museum/tcp-ip-digest/tcp-ip-digest.v1n10.1, last accessed 2 May 2009).

8 Lawrence Landweber, 'CSNET' (29 November 2007) (URL: www.nsfnet-legacy.org/archives/02—Beginnings.pdf, last accessed 8 May 2009).

9 Peter J. Denning, Anthony Hearn and C. William Kern, 'History and overview of CSNET', ACM SIGCOMM *Computer Communication Review* (March 1983), pp. 138–45.

10 Lawrence Landweber, 'CSNet: A Brief History' (22 September 1991) (URL: dis-www.mit.edu/MENELAUS.MIT.EDU/com-priv/1395, last accessed 30 April).

11 'CREN history', CREN (URL: http://www.cren.net/cren/cren-hist-fut.html, 31 August 2009).

12 'BITNET history', Living Internet (URL: http://www.livinginternet.com/u/ui_bitnet.htm, 31 August 2009).

13 David Roessner et al., *The Role of NSF's Support of Engineering in Enabling Technological Innovation, First Year Final Report* (January 1997), prepared for the

<213>

National Science Foundation (URL: www.sri.com/policy/csted/reports/techin/inter3.html, last accessed 4 May 2009).

14 *Merit's History: The NSFNET Backbone Project, 1987–1995* (URL: www.livinginternet.com/doc/merit.edu/partnership.html, last accessed 5 May 2009).

15 MERIT statistical data, 3 February 1994 (URL: www.textfiles.com/INTERNET/hosts.hst, last accessed 2 May 2009).

16 *Merit's History: The NSFNET Backbone Project, 1987–1995.*

17 J.C.R. Licklider, 'Computers and Government' in Michael Dertouzos and Joel Moses, *The Computer Age: a Twenty-year View* (London, 1980), p. 117.

18 Mark Pullen and Brian Boesch, 'Death of ARPANET and Other Paranoia', internal DARPA memorandum, quoted in Gregory M. Vaudreuil, 'The Federal Research Internet Committee and the National Research Network' (27 April 1988), ACM SIG-COMM *Computer Communication Review*, XVIII/3 (May/June, 1988) p. 8.

19 MERIT statistical data, 3 February 1994.

20 Eric Boehlert, *Wired Owes Al Gore an Apology*, HuffingtonPost.com, 28 April 2006 (URL:www.huffingtonpost.com/eric-boehlert/wired-owes-al-gore-an-apo_b_19980.html, last accessed 8 May 2009).

21 'A Study of Critical Problems and Future Options: A Report to the Office of Science and Technology Policy on Computer Networks to Support Research In the United States', vol. 1, Federal Coordinating Council on Science, Engineering and Technology (November 1987).

22 'Al Gore and the Internet', in e-mail from Vint Cerf to various recipients (30 September 2008).

23 Transcript of Al Gore interview with Wolf Blitzer, CNN *Late Edition* (9 March 1999) (URL: www.cnn.com/ALLPOLITICS/stories/1999/03/09/president.2000/transcript.gore/, last accessed 8 May 2009).

24 'Al Gore and the Internet'.

25 Anton A. Huurdeman, *The Worldwide History of Telecommunications* (New York, 2003), p. 87.

26 José Chesnoy, ed., *Undersea Fiber Communication Systems* (London, 2002), p. 19.

27 Tom Standage, *The Victorian Internet* (London, 1999), p. 84.

28 Vint Cerf, interviewed by Judy O'Neill, Charles Babbage Institute (24 April 1990).

29 Barry Leiner, 'Globalization of the Internet' in Daniel C. Lynch and Marshall T. Rose, *Internet System Handbook* (Greenwich, CT, 1993), pp. 16–38.

30 Fred Rounds, 'NSI Directed to continue SPAN's functions', NASA memorandum, 1 May 1991.

31 Bernhard Stockman, 'EBONE, a technical overview', 1993 (URL: ftp://ftp.cuhk.hk/pub/doc/inet93/GED.Stockman.gz, last accessed 22 August 2009).

32 Peter Quennell, *Byron: The Years of Fame* (New York, 1935), pp. 49–50.

33 Steven Levy, *Hackers: Heroes of the Computer Revolution* (New York, 2001), p. 84.

34 Po Bronson, *The Nudist on the Late Shift* (London, 2000), pp. xiv–xvi.

35 Katie Hafner and Matthew Lyon, *Where Wizards Stay Up Late: The Origins of the Internet* (London, 2003), pp 94–5.

36 Leo Beranek, 'Roots of the Internet: A Personal History', *Massachusetts Historical Society*, II (2000) (URL: www.historycooperative.org/journals/mhr/2/beranek.html, last accessed 13 January 2009).

37 Lawrence G. Roberts, interviewed by Arthur L. Norberg (4 April 1989), Charles Babbage Institute, p. 8.

< 214 >

38 '"God of the Internet" is dead', BBC *News* (19 October 1998).

39 'Battle for the Soul of the Internet', *Time* magazine (18 March 2005).

40 Steve Crocker, RFC 3 (April 1969) (URL: www.faqs.org/rfcs/rfc3.html, last accessed 23 April 2009).

41 Dave Clarke, quoted in P. Hoffman, *The Tao of IETF: A Novice's Guide to the Internet Engineering Task Force*, IETF Internet draft (16 February 2009) (URL: www.ietf. org/tao.html, last accessed 26 May 2009).

42 Robert Kahn, 'The Role of Government in the Evolution of the Internet', *Communications of the ACM*, XXXVII/8 (August 1994), p. 16.

43 Vint Cerf, 'Internet Activities Board', RFC1160 (May 1990).

44 Scott Bradner, e-mail to author (21 April 2009); Steve Crocker, e-mails to author, (18–19 April 2009).

45 Steve Crocker, e-mails to author (18–19 April 2009).

46 Scott Bradner, 'IETF Working Group Guidelines and Procedure', Network Working Group RFC 2418 (September 1998) (URL:tools.ietf.org/html/rfc2418, 20 April 2009), p.10.

47 Ibid., pp. 12, 16–19.

48 Ibid., pp. 2–3.

49 Ibid., pp. 9–10.

50 Paul Mockapetris, RFC 882, 'Domain names – concepts and facilities' (November 1983).

51 'Cooperative agreement between NSI and US Government: Network Information Services Manager(s) for NSFNET and the NREN: INTERNIC Registration Services' (1 January 1993).

52 'David Bennahum interview with Jon Postel 1995', Memex (URL: http://memex. org/meme4-01.html, last accessed 27 August 2009).

53 Author's exchange with Vint Cerf (29 August 2009).

54 'Management of Internet Names and Addresses', NTIA statement of policy, US Department of Commerce (5 June 1998).

55 'Articles of Incorporation of Internet Corporation for Assigned Names and Numbers' (21 November 1998).

56 'US Statement of Principles on the Internet's Domain Name and Addressing System', NTIA (30 June 2005).

57 Victoria Shannon, 'Other Nations Hope to Loosen US Grip on Internet', *New York Times* (15 November 2005).

8 THE WEB!

1 Vannevar Bush, 'As We May Think', *The Atlantic* (July 1945), p. 8.

2 Ibid., p. 6.

3 Theodore Nelson, 'Complex Information Processing: A File Structure for the Complex, the Changing and the Indeterminate', Proceedings of the 1965 20th National Conference (24–6 August 1965), Cleveland, Ohio.

4 See the manual for the Enquire program (URL: www.w3.org/History/1980/ Enquire/ manual/, last accessed 25 January 2009).

5 Tim Berners-Lee, 'The World Wide Web: A Very Short Personal History', w3.org (7 May 1998) (URL:www.w3.org/People/Berners-Lee/ShortHistory, last accessed 25 January 2009).

< 215 >

6 Tim Berners-Lee, *Weaving the Web: The Past, Present and Future of the World Wide Web by its Inventor* (London, 1999), p. 25.

7 Ibid., p. 47.

8 Ibid., pp. 30–31.

9 Perry Pei Wei, e-mail to author (21 July 2009).

10 Tom Bruce, e-mail to author (27 July 2009).

11 'Netscape Communications Corporation Announces Initial Public Offering of 5,000,000 Shares of Common Stock', press release (9 August 1995).

12 Author's conversation with Shih-Pau Yen (1 May 2009).

13 The Minnesota Gopher Team to Usenet community, regarding University of Minnesota Gopher software licensing policy (11 March 1993) (URL: www.nic.funet.fi/pub/vms/networking/gopher/gopher-software-licensing-policy.ancient, last accessed 28 February 2009).

14 Author's conversation with Shih-Pau Yen (1 May 2009).

15 Berners-Lee, *Weaving the Web*, p. 80.

16 Ibid., p. 84.

17 Richard Stallman, 'The GNU project', in *Free Software, Free Society: Selected Essays of Richard M. Stallman* (Boston, 2002), p. 18.

18 John Markoff, 'One Man's Fight for Free Software', *New York Times*, 11 January 1989.

19 Richard Stallman, 'Why Software Should Be Free' in *Free Software, Free Society*, p. 124.

20 Author's exchange with Richard Stallman (June 2009).

21 Denis Ritchie, 'A Unix Ad' (URL: http://cm.bell-labs.com/cm/cs/who/dmr/unixad.html, last accessed 16 June 2009).

22 Richard Stallman to net.unix-wizards.net and usoft newsgroups, 'New Unix implementation' (27 September 1983).

23 Linus Torvalds, 'The Origins of Linux', speech at the Computer History Museum (19 September 2001) (URL:http://videos.linuxfoundation.org/video/1110, last accessed 22 June 2009).

24 Linus Torvalds quoted in Thomas Goetz, 'Open Source Everywhere', *Wired* (November 2003) (URL:www.wired.com/wired/archive/11.11/opensource.html, last accessed 29 June 2008).

25 Linus Torvalds, posting to comp.os.inix usenet group (26 August 1991) (URL: http://groups.google.co.uk/group/comp.os.minix/browse_thread/thread/76536d1fb451ac60/b813d52cbc5a044b?pli=1, last accessed 22 June 2009).

26 Lars Wirzenius, 'Linux Anecdotes', speech at the 1998 Linux Expo (27 April 1998) (URL: http://liw.iki.fi/liw/texts/linux-anecdotes.html, last accessed 23 June 2009).

27 Linus Torvalds, posting to comp.os.inix usenet group (5 October 1991) (URL: http://groups.google.com/group/comp.os.minix/msg/2194d253268b0a1b?pli=1, last accessed 22 June 2009).

28 Preamble, GNU General Public License Version 2 (June 1991), Free Software Foundation.

29 Glyn Moody, 'The Greatest os that (N)ever was', *Wired*, 5.08 (August 1997).

30 'Linux: The Making of a Global Hack', *Forbes* (10 August 1998).

31 Charles Babcock, 'Linux Will Be Worth $1 Billion In First 100 Days of 2009', *InformationWeek*'s Open Source Weblog (19 October 2007).

32 J.C.R. Licklider and Robert W. Taylor, 'The Computer as a Communication Device', reprinted from *Science and Technology* (April 1968), p. 32.

< 216 >

33 'Linus Torvalds' Benevolent Dictatorship', *Business Week*, 18 August 2004.

34 Thomas Goetz, 'Open Source Everywhere', *Wired* (November 2003).

35 Eric S. Raymond, *The Cathedral and the Bazaar* (Cambridge, MA, 2000) (URL: www.catb.org/~esr/writings/cathedral-bazaar/cathedral-bazaar/ar01s04.html, last accessed 16 June 2009).

36 'About the Apache HTTP Server Project', Apache.org (URL: http://httpd.apache.org/ABOUT_APACHE.html, last accessed 17 August 2009).

37 'Link Letter', Merit Computer Network/NSFNET Information Services, Ann Arbor, MI, VII/1 (July 1994).

38 *Merit's History: The NSFNET Backbone Project, 1987–1995* (URL: www.livinginternet.com/doc/merit.edu/phenom.html, last accessed 5 May 2009).

39 Berners-Lee, *Weaving the Web*, p. 81.

40 Berners-Lee, 'The World Wide Web: A Very Short Personal History'.

41 *Merit's History: The NSFNET Backbone Project, 1987–1995*.

42 MERIT statistical data (1 September 1997) (URL: www.ccwhois.org/ccwhois/cctld/merit.history.hosts.txt, last accessed 3 May 2009).

43 Thomas Vanderwal, 'The Come to Me Web', Personal InfoCloud (19 January 2006) (URL:www.personalinfocloud.com/2006/01/the_come_to_me_.html, last accessed 25 January 2009).

44 Alan Emtage, e-mail to author (16 July 2009).

45 Brian Pinkerton, e-mail to author (14 May 2009).

46 John Batelle, *Search: How Google and its Rivals Rewrote the Rules of Business and Transformed Our Culture* (London, 2005), p. 58.

47 Ibid., p. 61.

48 Ibid., pp. 51–3.

49 'Sergey Brin's home page', 1999 (URL: http://web.archive.org/web/19991010223952/www-db.stanford.edu/~sergey/, last accessed 15 July 2009).

50 Sergey Brin and Lawrence Page, 'The Anatomy of a Large-Scale Hypertextual Web Search Engine', *Computer Networks and ISDN Systems*, xxx/1–7 (April 1998) (URL:http://infolab.stanford.edu/~backrub/google.html, last accessed 15 July 2009).

51 'Our Philosophy: Ten Things That Google Had Found to be True', Google.com (URL: www.google.com/corporate/tenthings.html, last accessed 11 August 2009).

52 'Corporate Information', Google (URL: www.google.com/corporate/history.html, last accessed 7 August 2009).

9 A PLATFORM FOR TRADE AND THE PITFALLS OF THE DOT-COM

1 'Our history', eBay.com (URL: news.ebay.com/history.cfm, last accessed 9 July 2008).

2 Thomas Jones, 'Diary', *London Review of Books* (19 June 2008).

3 Paul Baran, 'Some Changes in Information Technology Affecting Marketing in the Year 2000', RAND (1968), p. 20.

4 Brian Kahin, 'Commercialization of the Internet: Summary Report', RFC 1192 (November 1990), p. 3.

5 Laurence A. Carter and Martha S. Siegel, *How to Make a Fortune on the Information Superhighway: Everyone's Guerrilla Guide to Marketing on the Internet and Other On-line Services* (New York, 1994), p. 21.

6 Kahin, 'Commercialization of the Internet', p. 4.

< 217>

7 'NSF 93-52 – Network access point manager, routing arbiter, regional network providers, and very high speed backbone network services provider for NSFNET and the NREN(SM) program', National Science Foundation (6 May 1993) (URL: w2.eff.org/Infrastructure/Govt_docs/nsf_nren.rfp, last accessed 5 May 2009).

8 Anne Goldgar, *Tulipmania: Money, Honor, and Knowledge in the Dutch Golden Age* (Chicago, 2007), p. 31.

9 Charles Mackey, *Extraordinary Popular Delusions and the Madness of Crowds* (London, 1841, reprint 1932), p. 90.

10 Peter M. Garber, *Famous First Bubbles: The Fundamentals of Early Manias* (Cambridge, MA, 2001), pp. 29–36.

11 Mackey, *Extraordinary Popular Delusions*, p. 91.

12 'When Bubbles Burst Tulips. Dot-coms', *Fortune* (11 June 2001).

13 'Internet Worth: Why the Frenzy Won't Stop Soon', *Fortune*, 11 December 1995.

14 John Doerr quoted in 'The Little Creepy Crawlers Who Will Eat You In The Night', *New York Times* (1 March 1998).

15 Peter Schwartz and Peter Leyden, 'The Long Boom, 1980–2020', *Wired* (July 1997).

16 'Chart-topping "pops": statistics on the Internet bubble', PBS Frontline (URL: www.pbs.org/wgbh/pages/frontline/shows/dotcon/thinking/stats.html, last accessed 16 June 2008); see also Jay Ritter, 'Big IPO runups of 1975–2005', working paper (January 2008) (URL:bear.cba.ufl.edu/ritter/Runup7504.pdf, last accessed 16 June 2008).

17 Vince Heaney, 'Technical Analysis: Clear Signs of a Bursting Nasdaq', *Financial Times* (23 May 2003).

18 Richard Nolan, *Dot Vertigo: Doing Business in a Permeable World* (New York, 2001), p. 7.

19 'The $1.7 Trillion Dot Com Lesson', CNN *Money* (9 November 2000).

20 'Will Dotcom Bubble Burst Again?', *Los Angeles Times* (17 July 2006).

21 'The Challenge of Central Banking in a Democratic Society', remarks by Chairman Alan Greenspan at the Annual Dinner and Francis Boyer Lecture of The American Enterprise Institute for Public Policy Research, Washington, DC (5 December 1996).

22 Warran Buffett to shareholders of Berkshire Hathaway Inc. (28 February 2001).

23 Peter Garber, *Famous First Bubbles* (Cambridge, MA, 2001), pp. 43–9.

24 'eBay Marketplace Fast Facts', eBay.com (URL: news.ebay.com/fastfacts_ebay_marketplace.cfm, last accessed 9 July 2008).

25 'eBay: A Short History', eBay.com (URL: news.ebay.com/about.cfm, last accessed 9 July 2008).

26 'Going once, going twice . . .', ComputerUser.com (17 September 2000).

27 'What Webvan Could Have Learned from Tesco', Knowledge@Wharton (10 October 2001).

28 James Marcus, *Amazonia: Five Years at the Epicentre of the Dot.com Juggernaut* (New York, 2004), p. 91.

29 Ibid., p. 47.

30 Gary Rivlin, *The Godfather of Silicon Valley: Ron Conway and the Fall of the Dot-coms* (New York, 2001), p. 61.

31 Nicholas Negroponte, *Being Digital* (New York, 1996), p. 2.

32 Philip Kaplan, *F'd Companies: Spectacular Dot-com Flameouts* (New York, 2002), p. 50.

33 'Webvan is Delaying its Offering of Stock', *New York Times*, 8 October 1999.

< 218 >

34 Joel Spolsky, 'Ben and Jerry's vs. Amazon', Joel on Software blog, 12 May 2000 (URL: www.joelonsoftware.com/articles/fog0000000056.html, last accessed 13 January 2009).

35 Lawrence Fisher, 'On-Line Grocer is Setting up Delivery System for $1 Billion', *New York Times* (10 July 1999).

36 Victoria Shannon, 'WebVan Shuts', *New York Times* (11 July 2001).

37 'What Webvan Could Have Learned from Tesco'.

38 Tesco Plc Interim results (18 September 2001), pp. 2, 5.

39 Andy Reinhardt, 'Tesco Bets Small – and Wins Big', *Business Week* (1 October 2001).

40 Troy Wolverton, 'Pet Sites Bark Up the Wrong Tree', CNet *News* (3 November 1999).

41 'The E-Commerce Survivors', *The Industry Standard* (16 July 2001).

42 Chip Bayers, 'The Great Web Wipeout', *Wired* (April 1996).

43 Kaplan, *F'd Companies*, p. 72.

44 Rivlin, *The Godfather of Silicon Valley*, p. 55.

45 Randall E. Stross, *eBoys* (New York, 2001), p. vi.

46 Tom Herman, 'Entrepreneurship in Difficult Times' (date unknown) (URL: www.windsormountain.org/pds/pres_exrpt.pdf, last accessed 10 January 2009).

47 Ibid.

48 John Heilemann, 'Andy Grove's Rational Exuberance', *Wired* (June 2001).

49 Brent Goldfarb, David Kirsch and David A. Miller, 'Was There Too Little Entry During the Dot Com Era?', *Journal of Financial Economics*, v. 86, no. 1 (October 2007), p. 2.

50 Marcus, *Amazonia*, pp. 104–5.

51 'Quarterly Retail e-commerce Sales, 4th quarter 2008', US Census Bureau, US Department of Commerce (17 February 2009), p. 1.

52 Dixon Ryan Fox and Arthur M Schlesinger, eds, *The Cavalcade of America* (Springfield, MA, 1937), pp. 30–31.

53 'Our Philosophy', Google.com (URL: www.google.com/corporate/tenthings.html, last accessed 11 August 2009).

54 Alan Levenson, e-mail to author (19 April 2009).

55 Frederick Taylor, *The Principles of Scientific Management* (New York, 1911), pp. 31–4.

56 Ibid., p. 35.

57 Don Tapscott and Art Caston, *Paradigm Shift: The New Promise of Information Technology* (New York, 1993), p. 11.

58 Alan Greenspan, *Age of Turbulence* (London, 2008), pp. 183–4.

59 Edgar H. Schein, DEC *Is Dead, Long Live* DEC: *The Lasting Legacy of Digital Equipment Corporation* (San Francisco, 2003), p. 3.

60 Nolan, *Dot Vertigo*, p. 62.

61 D. Calvin Andrus, 'The Wiki and the Blog: Toward a Complex Adaptive Intelligence Community', *Studies in Intelligence*, XLIX/3 (September 2005), p. 26.

62 Massimo Calabresi, 'Wikipedia for Spies: The CIA Discovers Web 2.0', *Time* (8 April 2009).

10 WEB 2.0 AND THE RETURN TO THE ORAL TRADITION

1 Ted Nelson, text on front page of Xanadu project (URL: www.xanadu.com/, last accessed 9 February 2009).

2 Robert Cailliau, e-mail to author (2 March 2009).

3 'Size of Wikipedia', Wikipedia (URL: http://en.wikipedia.org/wiki/Wikipedia: Size_of_Wikipedia, last accessed 15 June 2009).

4 John Perry Barlow, 'The Economy of Ideas', *Wired* (March 1994).

5 Wikipedia most frequently edited pages (URL: http://en.wikipedia.org/wiki/ Wikipedia:Most_frequently_edited_articles, last accessed 15 June 2009).

6 Wikipedia, archive of talk on George W. Bush page (URL: http://en.wikipedia. org/wiki/Talk:George_W._Bush/Archive_index, last accessed 15 June 2009).

7 H.F.D. Sparks, 'Jerome as Biblical Scholar', *The Cambridge History of the Bible*, vol. 1, *From the Beginnings to Jerome* (London, 1970), p. 513.

8 'Decree Concerning the Edition and the Use of the Sacred Books', Canons and Decrees of the Council of Trent, The Fourth Session, Celebrated on the eighth day of the month of April, in the year 1546.

9 John Sandys-Wunsch, *What Have They Done to the Bible?: A History of Modern Biblical Interpretation* (Collegeville, MN, 2005), p. 6.

10 Steve Crocker, e-mail to author (18 April 2009).

11 Tim O'Reilly, 'What Is Web 2.0: Design Patterns and Business Models for the Next Generation of Software', 30 September 2005 (URL: www.oreillynet.com/pub/a/ oreilly/tim/news/2005/09/30/what-is-web-20.html?page=4, last accessed 12 August 2009).

12 J.C.R. Licklider contributing to the Carnegie Commission report on educational television, January 1967, quoted in Patrick Parsons, *Blue Skies: A History of Cable Television* (Philadelphia, PA, 2008), p. 242.

13 'Notice of Inquiry and Notice of Proposed Rulemaking in Docket 18397, 15 FCC 2d 417', FCC (1968), quoted in ibid., p. 254.

14 Thomas Streeter, 'The Cable Fable Revisited: Discourse, Policy, and the Making of Cable Television,' in *Critical Studies in Mass Communication* (June 1987), pp. 174– 200.

15 'The User Revolution: The New Advertising Ecosystem and the Rise of the Internet as a Mass Medium', PiperJaffray Investment Research (February 2007), pp. 55–6.

16 'Teens and Social Media', Pew Internet & American Life Project (19 December 2007), p. i.

17 Alexa web service rankings (24 January 2009).

18 'Craigslist factsheet' (URL: www.craigslist.org/about/factsheet, last accessed 26 August 2009).

19 Gary Wolf, 'Why Craigslist Is Such a Mess', *Wired* (September 2009).

20 'Craigslist factsheet'.

21 Craig Newmark, quoted in '"Nerd Values" Help Propel Tiny Craigslist Into Classi- fieds Treat', USC Annenberg Online Journalism Review, 3 July 2004 (URL: www.ojr.org/ojr/business/1086222946.php, last accessed 23 January 2009).

22 Wolf, 'Why Craigslist Is Such a Mess'.

23 'An Ad (Gasp!) in Cyberspace', *New York Times* (19 April 1994).

24 Laurence A. Carter and Martha S. Siegel, *How to Make a Fortune on the Informa- tion Superhighway: Everyone's Guerrilla Guide to Marketing on the Internet and Other On-line Services* (New York, 1994), p. 24.

25 Ibid., p. 6.

26 Kevin Kelly, 'Pro-choice: The Promise of Technology', *Organisation & Environment*, XII/4 (December 1999), p. 28.

< 220 >

27 Craig Newmark, quoted in "'Nerd Values'".

28 Craig Newmark, quoted in 'On the Record: Craig Newmark', *San Francisco Chronicle* (15 August 2004).

29 'Manuscript Peer Review – A Guide for Health Care Professionals: What is Peer Review?', *Pharmacotherapy*, XXI/4 (2001) (URL: www.medscape.com/viewarticle/ 409692, last accessed 26 April 2009).

30 Daryl E. Chubin and Edward J. Hackett, *Peerless Science: Peer Review and US Science Policy* (New York, 1990), p. 4.

31 'eBay Marketplace Fast Facts', eBay.com (URL: news.ebay.com/fastfacts_ebay_ marketplace.cfm, last accessed 9 July 2008).

32 'Jeff Bezos on Word-of-Mouth Power', *Business Week* (2 August 2004).

33 Kevin Kelly, 'Tools Are the Revolution', *Whole Earth*, issue 103 (Winter 2000) (URL: www.wholeearth.com/issue/103/article/126/tools.are.the.revolution, last accessed 6 October 2008).

34 See Thomas Vanderwal, 'Folksonomy Coinage and Definition', Vanderwal.net (2 February 2007) (URL: vanderwal.net/folksonomy.html, last accessed 25 January 2009).

35 Nicholas Negroponte and Pattie Maes, 'Electronic Word of Mouth', *Wired* (October 1996).

36 Brian Morrissey, 'Brands Tap Web Elite for Advertorial 2.0', *Adweek* (12 January 2009).

37 'Sponsored Conversations', Izea.com (URL: http://izea.com/social-media-marketing/sponsored-conversations/, last accessed 25 July 2009).

38 Jimmy Wales interview on Slashdot (24 July 2004) (URL: http://interviews.slashdot. org/article.pl?sid=04/07/28/1351230, last accessed 24 June 2009).

39 Friedrich Hayek, 'The Use of Knowledge in Society', *The American Economic Review*, XXXV/4 (September 1945), pp. 519–21.

40 Ibid., p. 524.

41 Jimmy Wales quoted in Stacy Schiff, 'Annals of Information: Know it All', *The New Yorker* (31 July 2006).

42 'Welcome newcomers', Wikipedia (February 2003) (URL: http://web.archive. org/web/20030210054132/www.wikipedia.org/wiki/Welcome,_newcomers, last accessed 24 June 2009).

43 'Nupedia.com Editorial Policy Guidelines, version 4' (May 2000) (URL: http://web. archive.org/web/20010607080354/www.nupedia.com/policy.shtml, last accessed 24 June 2009).

44 'Announcements for January 2001', Wikipedia, (URL: http://web.archive.org/web/ 20021102155538/www.wikipedia.org/wiki/Wikipedia:Announcements_January_ 2001, last accessed 24 June 2009).

45 'Policy and guidelines', Wikipedia (October 2002) (URL: http://web.archive.org/ web/20021029025626/www.wikipedia.org/wiki/Wikipedia_policy, last accessed 24 June 2009).

46 Larry Sanger, 'The Origins of Wikipedia' in *Open Sources 2.0*, ed. Chris DiBona, Danese Cooper and Mark Stone (Sebastopol, CA, 2005), p. 315.

47 'Rules to Consider', Wikipedia (2 April 2001) (URL: http://web.archive.org/web/ 20010416035716/www.wikipedia.com/wiki/RulesToConsider, last accessed 24 June 2009).

48 Marc Andreessen, presentation on Mosaic at the First Internet Marketing Con-

< 221 >

ference, San Francisco (November 1994) (URL: video.google.com/videoplay?docid=
-5046297730700144952, 26 October 2008).

49 'Idea for Online Networking Brings Two Entrepreneurs Together', *New York Times*
(1 December 2003).

50 Author's conversation with Andrew Weinreich (14 August 2009).

51 Max Chafkin, 'How to Kill a Great Idea', *Inc.* (1 June 2007).

52 Nielsen Online, 'Nielsen Online Provides Fastest Growing Social Networks for
September 2008' (22 October 2008).

53 Jesse James Garrett, 'Ajax: A New Approach to Web Applications' (18 February 2005)
(URL: www.adaptivepath.com/ideas/essays/archives/000385.php, last accessed 22
July 2009).

54 'Zoinks! 20 Hours of Video Uploaded Every Minute!', YouTube blog (21 May
2009) (URL: www.youtube.com/blog, last accessed 15 June 2009).

11 NEW AUDIENCES, THE FOURTH WALL AND EXTRUDED MEDIA

1 'The Scene Archives: The Scene Timeline', Defacto2.net (URL: www.defacto2.net/
timeline.cfm?startMonth=8&startYear=1996&endMonth=8&endYear=1996&
events=true&magazines=true&display=Submit&docText=true&docNonPC=true,
last accessed 27 April 2009).

2 NetFrack interviewed by Mr Mister (19 August 1996), *Affinity* (diskmag), issue 3
(URL: www.defacto2.net/magazines.cfm?id=63&reader=raw, last accessed 27 April
2009).

3 *Digital Music Report 2009*, International Federation of the Phonographic Industry (16 January 2009), p. 3.

4 William M. Hartmann, *Signals, Sound, and Sensation* (New York, 1997), p. 7.

5 'The story of MP3', Fraunhofer IIS (URL: www.iis.fraunhofer.de/EN/bf/amm/mp3
history/mp3history01.jsp, last accessed 27 April 2009).

6 Karlheinz Brandenburg, interviewed by Bruno Giussani (15 January 2007) (URL:
www.lunchoverip.com/2007/01/meet_the_mp3_ma.html, last accessed 27 April
2009).

7 Bruce Haring, 'Sound Advances Open Doors to Bootleggers Albums on Web Sites
Proliferate', *USA Today* (27 May 1997).

8 Opinion by Judge Diarmuid O'Scannlain in the case of RIAA and AARC v Diamond
Multimedia Systems, Appeal from the US District Court for the Central District of
California (15 June 1999).

9 Christopher Mitten, *Shawn Fanning: Napster and the Music Revolution* (Min-
neapolis, MN, 2002), p. 11.

10 Giancarlo Varanini, 'Q&A: Napster Creator Shawn Fanning', ZDNet (3 March
2000).

11 Steve Jobs, presentation launch of the iPod (23 October 2001).

12 Clive Thompson, 'The BitTorrent Effect', *Wired* (January 2005).

13 Figures from Nielsen Soundscan end of year music industry report 1999 and
2008.

14 'Billboard / Soundscan: Digital Album Sales Up 32% in 2008', *Nielsen Wire* (7 January 2009).

15 *Digital Music Report 2009*, the International Federation of the Phonographic
Industry, p. 6.

< 222 >

16 Ibid.
17 'iTunes Store Top Music Retailer in the US', Apple press release (3 April 2008).
18 Fred Goodman, 'Rock's New Economy: Making Money When CDS Don't Sell', *RollingStone* (29 May 2008).
19 *Digital Music Report 2009*, International Federation of Phonographic Industry, p. 6.
20 'Billboard / Soundscan' (7 January 2009).
21 William M. Bulkeley, 'The Internet Allows Consumers to Trim Wasteful Purchases', *Wall Street Journal* (29 November 2006).
22 Paul Baran, 'Some Changes in Information Technology Affecting Marketing in the Year 2000', RAND (1968), pp. 18–28.
23 Nicholas Negroponte, 'Prime Time is My Time', *Wired* (March/April 1993).
24 John Batelle, 'How Viacom is Leveraging its Brand Strength to Create the First 21st-century (New) Media Company', *Wired* (April 1995).
25 Nicholas Johnson, *How to Talk Back to Your Television Set* (New York, 1970), p. 140.
26 'Media Kit: Timeline & History', Amazon.com (June 2009).
27 Chris Anderson, 'The Long Tail', *Wired* (October 2004).
28 Chris Anderson, *The Long Tail: Why the Future of Commerce is Selling Less of More* (London, 2006), p. 7.
29 Anderson, 'The Long Tail', *Wired*.
30 'iTunes Music Store Downloads Top a Quarter Billion Songs', Apple press release (24 January 2005).
31 Jeff Bezos, interviewed by Chris Anderson, *Wired* (January 2005).
32 Subscription details, *World of Warcraft* (URL: www.wow-europe.com/en/requirements/subscription.html, last accessed 27 April 2009).
33 'World of Warcraft: Wrath of the Lich King Midnight Store Openings', press release (30 October 2009) (URL: eu.blizzard.com/en/press/081030.html, last accessed 1 May 2009); Blizzard company profile (URL:http://eu.blizzard.com/en/inblizz/profile.html, last accessed 1 May 2009).
34 Alex Pham, 'Guitar Hero and Rock Band Try to Drum Up New Players', *Los Angeles Times* (16 March 2009).
35 Yezdi Lashkari, Max Metral and Pattie Maes, 'Collaborative Interface Agents', Proceedings of AAAI '94 Conference, Seattle (August 1994) (URL: agents.media.mit.edu/publications/aaai ymp/aaai.html, last accessed 10 January 2008).
36 Paul C. Judge, 'Firefly: The Web Site that has Mad Ave. Buzzing', *Business Week* (7 October 1996).
37 Newspaper Association of America, advertising expenditures data (updated May 2009) (URL: www.naa.org/TrendsandNumbers/Advertising-Expenditures.aspx, last accessed 28 June 2009).
38 Newspaper Association of America, total paid circulation data (URL: www.naa.org/TrendsandNumbers/Total-Paid-Circulation.aspx, last accessed 28 June 2009).
39 MERIT statistical data (1 September 1997) (URL: www.ccwhois.org/ccwhois/cctld/merit.history.hosts.txt, last accessed 3 May 2009).
40 David Simon, 'Does the News Matter To Anyone Anymore?', *Washington Post* (20 January 2008).
41 John Horrigan, 'Online News: For Many Home Broadband Users, the Internet is a Primary News Source', *Pew Internet & American Life Project* (22 March 2006).
42 Rupert Murdoch, speech to the American Society of Newspaper Editors Conference (13 April 2005).

43 Yochai Benkler, *The Wealth of Networks: How Social Production Transforms Markets and Freedom* (New Haven, 2006), p. 277.

44 Cass Sunstein, *Republic.com* (Princeton, NJ, 2001).

45 Gary Kamiya, 'The Death of News', Salon.com (17 February 2009) (URL: www.salon.com/opinion/kamiya/2009/02/17/newspapers/print.html, last accessed 28 June 2009).

46 'Who Killed the Newspaper?', *The Economist* (24 August 2006).

47 Tim Wu, speaking at the Institute of International & European Affairs (25 May 2009).

12 TWO-WAY POLITICS

1 Author's e-mail correspondence with Phil Madsen (June 2009).

2 Ibid.

3 'Former Wrestler's Campaign Got a Boost from the Internet', *Politics Online* (6 November 1998) (URL: www.politicsonline.com/coverage/nytimes2/06campaign.html, last accessed 8 January 2009).

4 Phil Madsen, 'Notes Regarding Jesse Ventura's Internet Use in his 1998 Campaign for Minnesota Governor', distributed by DOWire (10 December 1998) (URL: www.dowire.org/notes/?p=413, last accessed 8 January 2009).

5 Bill McAuliffe, 'Ventura Riding the Web', *Minnesota Star Tribune* (1 March 1999).

6 Rebecca Fairley Raney, 'Former Wrestler's Campaign Got a Boost from the Internet', *New York Times* (6 November 1998).

7 Phil Madsen, quoted in McAuliffe, 'Ventura Riding the Web'.

8 Jesse Ventura, quoted in 'Minnesota's New Chief Pushes Net as Political Tool', *New York Times* (28 January 1999).

9 Madsen, 'Notes regarding Jesse Ventura's Internet Use'.

10 Phil Madsen, 'The E-Democracy – Alternative Methods for Engaging Citizens', Pew Centre for Civic Journalism 1999 Batten Symposium Panel Presentation (URL: www.pewcenter.org/batten/edem.html, last accessed 8 January 2009).

11 Joe Trippi in *Campaign for President: The Managers Look at 2004* (Cambridge, MA, 2005), p. 2.

12 Joe Trippi, *The Revolution Will Not Be Televised: Democracy, the Internet, and the Overthrow of Everything* (New York, 2004) p. 85.

13 Lawrence Lessig interview with Joe Trippi, Lessig's blog (16 August 2003) (URL: lessig.org/blog/2003/08/interview_with_joe_trippi.html, last accessed 10 December 2008).

14 Ibid.

15 Ibid.

16 Lawrence Lessig, 'The New Road to the White House: How Grass Roots Blogs Are Transforming Presidential Politics', *Wired* (November 2003).

17 Joe Trippi, comment on 'Howard Dean to Guest Blog for Lawrence Lessig', *Slashdot* (13 July 2003), (URL: http://slashdot.org/comments.pl?sid=70875&cid=6428904, last accessed 25 June 2009).

18 Joe Trippi, 'The Perfect Storm', blog post (17 May 2003) (URL: joetrippi.com/blog/?page_id=1378, last accessed 10 December 2008).

19 Trippi, *The Revolution Will Not Be Televised*, p. 103.

20 Doc Searls, 'The Open Source Force Behind the Obama Campaign', *Linux Journal* (November 2008).

< 224 >

21 Lessig interview with Trippi.
22 Trippi, *The Revolution Will Not Be Televised*, pp. 48–50.
23 Lessig interview with Trippi.
24 Trippi, *The Revolution Will Not Be Televised*, pp. 133–4.
25 Doc Searls, 'Hacking Democracy', *Linux Journal* (1 June 2004).
26 Trippi, *The Revolution Will Not Be Televised*, p. 154.
27 Ibid.
28 Walter Shapiro, *One Car Caravan: On the Road with the 2004 Democrats Before America Tunes In* (New York, 2003), p. 1.
29 Walter Shapiro, 'Until Next Year, Just Enjoy Dem's Show', *usa Today* (17 July 2003).
30 Trippi quoted in Searls, 'The Open Source Force Behind the Obama Campaign'.
31 Micah Sifry, 'Open-Source Politics 1.0: Lessons from Advocates for Rasiej, 2005 Campaign for nyc Public Advocate' (url: www.gomaya.com/glyph/archives/001478.html, last accessed 11 December 2008).
32 Ibid.
33 Ibid.
34 Trippi, *The Revolution Will Not Be Televised*, p. 255.
35 Marc Andreessen's blog post about his meeting with Barack Obama (url: blog.pmarca.com/2008/03/an-hour-and-a-h.html, last accessed 26 November 2008).
36 Jascha Franklin-Hodge quoted in Searls, 'The Open Source Force Behind the Obama Campaign'.
37 'Clinton fundraising for March', abc News political radar (3 April 2008).
38 'Obama Raises More Than $40 Million in March', cnn (3 April 2008).
39 Donor Demographics: Barack Obama, opensecrets.org (url: www.opensecrets.org/pres08/donordemcid.php?cycle=2008&cid=N00009638, last accessed 13 August 2009).
40 'Donors', Change.gov; the Obama-Biden Transition Team (url: http://change.gov/page/content/donors/, last accessed 25 June 2009).
41 Declan McCullagh, 'The Cyberbrains Behind Howard Dean', cnet (16 January 2008).
42 ActBlue about page (url: www.actblue.com/about, last accessed 12 December 2008).
43 Joe Trippi, 'From Linux to Obama', blog post (25 November 2008) (url: joetrippi.com/blog/?p=2544, last accessed 10 December 2008).
44 Andrew Rasiej and Micah L. Sifry, 'Politics 2.0', *Politico* (url: www.politico.com/news/stories/0107/2456.html, last accessed 15 July 2009).
45 Thomas Streeter, 'Blue Skies and Strange Bedfellows: The Discourse of Cable Television', in Lynn Spigel and Michael Curtin, eds, *The Revolution Wasn't Televised: Sixties Television and Social Conflict* (New York, 1997), pp. 221–42.
46 Ralph Lee Smith, 'The Wired Nation', *The Nation* (18 May 1970).
47 Ralph Lee Smith, e-mail to author (5 August 2009).
48 Peter I. Bogucki, *The Origins of Human Society* (Hoboken, nj, 1999), p. 74.
49 Eleanor Burke Leacock and Richard B. Lee, *Politics and History in Band Societies* (Cambridge, 1982), p. 1.
50 Peter Bellwood, *First Farmers: The Origins of Agricultural Societies* (Hoboken, nj, 2005), p. 54.
51 William M. Dugger, *Howard J. Sherman Evolutionary Theory in the Social Sciences*, vol. 3 (London, 2003), pp. 48–9.

<225>

52 John Gray Geer, *Public Opinion and Polling Around the World: A Historical Encyclopedia*, vol. 1 (Santa Barbara, CA, 2004), p. 408.

53 Ibid., p. 409.

54 Kevin Kelly, *New Rules for the New Economy: 10 Radical Strategies for a Connected World* (London, 1999), p. 14.

55 'Consolidated sales transition by region', Nintendo.co.jp (June 2009) (URL: www.nintendo.co.jp/ir/library/historical_data/pdf/consolidated_sales_e0906.pdf, last accessed 17 August 2009).

56 'Everybody Votes Channel', Wii.com (URL: http://uk.wii.com/wii/en_GB/channel/everybody_votes_channel_859.html, last accessed 17 August 2009).

57 Ibid.

58 'Obama Leads By 20%: Xbox Live a Blue State', Xbox 360 Press (4 November 2008) (URL: http://gamerscoreblog.com/press/archive/2008/11/04/562228.aspx, last accessed 27 August 2009).

59 Howard Rheingold, 'The Tragedy of the Electronic Commons', *San Francisco Examiner* (19 December 1994).

60 J.C.R. Licklider, 'Computers and Government' in Michael Dertouzos and Joel Moses, *The Computer Age: A Twenty-year View* (London, 1980), pp. 114–15.

61 Jeremy Caplan, 'The Citizen Watch-dogs of Web 2.0', *Time* (30 June 2008).

62 Earmarkwatch.org (URL: http://earmarkwatch.org/, last accessed 17 August 2009).

63 Josh Tauberer, e-mail to author (17 August 2009).

64 Eric S. Raymond, *The Cathedral and the Bazaar* (Cambridge, MA, 2000) (URL: www.catb.org/~esr/writings/cathedral-bazaar/cathedral-bazaar/ar01s05.html, p. 33.

13 PROMISE AND PERIL

1 Steve Jobs interviewed by Gary Wolf, *Wired* (February 1996) (URL: www.wired.com/wired/archive/4.02/jobs.html?pg=3&topic=, last accessed 28 June 2008).

2 Note to author included in delivery from Chinese retailer on eBay (2009).

3 Quoted in 'Whose Internet is it Anyway?', *Fortune* (11 December 1995).

4 Leo Beranek, 'Roots of the Internet: A Personal History', *Massachusetts Historical Society*, 11 (2000) (URL: www.historycooperative.org/journals/mhr/2/beranek.html, last accessed 13 January 2009).

5 Marc Benioff and Carlye Adler, *Behind the Cloud: The Untold Story of How Salesforce.com Went From Idea to Billion-Dollar Company – and Revolutionized an Industry* (San Francisco, 2009), p. 4.

6 Nicholas Carr, 'Open Source and the Utility Revolution', presentation, 2006 (URL: www.nicholasgcarr.com/download/carrosBC.pdf, last accessed 6 September 2009).

7 Thomas Friedman, *The World is Flat: A Brief History of the Twenty-first Century* (New York, 2005).

8 Richard Florida, 'The World is Spikey', *The Atlantic* (October 2005), p. 48.

9 J.A.S. Evans, *The Age of Justinian* (New York, 1996), p. 235.

10 Kym Anderson, *The World's Wine Markets* (Cheltenham, 2004), p. 111.

11 James H. Crees, *The Reign of the Emperor Probius* (London, 2005), p. 91.

12 'Total Share: 20 Years of Personal Computer Market Share Figures', *Ars Technica* (14 December 2005) (URL: arstechnica.com/articles/culture/total-share.ars/, last accessed 21 January 2009).

13 S. J. Liebowitz and S. E. Margolis, 'Network Externalities (Effects)', *The New Pal-*

< 226 >

grave's *Dictionary of Economics and the Law* (Basingstoke, 1998) (URL: www.
utdallas.edu/~liebowit/palgrave/network.html, last accessed 15 June 2008).

14 'Apple's App Store downloads Top 1.5 Billion in First Year', Apple press release
(14 July 2009).

15 Jeffrey Long, 'On the Shoulders of Giants' (24 July 2008), banterability blog (URL:
blog.banterability.com/post/43413265/on-the-shoulders-of-giants, last accessed 20
January 2009).

16 Chris Foresman, 'iPhone NDA: Doing More Harm Than Good', *Ars Technica* (28 July
2008) (URL: arstechnica.com/news.ars/post/20080728-iphone-nda-doing-more-
harm-than-good.html, last accessed 20 January 2009).

17 Justin Williams, in correspondence with author (20 January 2009).

18 Paul Baran, 'Communications, Computers and People', American Federation of
Information Processing Societies (Fall 1965), p. 48.

19 FCC submission of Professor Mark A. Lemley and Professor Lawrence Lessig,
'Application for Consent to the Transfer of Control of Licenses MediaOne Group,
Inc. to AT&T' (December 1999) p. 20.

20 Lawrence Lessig and Robert W. McChesney, 'No Tolls on the Internet', *Washington Post* (8 June 2005).

21 Tim Wu, testimony, House Committee on the Judiciary Telecom & Antitrust Task
Force Hearing on 'Network Neutrality: Competition, Innovation, and Non-dis-
criminatory Access' (24 April 2006).

22 Jonathan Zittrain, 'The Generative Internet', *Harvard Law Review*, CXIX (May
2006), pp. 1981–2.

23 Tim Wu, *Open: The Fate of an Idea* (working title) (2010 forthcoming), pp. 58–60.

24 Author's interview with Tim Wu, at the IIEA in Dublin (25 May 2009).

25 Quoted in David Welch, *The Third Reich: Politics and Propaganda* (New York, 2002),
p. 23.

26 Paul Baran, 'Summary Overview: On Distributed Communications' (Santa Monica, CA, 1964), p. 4 (URL: rand.org/pubs/research_memoranda/RM3767/, last accessed 22 October 2008).

27 Richard Clayton, Steven J. Murdoch and Robert N. M. Watson, 'Ignoring the
Great Firewall of China', 6th Workshop on Privacy Enhancing Technologies, Cambridge (June 2006).

28 'PRC Regulations on Safeguarding Computer Information Systems', from Beijing
XINHUA Domestic Service (23 February 1994) (URL: www.interesting-people.org/
archives/interesting-people/199404/msg00001.html, 20 January 2009).

29 Johnny Ryan, *Countering Militant Islamist Radicalization on the Internet: A User-
Driven Strategy to Recover the Web* (Dublin, 2007); see also Johnny Ryan, Caitri-
ona Heinl, Oisin Suttle, Gilbert Ramsay and Tim Stevens, '(NLM-RFC2) Initial
Overview of Measures Against Illegal Content on the Internet in Each of the 27 EU
Member States, RFC from the IIEA' (22 December 2009) (URL: http://www.iiea.com/
documents/non-legislative-measures-rfc2, last accessed 22 December 2009).

30 Chronology of events in David Ronfeldt, John Arquilla, Graham Fuller and Melissa
Fuller, *The Zapatista 'Social Netwar' in Mexico* (Santa Monica, CA, 1998), p. 133.

31 Ronfeldt, Arquilla, Fuller and Fuller, *The Zapatista 'Social Netwar'*, p. 62.

32 Quoted in ibid., pp. 69–70.

33 Quoted in ibid.

34 *The Times* (18 May 2007).

<227>

35 'We're Teen, We're Queer, and We've Got e-mail', *Wired* (November 1994) (URL: www.wired.com/wired/archive/2.11/gay.teen.html, last accessed 30 October 2008).

36 The Mentor, 'The Conscience of a Hacker', *Phrack*, 1/7, phile 3 of 10 (8 January 1986) (URL: www.phrack.org/issues.html?issue=7&id=3&mode=txt, last accessed 9 January 2009).

37 Ibid.

38 Paul Craig, Ron Honick and Mark Burnett, *Software Piracy Exposed* (Boston, MA, 2005), p. 8.

39 'Joybubbles, 58, Peter Pan of Phone Hackers, Dies', *New York Times* (20 August 2007).

40 Bill Gates, 'Open letter to hobbyists' in 'Homebrew Computer Club newsletter', 11/1 (3 February 1976), (URL: www.digibarn.com/collections/newsletters/homebrew/V2_01/index.html, last accessed 6 November 2007)

41 David Drummond, 'A new approach to China', Google Blog, 12 January 2010 (URL: http://googleblog.blogspot.com/2010/01/new-approach-to-china.html, last accessed 11 February 2010).

42 Johnny Ryan and Stefan Halper, 'Google vs China: capitalist model, virtual wall', OpenDemocracy, 22 January 2010 (URL: http://www.opendemocracy.net/johnny-ryan-stefan-halper/google-vs-china-capitalist-model-virtual-wall, last accessed 11 February 2010).

43 Stefan Halper, *The Beijing Consensus: How China's Authoritarian Model Will Dominate the Twenty-first Century* (New York, 2010).

44 'Our philosophy: ten things that Google had found to be true', Google.com (URL: www.google.com/corporate/tenthings.html, last accessed 11 August 2009).

45 'The Internet timeline of China (2008)', China Internet Network Information Center (URL: http://www.cnnic.net.cn/html/Dir/2009/05/18/5600.htm, last accessed 11 February 2010).

46 'China Internet population hits 384 million', Reuters, 15 January 2010.

47 David Drummond, 'A new approach to China', Google Blog, 12 January 2010 (URL: http://googleblog.blogspot.com/2010/01/new-approach-to-china.html, last accessed 11 February 2010).

48 Hillary Clinton, 'Remarks on Internet Freedom', The Newseum, 21 January 2010 (URL: http://www.state.gov/secretary/rm/2010/01/135519.htm, last accessed 9 February 2010).

49 Toomas Hendrik Ilves, President of the Republic of Estonia, interview with author, Dublin (15 April 2008) (URL: www.youtube.com/watch?v=jIK4gcT115Q, last accessed 18 May 2008.)

50 J.C.R. Licklider, 'Computers and Government' in Michael Dertouzos and Joel Moses, *The Computer Age: A Twenty-Year View* (London, 1980), p. 118.

< 228 >

Bibliography

Abbate, Janet, *Inventing the Internet* (Cambridge, MA, 2000)

'A History of ARPANET: The First Decade', Report 4799, BBN, April 1981

Anderson, Chris, *The Long Tail: Why the Future of Commerce is Selling Less of More* (London, 2006)

Andrus, D. Calvin, 'The Wiki and the Blog: Toward a Complex Adaptive Intelligence Community', *Studies in Intelligence*, XLIX/3, September 2005

Baran, Paul, 'On Distributed Communication Networks' (Santa Monica, CA, 1962)

—, 'Some Changes in Information Technology Affecting Marketing in the Year 2000', RAND, 1968.

Bardini, Thierry, *Bootstrapping: Douglas Engelbart, Coevolution, and the Origins of Personal Computing* (Palo Alto, CA, 2000)

Barlow, John Perry, 'The Economy of Ideas', *Wired*, March 1994

Batelle, John, *Search: How Google and its Rivals Rewrote the Rules of Business and Transformed out Culture* (London, 2005)

Benioff, Marc, and Carlye Adler, *Behind the Cloud: The Untold Story of how Salesforce.com Went from Idea to Billion-dollar Company – and Revolutionized an Industry* (San Francisco, 2009)

Benkler, Yochai, *The Wealth of Networks: How Social Production Transforms Markets and Freedom* (New Haven, CT, 2006)

Berners-Lee, Tim, *Weaving the Web: The Past, Present and Future of the World Wide Web by its Inventor* (London, 1999)

Bradner, Scott, 'IETF Working Group Guidelines and Procedure', Network Working Group RFC 2418, September 1998 (URL: tools.ietf.org/html/rfc2418, 20 April 2009)

Brin, Sergey, and Lawrence Page, 'The Anatomy of a Large-Scale Hypertextual Web Search Engine', *Computer Networks and ISDN Systems*, XXX/1–7, April 1998 (URL: http://infolab.stanford.edu/~backrub/google.html, last accessed 15 July 2009)

Brockman, John, *Digerati: Encounters with the Cyber Elite*, 1996 (URL: www.edge.org/documents/digerati/Brand.html, last accessed 20 May 2009)

Buffett, Warren, to shareholders of Berkshire Hathaway Inc., 28 February 2001

Bush, Vannevar, 'As We May Think', *The Atlantic*, July 1945

—, 'Science: The Endless Frontier', July 1945, United States Government Printing Office, Washington: 1945 (URL: www.nsf.gov/od/lpa/nsf50/vbush1945.htm, last accessed 25 November 2008)

Campbell-Kelly, Martin, *From Airline Reservations to Sonic the Hedgehog: A History of the Software Industry* (London, 2003)

< 229 >

—, and Daniel D. Garcia-Swartz, 'The History of the Internet: The Missing Narratives', 2 December 2005 (URL: ssrn.com/abstract=867087, last accessed 3 April 2009)

Caplan, Jeremy, 'The Citizen Watch-dogs of Web 2.0', *Time*, 30 June 2008

Carr, Nicholas, *The Big Switch: Rewiring the World, from Edison to Google* (New York, 2008)

Carter, Laurence A., and Martha S. Siegel, *How to Make a Fortune on the Information Superhighway: Everyone's Guerrilla Guide to Marketing on the Internet and Other On-Line Services* (New York, 1994)

Cerf, Vinton, and Robert E. Kahn, 'A Protocol for Packet Network Intercommunication', IEEE *Transactions on Communications*, XXII/5 (May 1974)

—, 'How the Internet Came to Be', in *The Online User's Encyclopedia*, ed. Bernard Aboba, November 1993

Charles Babbage Institute, oral histories (www.cbi.umn.edu/).

Chesnoy, José, ed., *Undersea Fiber Communication Systems* (London, 2002)

Christensen, Clayton M., *The Innovator's Dilemma: When New Technologies Cause Great Firms to Fail* (Cambridge, MA, 1997)

Coon, Horace, *American Tel & Tel: The Story of a Great Monopoly*, reprint of 1939 edn (Manchester, NH, 1971)

Denning, Peter J., Anthony Hearn, C. William Kern, 'History and Overview of CSNET', ACM SIGCOMM *Computer Communication Review*, XIII/2 (April 1983)

Ditlea, Steve, ed., *Digital Deli: The Comprehensive, User-Lovable Menu of Computer Lore, Culture, Lifestyles and Fancy* (New York, 1984)

Engelbart, Douglas, 'Augmenting Human Intellect: A Conceptual Framework', summary report prepared for the Director of Information Science, Air Force Office of Scientific Research, October 1962

Garber, Peter M., *Famous First Bubbles: The Fundamentals of Early Manias* (Cambridge, MA, 2001)

Garrett, Jesse James, 'Ajax: A New Approach to Web Applications', 18 February 2005 (URL: www.adaptivepath.com/ideas/essays/archives/000385.php, last accessed 22 July 2009).

Gilder, George, "Metcalfe's Law and its legacy", *Forbes* ASAP, 13 September 1993 (URL: www.seas.upenn.edu/~gaj1/metgg.html, last accessed 22 April 2009)

Goetz, Thomas, 'Open Source Everywhere', *Wired*, (URL: www.wired.com/wired/archive/11.11/opensource.html, last accessed 29 June 2008)

Goldfarb, Brent, David Kirsch, David A. Miller, 'Was There Too Little Entry During the Dot Com Era?', *Journal of Financial Economics*, LXXXVI/1

Hafner, Katie, and Matthew Lyon, *Where Wizards Stay Up Late: The Origins of the Internet* (London, 2003)

Hauben, Ronda, 'The Evolution of USENET News: The Poor Man's ARPANET', speech at the Michigan Association for Computer Users in Learning (MACUL), 3 December 1993 (URL: http://neil.franklin.ch/Netizen/ch.1 _poorman_ARPA, last accessed 12 June 2009)

—, and Michael Hauben, *Netizens*, netbook last updated 6 December 1996 (URL: www.columbia.edu/~hauben/book/, last accessed 20 January 2009)

Hayek, Friedrich, 'The Use of Knowledge in Society', *The American Economic Review*, XXXV/4, September 1945

Herken, Gregg, *Counsels of War* (New York, 1985)

Hoffman, P., *The Tao of* IETF: *A Novice's Guide to the Internet Engineering Task Force*,

< 230 >

IETF internet draft, 16 February 2009 (URL: www.ietf.org/tao.html, last accessed 26 May 2009)

Huber, Peter William, Michael K. Kellogg, John Thorne, *Federal Telecommunications Law* (New York, 1999)

Huurdeman, Anton A., *The Worldwide History of Telecommunications* (New York, 2003)

'Jeff Bezos on Word-of-mouth Power', *Business Week*, 2 August 2004

Jimmy Wales interview on Slashdot, 24 July 2004 (URL: http://interviews.slashdot.org /article.pl?sid=04/07/28/1351230, last accessed 24 June 2009)

Johnson, Nicholas, 'Carterfone: My Story', *Santa Clara Computer & High Tech. Law Journal*, xxv, 2009

—, *How to Talk Back to Your Television Set* (New York, 1970)

Kelly, Kevin, *New Rules for the New Economy: 10 Radical Strategies for a Connected World* (London, 1999)

Kleinrock, Leonard, 'Information Flow in Large Communication Nets', Proposal for a PhD Thesis, MIT, 31 May 1961 (URL: www.cs.ucla.edu/~lk/LK/BIB/REPORT/PHD/, last accessed 10 July 2009)

Landweber, Lawrence, 'CSNET', 29 November 2007 (URL: www.nsfnet-legacy.org/ archives/02—Beginnings.pdf, last accessed 8 May 2009)

Leadbeater, Charles, *We-think: Mass Innovation, Not Mass Production: The Power of Mass Creativity* (London, 2008)

Lee Smith, Ralph, 'The Wired Nation', *The Nation*, 18 May 1970

Lessig, Lawrence, 'The New Road to the White House: How Grass Roots Blogs are Transforming Presidential Politics', *Wired Magazine*, November 2003

Levy, Steven, *Hackers: Heroes of the Computer Revolution* (New York, 2001)

Licklider, J.C.R., and Robert W. Taylor, 'The Computer as a Communication Device', reprinted from *Science and Technology*, April 1968

—, 'Man-Computer Symbiosis', IRE *Trans-actions on Human Factors in Electronics*, March 1960

—, *Libraries of the Future* (Cambridge, MA, 1965)

—, and Albert Vezza, 'Applications of Information Networks', *Proceedings of the IEEE*, LXVI/11, November 1978

—, and Robert W. Taylor, 'The Computer as a Communication Device', reprinted from *Science and Technology*, April 1968 (URL: memex.org/licklider.pdf, last accessed 22 October 2008)

'Linus Torvalds' Benevolent Dictatorship', *Business Week*, 18 August 2004.

Living Internet (URL: www.livinginternet.com, 31 August 2009)

Locke, Christopher, Rick Levine, Doc Searls, David Weinberger, *The Cluetrain Manifesto: The End of Business as Usual* (Cambridge, MA, 2000)

Lynch, Daniel C., and Marshall T. Rose, *Internet System Handbook* (Greenwich, CT, 1993)

Madsen, Phil, 'Notes Regarding Jesse Ventura's Internet use in his 1998 Campaign for Minnesota Governor', distributed by DOWire, 10 December 1998 (URL: www. dowire.org/notes/?p=413, last accessed 8 January 2009

Merit's History: The NSFNET Backbone Project, 1987–1995 (URL: www.livinginternet. com/doc/merit.edu/partnership.html, last accessed 5 May 2009)

Marcus, James, *Amazonia: Five Years at the Epicentre of the Dot.com Juggernaut* (New York, 2004)

Mentor, The, 'The Conscience of a Hacker', *Phrack*, 8 January 1986, 1/7, phile 3 of 10

< 231>

(URL: www.phrack.org/issues.html?issue=7&id=3&mode=txt, last accessed 9 January 2009)

Metcalfe, Bob, 'Metcalfe's Law Recurses Down the Long Tail of Social Networks', VC Mike's Blog (URL: vcmike.wordpress.com/2006/08/18/metcalfe-social-networks/, 13 January 2009)

Naughton, John, *A Brief History of the Future: From Radio Days to Internet Years in a Lifetime* (New York, 2000)

Negroponte, Nicholas, *Being Digital* (New York, 1996)

Nielson, Don, 'The SRI Van and Computer Internetworking', *Core*, 3.1, February 2002

Nolan, Richard, *Dot Vertigo: Doing Business in a Permeable World* (New York, 2001)

O'Reilly, Tim, 'What Is Web 2.0: Design Patterns and Business Models for the Next Generation of Software', 30 September 2005 (URL: www.oreillynet.com/pub/a/oreilly/tim/news/2005/09/30/what-is-web-20.html?page=4, last accessed 12 August 2009)

Parsons, Patrick, *Blue Skies: A History of Cable Television* (Philadelphia, PA, 2008)

Pouzin, Louis, 'Presentation and Major Design Aspects of the CYCLADES Computer Network', *Proceedings of the Third ACM Symposium on Data Communications and Data Networks: Analysis and Design*, 1973

Raymond, Eric S., *The Cathedral and the Bazaar: Musings on Linux and Open Source by an Accidental Revolutionary* (Sebastopol, CA, 2001)

Reed, David, 'That Sneaky Exponential – Beyond Metcalfe's Law to the Power of Community Building', *Context*, Spring 1999 (URL: www.contextmag.com/archives/199903/digitalstrategyreedslaw.asp, last accessed 31 October 2009)

Rivlin, Gary, *The Godfather of Silicon Valley: Ron Conway and the Fall of the Dot-coms* (New York, 2001)

Rosenbaum, Ron, 'Secrets of the Little Blue Box', *Esquire*, October 1971

Ryan, Johnny, *Countering Militant Islamist Radicalization on the Internet: A User-driven Strategy to Recover the Web* (Dublin, 2007)

Sanger, Larry, 'The Origins of Wikipedia', in *Open Sources 2.0*, ed. Chris DiBona, Danese Cooper, Mark Stone (Sebastopol, CA, 2005)

Schein, Edgar H., *DEC Is Dead, Long Live DEC: The Lasting Legacy of Digital Equipment Corporation* (San Francisco, 2003)

Schwartz, Peter, and Peter Leyden, 'The Long Boom, 1980–2020', *Wired*, July 1997

Searls, Doc, 'The Open Source Force behind the Obama Campaign', *Linux Journal*, November 2008

Smith, Bruce, *The RAND Corporation: Case Study of a Non-Profit Advisory Corporation* (Cambridge, MA, 1966)

Smith, Douglas K., and Robert C. Alexander, *Fumbling the Future* (New York, 1988)

Stallman, Richard, *Free Software, Free Society: Selected Essays of Richard M. Stallman* (Boston, MA, 2002)

Standage, Tom, *The Victorian Internet* (London, 1999)

Strassmann, Paul A., *The Squandered Computer: Evaluating the Business Alignment of Information Technologies* (New Canaan, CT, 1997)

Streeter, Thomas, 'The Cable Fable Revisited: Discourse, Policy, and the Making of Cable Television,' in *Critical Studies in Mass Communication*, June 1987

Stross, Randall E., *eBoys* (New York, 2001)

Suess, Randy, 'The Birth of BBS', 1989 (URL: chinet.com/html/cbbs.html, last accessed 2 April 2009)

< 232 >

Sunstein, Cass, *Republic.com* (Princeton, NJ, 2001)

Surowiecki, James, *The Wisdom of Crowds: Why the Many Are Smarter Than the Few and How Collective Wisdom Shapes Business, Economies, Societies and Nations* (New York, 2004)

Sutherland, Ivan Edward, 'Sketchpad: A Man-machine Graphical Communication SYSTEM', PhD thesis, MIT 1963 (URL: www.cl.cam.ac.uk/techreports/UCAM-CL-TR-574.pdf, 1 May 2009)

Taft, Ed, and Bob Metcalfe, 'Pup Specifications; Inter-Office Memorandum, 30 June 1978, p. 1 (URL: www.bitsavers.org/pdf/xerox/alto/pupSpec.pdf, last accessed 1 December 2009)

Tapscott, Don, and Anthony D. Williams, *Wikinomics: How Mass Collaboration Changes Everything* (New York, 2006)

Taylor, Frederick, *The Principles of Scientific Management* (New York, 1911)

Trippi, Joe, *The Revolution Will Not be Televised: Democracy, the Internet, and the Overthrow of Everything* (New York, 2004)

Vanderwal, Thomas, 'Folksonomy Coinage and Definition', Vanderwal.net, 2 February 2007 (URL: vanderwal.net/folksonomy.html, last accessed 25 January 2009)

Winkler, David F., *Searching the Skies: The Legacy of the United States Cold War Radar Defence Program* (Champaign, IL, 1997)

Wu, Tim, *The Master Switch: The Rise and Fall of Information Empires* (New York, 2010)

< 233 >

Acknowledgements

I must thank my colleagues at the Institute of International & European Affairs (IIEA), most particularly its Director of Research, Jill Donoghue. Rarely has there been an institution so creatively chaotic within and respected without since the early days of RAND, ARPA and BBN. Many of the ideas in this book were prompted by the input of the stakeholders consulted during the 2008 Next Leap project at the IIEA. In particular I should highlight Jonathan Zittrain of the Berkman Centre at Harvard. His IIEA presentation prompted some of the ideas that led to the writing of this book.

I would also like to thank the O'Reilly Scholarship Foundation through whose generosity it was possible to return to the University of Cambridge.

A number of people were kind enough to respond to my enquiries during the research of this book including Vint Cerf, Robert Kahn, Leonard Kleinrock, Steve Crocker, Robert Cailliau, Bob Metcalfe, Dave Crocker, Heidi Heiden, Shih-Pau Yen (inventor of Gopher), Bill Thompson, Gregor Bailar, Ralph Lee Smith (author of 'The Wired Nation' in 1970), Brian Pinkerton (search engine innovator), Gordon Bell, Phil Madsen (the man behind Jesse Ventura's Internet-driven 1998 campaign), Thomas Bruce (creator of Cello, the first PC web browser), Alan Emtage (inventor of Archie), Perry Pei Wei (creator of the first Unix www browser), Andrew Weinreich (founder of the first social network, sixdegrees.com), Josh Tauberer (founder of GovTrack.us), Justin Williams (activist against the App Store NDA policy), Netfrack (the first MP3 pirate), Steven M. Bellovin (one of the founders of Usenet), Carlye Adler and Marc Benioff (founder of Salesforce.com). A range of people including Peter Kirstein, Howard Rheingold, Micah Sifry and Nick Yee, have helped with sources. Thanks are due also to Tim Wu, Bruce Hoffman, Andrew Jarvis, Oisin Suttle, Nikolai Jensen, Aidan Corbet and Chris Bollard for their input.

I would like to thank Martha Jay at Reaktion Books. Michael Leaman, the founder of Reaktion, deserves particular thanks, not only for initially approaching me to write this book, but for his forgiving my habit of going considerably beyond agreed word limits.

< 234 >

Index

Abrams, Jonathan 149
Abramson, Norman 35
advertising
Ad-Words 145
online 162
and protection of privacy 185
AJAX technology 150
Allen, Paul 55
AlohaNet 35, 37
Altair computer 54–5
AltaVista search engine 117–18
Alternet 121
Alto computer 37, 53
Amazon
dot-com success 125, 126–7, 128, 131, 133
employment numbers 141
and niche audiences 156–7
origins 98
and peer-review 144
personalized welcome page 161
and Toys'R'Us 130
Amiga 53, 55
Anderson, Chris 157
Anderson, Harlan 48
Andreessen, Marc 109, 131–2, 149, 150, 171
Andrus, D. Calvin 134
AOL (America OnLine) 71, 189
Apache web server 114–15
Apple
Apple II launch 57
hardware protection 59
hypercard program 147
iPhone see iPhone
iPod 153–4

iTunes 154–5, 157, 180
Mac 53, 55
Mac mouse 82
platform control 183–4
SAMBA browser for Mac 108
software development kit (SDK)
restrictions 184–5
spontaneous development by users
57–8
VisiCalc spreadsheet 58, 72
Archie search tool 94, 116–17
Arnold, General 'Hap' 19–20
ARPA (Advanced Research Projects
Agency) 24–5
'Aloha method' 35, 37
CPYNET file transfer protocol 77–8
'datagram' packets 43–4
and DNS (Domain Name System)
101–3
e-mail discussion groups 77–8, 80–81,
91–3, 149
funding issues 28–9, 35
'gateway' machines and routing
tables 39, 40
IMPS (Interface Message Processors)
27, 30, 38, 39, 49, 180
International Conference on Computer Communication expo 30
Internet Activities Board (IAB) 100,
101
Internet Architecture Board 100
Internet Assigned Numbers Authority (IANA) 101, 102, 103
Internet Configuration Control
Board (ICCH) 100

Internet Engineering Task Force
(IETF) 100–1
Internet Research Task Force (IRTF)
100
Internet Society 100, 101, 102
internetwork protocol 37–41
IP (Internet Protocol) 40, 73, 90–91,
92, 93, 96, 97, 121
IPTO (Information Processing
Techniques Office) 25–6, 49
and Lycos 118
NCP (Network Control Protocols) 33,
38, 100
and networking research 25–30, 71
networking research, lack of
enthusiasm for 27
NSF (National Science Foundation)
see NSF (National Science
Foundation)
PRNET (packet radio network) 34–5,
37, 40
and research community 80, 90, 91–2
RFC (Request for Comments)
documents 32–3, 37, 77, 99, 100,
101
SATNET Atlantic networking
programme 36, 37, 40, 96
and Stanford Research Institute (SRI)
see Stanford Research Institute
(SRI)
TCP (Transmission Control Protocol)
38–40, 73, 85, 90–91, 92, 93, 96, 97,
121
technical protocols development
31–3
and telephone industry standards see
telephone industry standards
see also BBN (Bolt, Beranek and
Newman)
ARPANET 26, 27, 28, 29, 31–3, 34–5
and Defense Communications
Agency (DCA) 17, 89–91
first transmission 30
international connection, first 36, 95–6
and NORSAR satellite link 36, 95
and satellites 35–6, 37
and screen to screen messages 77
Ashby, Ross 50

AT&T
and Carterfone 67–8
as centralized network 13, 16–17, 84
digital communication, lack of
interest in 17, 42, 88–9
and Hush-A-Phone 66–7
long-distance phone calls 74–5
and MediaOne merger 185–6
as monopoly 41–2, 43, 66, 111
and network deregulation 67–8
and Skype 186
survey on Internet overload 130
Atari 53, 55
Atari Democrats 94
AUTODIN 90–91

Babbage, Charles 98
BackRub system 118–19
Baidu search engine 192, 193
Baran, Paul
digital communication as unexplored
technology 15
mass market predictions 155
nuclear war concern 13–14
'On Distributed Communication
Networks' 14–15
online shopping prediction 120
and packet-switching concept 21–2,
27–8, 43, 48, 96, 99, 187
and RAND see RAND
user-to-user operation 16–17
Barlow, John Perry 138
Baron, Ron 122–3
BASIC programming language 55
Battlestar Galactica 145, 158
BBN (Bolt, Beranek and Newman)
and e-mail 77–8
file transfer protocol 77
IMP machines 29–30, 31, 39
and networking 80
working practices 98–9
Bell, Gordon 94
Bell telephone system see AT&T
Benioff, Marc 180–81
Benkler, Yochai 163
Beranek, Leo 180
Berkeley Unix Distribution 113
Berners-Lee, Tim

Enquire software 105, 106
and World Wide Web 106–7, 109,
110–11, 115
Bezos, Jeff 98, 128, 144, 157
Big Bunch 54, 55
BITNET 92–3, 96, 97
BitTorrent peer-to-peer software 154
Blankenship, Loyd 'The Mentor' 190,
191
Blue State Digital 172
Boo.com 129
Border, Louis 127–8
botnets 195, 196
Bowles, Edward 20
Brand, Stewart 82, 83
Brandenburg, Karlheinz 152
Bricklin, Dan 57–8
Brilliant, Larry 82, 143
Brin, Sergey 118, 119
Bronson, Po 98
Brown, Jerry 168–9
Bruce, Tom 108
Buckmaster, Jim 142
Buffet, Warren 124–5, 126
Bush, George W., and Wikipedia 138
Bush, Vannevar 18, 19, 105–6, 118
Memex device 106
Science: the endless frontier report 19
Byron (Lovelace), Ada 98

cable TV
and narrowcasting 140
pay-per-view 156
and political participation 173
Cailliau, Robert 107, 137
Campbell, Clive 'Kool DJ Herc' 160
Carter, Thomas 67–8
Carter & Siegel, and first commercial
spam 121, 142
CCIRN (Coordinating Committee for
Intercontinental Research Networks)
96
Cello browser for personal computers
108, 115
censorship 187–8, 191–4
Cerf, Vint 32–3, 37, 38–9, 40, 44, 95, 96,
100, 102
CERFnet 121

CERN see European Organization for
Nuclear Research (CERN)
Champion Ventures 126
Cheney, Dick 169–70
China
Internet users 192–3
online censorship 187–8, 191–3
Christensen, Ward 68
Cisco Systems 123
CIX 121
Clark, Jim 109
Clark, Wesley 27, 46, 47–8, 49, 99
Clarke, Dave 32, 100
Clinton, Hillary 172, 193
cloud computing 180–81
Cohen, Danny 39
Cold War
analogue systems, comparison with
13, 16, 17
communication and centrifugal distribution of control points 14–17
and communications network,
importance of 11–14
and MAD (mutually assured destruction) 13
military experiment 23–30
nuclear-proof communications 14–17
research and development see RAND
and satellite communication 23, 24, 28
Columbia Data Products, 'Multi
Personal Computer 1600' 59
Commodore 64 55
CompuServe 71
Computer Memory experiment and
social networking, California 56
computer networking
academic networks 91–3
businesses, slow take-up of 72–3
and community development 74–87
and e-mail see e-mail
globalization see globalization
and group application 84–7
information-finding services 94
international scientific collaborations
96–7
Internet connections (early 1990s) 94
military networks 89–91
and modem speeds, early 82–3

and Netizens 86–7
and NSFNET *see* National Science
Foundation (NSF)
online communities, intimacy of 81–3
programmer norms and recognised
authority 98–104
and SITA airline reservation system
70–71, 96
and subscription services 71–2
time-sharing *see* time-sharing
see also digital distribution; World
Wide Web
computers, connection to phone lines
65–9
Computer Bulletin Board System
(BBS) 68–9, 71, 81, 83, 149, 190
FidoNet 69, 97
network deregulation 67–8
phone attachments 66–8
XMODEM system 68
see also telecommunications
computers, cost and availability 45–61
affordability, improved 59
applications, development of new 58
'batch processing' of large computers
47, 48, 77
and cloned hardware 55–6
first commercially-available interactive computer 48
GUI (graphical user interface) 50, 53
hard drive capacity, improved 60
integrated circuit, first 53–4
interactive computing, start of 50, 51
and light pens 53
memory, increased 60
microprocessors, first 54–5
NLS (oN-Line System) development
50, 53, 82
personal computers, launch of 53,
54–5
personal computers in use, rise of
(1980s) 61
and source code publication 58
usability, improved 46–50, 53
Conway, Ron 127
CPYNET file transfer protocol 77–8
Craigslist.com 141–2, 143, 185, 193
CREN (Corporation for Research and

Educational Networking) 93
Crocker, Steve 32–3, 99, 100, 139
Crowther, Will 29
Cunningham, Ward 147
cybernetics 48, 50
cyberspace, origin of term 60
Cyclades 37, 95, 96

Darwinian meritocracy 52
Davies, Donald, packet-switched networking theory 15, 17, 28, 48, 95–6
Dean, Howard, presidential campaign
166–70, 171–2
DEC (Digital Equipment Corporation)
42, 48, 92, 94
and AltaVista 117–18
bottom-up approach 133
DECNET 96, 97
PDP computer 48, 51
Del.icio.us directory 144–5
Dennis, Jack 52
Deutsch, Peter 52
Diamond Multimedia, 'The Rio' MP3
player 152
digital distribution
choice and availability 154–5
community participation 159
and global media boom 158–60
high bandwidth connections 159
and mobile phones 158–9
and MP3s *see* MP3 music compression
and niche audiences 156–7
video and TV downloads 155–6
see also computer networking
Doerr, John 123
Domain Name System (DNS) 101–3
DOS (denial of service) attacks 194–7
DOS operating system 55, 58, 59, 73
dot-com industry 98, 122–30
Amazon success 125, 126–7, 128, 131,
133
business management lessons learned
from collapse of 131–4
change brought about by 126–30
Dougherty, Dale 137
Draper, John T. (Captain Crunch) 75
Drummond, David 191
e-mail 49

discussion groups 77–81, 91–3, 149
  first, and CPYNET 77–8
  free 118
  global 97
  Msg-Group (first discussion group) 78
  smiley face :-) debut 79
Earmarkwatch.org 176
eBay 120, 125–6, 141, 143, 180
EchoMail 69
Emtage, Alan 116–17
Engelbart, Douglas 50, 53, 82, 86–7, 106
Engressia, Joe 'Joybubbles' 74–5, 190–91
ENIAC (Army) computer 54
Enquire software 105, 106
entrepreneurial problems and 'get big
  fast' (GBF) strategies 127–30
Erwise browser 108
Estonia, DOS (denial of service) attacks
  194, 195, 196
Ethernet 37, 84
Europe
  EARN (European Research Network)
    92, 96–7
  EBONE 92 backbone project 97
  Eureka research fund 152
European Organization for Nuclear
  Research (CERN)
  and Enquire software 105, 106
  SAMBA browser for Apple Mac 108
  SGML hypertext language 107, 108–9
  and World Wide Web 107, 115
Excite search engine 117, 118

Fabian, Bill 99
Facebook 140, 181, 183, 185
  see also social networking
Fahlman, Scott 79
Fanning, Shawn 'Napster' 153
FidoNet 69, 97
Filo, David 98, 117
Finland, Erwise browser 108
France, Cyclades 37, 95, 96
Frankston, Bob 57
Friendster 149–50
FTP (file transfer protocol) 77–8, 109,
  115, 116–17
fuckingnda.com 184

Gallup, George 174–5
Gates, Bill 55, 59, 191
'gateway' machines and routing tables
  39, 40
Gibson, William, Neuromancer 60
Gilder, George 84
globalization
  and censorship 187–8, 191–4
  and cloud computing 180–81
  and digital instincts 182
  DOS (denial of service) attacks 194–7
  and global commons 194, 196–7
  global connection and international
    bodies 95–6
  and hackers 190–92
  international trade 178–80
  iWar 194–7
  and media boom 158–60
  micro-entrepreneurship 179–80,
    181–2
  network neutrality debate 185–7
  and platform control 183–5
  and protection of privacy 185
  terrorism and militant web forums
    189–90
  and Total Commerce 182
  and VOIP (voice over Internet proto-
    col) 186
GNU (GNU's Not Unix) 112, 113, 114
Google 52, 132
  Ad-Words 145
  Android platform 183
  bottom-up approach 133
  and Chinese censorship 191–4
  and opinion polling 175
  and PageRank 118–19
  as verb 119
Gopher search tool 94, 109–11, 117
Gore, Al 94–5
GovTrack.us 176
GovWorks.com 130
GPL (General Public License) 113, 114
Gray, Matthew 117
Greenblatt, Richard 98
Greenspan, Alan 124
Grif 108–9
Groove, Andrew 130
Guitar Hero 160

'hacker' culture 33
hackers 190–92
  and FidoNet 69
  MIT *see under* MIT (Massachusetts
    Institute of Technology)
Hart, Frank 82
Haughney, Major Joseph 89, 91
Hawn, Goldie 126
Hayek, Friedrich 146, 147, 148, 175
Heart, Frank 29–30, 46
Heiden, Colonel Heidi 91
HEPNET (High Energy Physics Network)
  96
Herzfeld, Charlie 26, 28–9
hip-hop culture 160
Home Box Office 156
Homebrew Computer Club 55–7, 58, 191
  and phone phreaks 75–6
Hotlinks 149
HTML hypertext language 107
Hush-A-Phone 66–7

IAB (Internet Advisory Board) 96
IAHC (International Ad Hoc Commit-
  tee) 102
IANW (International Academic Net-
  workshop) 96
IBM 30, 42, 48, 51
  5150 PC 58
  and AN/FSQ-7 47
  census tabulation 46
  cloning and IBM-compatible PCs
    59–60
  DOS operating system 58
  Linux investment 114
  Microsoft partnership 58–9
  personal computers 53, 55, 58–9,
    60–61
  RSCS (remote spooling communica-
    tions system) 92–3
  SABRE computerized reservations
    system 70–71
  SGML hypertext language 107
  source code publication 58
ICANN (Internet Corporation for
  Assigned Names and Numbers) 103–4
ICB (International Cooperation Board)
  96

IEPG (Intercontinental Engineering
  Planning Group) 96
IMPS (Interface Message Processors) 27,
  29–30, 31, 38, 39, 49, 180
Information Society World Summits
  103–4
Intel
  and dot-com bubble collapse 124, 130
  microprocessors, first 54, 55
  microprocessors, increased speed
    of 60
  Moore's Law 60
Intergalactic Computer Network 25
International Conference on Computer
  Communication expo 30
International Telecommunication
  Union 102
International Trademark Association
  102
Internet Governance Forum 104
INWG (International Network Working
  Group) 95–6
IP (Internet Protocol) 40, 73, 90–91, 92,
  93, 96, 97, 121
iPhone 49, 183–4
  App store 184
  connection speed 82–3
  and Skype 186
  see also Apple
IPO (initial public offering) 108, 123–5,
  133
iTunes 154–5, 157, 180
iWar 194–7

JenniCam.org 116
Jennings, Tom 69
Jobs, Steve 107, 179
Johnson, Nicolas 156
Johnson, Tony 108

Kahn, Robert 29, 30, 36, 37, 38–9, 92, 95
Kelly, Kevin 142, 144, 175
Kilby, Jack 53
Kleinrock, Leonard 17, 28, 32, 77–8
Korn, Hugo 18

LAN (Local Area Networking) 37, 73,
  84–5
< 240 >

Landweber, Lawrence 91–2
Leiner, Barry 100
Lelann, Gerard 37
LeMay, General Curtis 20–21
Lemley, Mark A. 185–6
Lessig, Lawrence 167, 168, 185–6
Levenson, Alan 132
Levy, Steve 52
Licklider, J.C.R. 25–6, 29, 46, 52, 93
    and cybernetics 48–9
    and global competition 197
    and interactive computing 50, 76, 82,
        113, 152
    and interactive politics 176
    and narrowcasting 140
    SAGE presentation group 47
light pens 53
Linux operating system 79–80, 113–15,
    146, 166, 167, 175, 177
    IPO 123, 124
Listserv 92
Loving Grace Cybernetics 56
Lycos search engine 117, 118

McElroy, Neil 24
McKenzie, John 51
Madsen, Phil 165
Maes, Pattie 144, 161
Magaziner, Ira 102
Mandel, Tom 83
Marill, Tomas 17
Marsh, Bob 55
MediaOne 185–6
MeetUp.com 166–7
Menabrea, General 98
MERIT (Michigan Educated Research
    Information Triad) 93, 115, 121
Metallica 151, 153
Metcalfe, Robert 37
Metcalfe's Law 84–5
Mexico, online censorship 188
MicroNet 71
microprocessors, first 54–5
Microsoft
    BASIC programming language 55
    DOS operating system 55, 58, 59, 73
    IBM partnership 58–9
    Internet Explorer 109

market value rise 59
platform control 183
Windows 53, 108, 183
Midas browser 108
MILNET 90
Minix 112–13
MIT (Massachusetts Institute of
    Technology) 17, 19, 46, 98
    agent programs 161
    hackers 51–2, 98, 111, 133, 191
    hackers and optimizing codes 52
    hackers and phone phreaks 75–6
    hackers and Spacewar! 52, 53
    RLE (Research Laboratory of
        Electronics) 50–51
    SAGE (Semi-Automatic Ground
        Environment) program 46–8, 70
    Tech Model Railroad Club (TMRC) 51,
        52, 191
    TX computers (transistorized) 48, 51,
        53
    Wanderer web crawler 117
    Whirlwind (AN/FSQ-7) computer 47,
        99
MITS, Altair computer sales 55
mobile phones 158–9
Monier, Louis 118
Moore, Gordon 54, 60
Moore, Ron D. 158
Morris Worm 194
MOS Technology 55
Mosaic browser 109, 117, 149
Motorola 55, 158
MP3 music compression
    and consumer choice 155
    and iPod 153–4
    MPMan F10 portable player 153
    music piracy 151–3, 160
    music sales 154–5
Murdoch, Rupert 150, 162–3
MySpace 150
MYSQL database 115

Napster, peer-to-peer software 153, 154
NASA Science Internet (NSI) 97
NASDAQ index 123–5
Naughton, John 76–7
Negroponte, Nicholas 127, 144, 156, 161

Nelson, Ted, Xanadu hypertext 106, 137
NetFrack 151, 153, 154
Netizens 86–7
Netscape 108, 109, 131–2
    IPO 123, 124
    open-source project 114
Network Solutions 102
Newman, Blair 83
Newmark, Craig 141–2, 143
newspaper circulation decline 161–3
    and trust model 163
NEXT computer 107, 108, 117
Nintendo
    platform control 183
    Wii, and online polling 175
NLS (oN-Line System) development 50,
    53, 82
Nokia 183
Norway, NORSAR satellite link 36, 95
Noyce, Robert 54
NSF (National Science Foundation) 19
    Acceptable Usage Policy and
        commercial trading 120
    and Computer Science Network
        (CSNET) 91–4, 97, 102, 115, 120, 121
    and Internet privatization 121
    NSFNET funding 120–21
    NSFNET and MERIT (Michigan
        Educated Research Information
        Triad) 93–4, 115
Nupedia 147, 148

Obama, Barack 171–2, 178
Olsen, Kenneth 46, 47–8
Omidyar, Pierre 120
open-source software 111–15, 133–4
OpenSecrets.org 176
Openshaw, Justice Peter 189
O'Reilly, Tim 109, 139
Ornstein, Severo 29, 46
Oxford English Dictionary, 'google' as
    verb 119

packet radio experiment, Stanford
    Research Institute (SRI) 29, 30, 34–5, 40
packet-switching concept
    Baran, Paul 21–2, 27–8, 43, 48, 96, 99,
        187

Davies, Donald 15, 17, 28, 48, 95–6
Page, Larry 118, 119
PageRank 119
Panasonic 145
PDP computer 48, 51
peer-to-peer software 153, 154
Pei Wei, Perry 108
People's Computer Company 56
Pets.com 129
PHP web application language 115
Pinkerton, Brian 117
politics
    campaign funding and grass-roots
        contributors 168–70, 172
    collective policy scrutiny 175–7
    network governance and
        participatory democracy 173–7
    online campaigning 164–6
    online polling 174–5, 176
    open-source campaigns and political
        blogs 166–72
Postel, Jon 39, 99, 101, 102, 103
PRNET (packet radio network) 34–5, 37,
    40
Prodigy 71
programmer norms and recognised
    authority 98–104
PSINet 120–21
psychoacoustics 152
publishing industry 126–7
    see also Amazon
PUP (PARC Universal Packet) (Alto
    Aloha) 37–8

RAND think tank
    and Cold War 13–14, 16
    as innovation incubator 17–22
    packet-switching research 21–2, 27–8,
        71
Rasiej, Andrew 170–71
    'Politics 2.0' 173
Raymond, Eric 114, 146, 177
Rechtin, Eberhardt 29
Reed, David 85
    Group Forming Law 85, 86
RFC (Request for Comments)
    documents 32–3, 37, 77, 99, 100, 101
Rheingold, Howard 86–7

< 242 >

Ringley, Jennifer 116
Ritchie, Denis 111
Roberts, Ed 54–5
Roberts, Lawrence 17, 26, 27–8, 29, 30, 46, 71, 79, 80, 113
Rock Band 160
Roosevelt, Franklin D. 18, 19
RSCS (remote spooling communications system) 92–3
RSS (really simple syndication) 161
Ruina, Jack 25
Rush, Jess 69

SABRE computerized reservations system 70–71
SAGE (Semi-Automatic Ground Environment) program 46–8, 70
Salesforce.com 181
SAMBA browser 108
Sanger, Larry 147–8
Sarnoff, David 84, 85–6
satellites 23–4, 33–41, 95
SATNET Atlantic networking programme 36, 37, 40, 96
Scantlebury, Roger 28, 96
Schmidt, Eric 180
Schracter, Joshua 144
Searls, David 'Doc' 167
Seitzer, Dieter 152
SGML hypertext language 107, 108–9
Shaheen, George 128
share dealing 123–5, 133
Sifry, Micah 171, 173
    'Politics 2.0' 173
Simon, David 162
SITA airline reservation system 70–71, 96
sixdegrees.com 149
Skype 186
Smith, Ralph Lee 173
social networking 148–50
    and Computer Bulletin Board System (BBS) 69
    and 'Computer Memory' 56
    see also Facebook; YouTube
source code publication 58
Spacewar! 52, 53
spam, first commercial 121, 142
Stallman, Richard, GNU 111–12, 113

Stanford Research Institute (SRI) 50
    Augmented Human Intellect Research Center 50
    and free e-mail 118
    NLS (oN-Line System) 50
    packet radio experiment 29, 30, 34–5, 40
    Stanford AI Lab (SAIL) 52
    and TCP protocol 96
Strassmann, Paul 73
subscription services 71–2
Suess, Randy 68
Sun Microsystems 180
Sunstein, Cass 163
Sutherland, Ivan 52–3
    'Sketchpad' graphics system 25–6, 53
SwapIt.com 127

Tanenbaum, Alan 79–80
Taylor, Bob 24, 26–7, 29, 46, 76, 77, 82
Taylor, Frederick, *The Principles of Scientific Management* 132–3
TCP (Transmission Control Protocol) 38–40, 73, 85, 90–91, 92, 93, 96, 97, 121
Teachout, Zephyr 172
telecommunications
    2111 Conference open line 75
    long-distance phone calls 74–5
    and phone phreaks 75–6
    Phonenet 92
    see also computers, connection to phone lines
telephone industry standards 41–2
    and Consultative Committee on International Telegraphy and Telephony (CCITT) 43, 44
    and monopolies 42–3
    open standards network development 42–3
    and x.25 networks 43–4, 96, 97, 185
Telnet 71
terrorism and militant web forums 189–90
Tesco 129
Texas Instruments 53
    integrated circuit, first 53–4
Thompson, Ken 111
3Com 84

time-sharing approach 26, 71–2, 77
Tomlinson, Ray 77, 78, 178
Torvalds, Linus, Linux 79–80, 112–14
Toys'R'Us 130
Trippi, Joe 166, 167, 168, 169, 170, 171, 172
Tsouli, Younis 'Irhabi 007' 189–90, 191
tulip mania 121–2
TX computers (transistorized) 48, 51, 53

UK
 Cambridge University time-share
  computer (1950s) 76–7
 Cambridge University web cam
  invention 116
 Goonhilly Downs and SRI test 40
 NPL (National Physics Laboratory)
  28, 95–6
 Post Office and satellite connection
  costs 36
Unix operating system 80–81, 92, 108,
 111–12
 Berkeley Unix Distribution 113
 and GNU (GNU's Not Unix) 112, 113,
  114
 and Minix 112–13
US
 air defence and use of computers
  45–8
 ARPA (Advanced Research Projects
  Agency) see ARPA (Advanced
  Research Projects Agency
 AT&T see AT&T
 Computer Memory experiment
  and social networking, California
  56
 DCA (Defense Communications
  Agency) 17, 89–91
 ENIAC (Army) computer 54
 Federal Communications Commis-
  sion (FCC) 41, 66–8, 140
 'Framework for Global Electronic
  Commerce' 102–3
 High Performance Computing and
  Communication Act (Gore Act)
  94–5
 and ICANN (Internet Corporation
  for Assigned Names and Numbers)
  103–4

MERIT (Michigan Educated Research
 Information Triad) 93, 115, 121
'National Roster of Scientific and
 Specialized Personnel' (Second
 World War) 18
NCSA (National Centre for Super-
 computing Applications) 109
NSF (National Science Foundation)
 see NSF (National Science Founda-
 tion)
RIAA (Recording Industry Associa-
 tion of America) 153
SAGE (Semi-Automatic Ground
 Environment) program 46–8, 70
satellite launches 24, 36
Second World War, scientific
 invention and research 18–20
Second World War, and seeds of
 Internet 17–19
Stanford Research Institute (SRI) see
 Stanford Research Institute (SRI)
University of Hawaii, AlohaNet 35, 37
University of Minnesota and Gopher
 109–11
Zott's ('The Alpine Inn'), San
 Francisco 33–4
Usenet 80, 81, 86–7, 109, 112, 113, 175–6
 and first commercial spam 121
user-driven websites see Web 2.0
USSR, satellite launches 23–4, 36
UUNET 120

Vail, Theodore 41, 65, 84, 185
Valley, George 45–7
Ventura, Jesse 164–5, 178
Veronica search tool 94, 117
video
 downloads 155–6
 uploading 150
Viola programming language 108
VisiCalc spreadsheet 58, 72
VOIP (voice over Internet protocol) 186

WAIS (Wide Area Information Servers)
 109
Walden, Dave 29, 30
Wales, Jimmy 146–7
Walker, Steven 78

Wanderer web crawler 117
Web 2.0
  AJAX technology 150
  bloggers and conversational
    marketing 145
  bookmarking websites 161
  and broadband connections,
    improved 150
  collaborative filtering (the daily me)
    161, 163
  content creation by users 137–41
  and digital cameras 150
  and hip-hop culture 160
  and mass collaboration 146–8
  niche audiences and producer
    interaction 157–8
  and online citizen journalism 163
  and opinion polling 175
  Saint Jerome's Vulgate Bible,
    comparisons with 138–9
  and social networking 148–50
  and tagging 144–5
  user-driven websites, and nerd norms
    141–3
  user-driven websites and peer-review
    143–5, 148, 150
  user-driven websites, popularity of
    140–41
  video content, uploading 150
  see also computer networking; World
    Wide Web
web cam 116
WebCrawler 117
website URLS 102, 108
Webvan 127–9
Weiner, Norbert 48
Weinreich, Andrew 149
The Well online community 82–3, 86–7,
  143, 149
Western Union 65, 88–9
Whirlwind (AN/FSQ-7) computer 47, 99
Whole Earth Catalog 82
Wikipedia 133–4, 140, 147, 175
  and George W. Bush 138
  'Rules To Consider' guidelines 148
  3R rule 148
WikiWikiWeb 147–8
Williams, Justin 184

Windows 53, 108, 183
  see also Microsoft
WinPlay3 152
Wired 114, 123, 142, 156, 189
World Altair Computer Convention 55
World Intellectual Property Organization 102
World of Warcraft 159
World Wide Web
  and BackRub system 118–19
  browser war 109
  dot-com industry see dot-com
    industry
  and Enquire software 105, 106
  entrepreneurial problems and 'get
    big fast' (GBF) strategies 127–30
  and Gopher, demise of 109–11
  and GPL (General Public License) 113,
    114
  HTML hypertext language 107
  and hypertext 106–7
  and intellectual property rights 110
  and Intelligence Community 134
  Internet privatization 121–2
  and knowledge arrangement 105–7
  lack of interest in, initial 107–9
  and open-source software 111–15,
    133–4
  overload and technical teething
    problems 130
  perpetual beta approach 109
  and physical distribution problems
    127–9, 130
  and publishing industry 126–7
  rise in connected networks (1990s)
    115
  search tools, improvements in 116–19
  share dealing in 123–5, 133
  spam, first commercial 121
  and tulip mania 121–2
  URI (universal resource identifier) 107
  W3C standardization Consortium 111
  and web cam 116
  see also computer networking; Web
    2.0
Wozniak, Steve 57
Wu, Tim 186

x.25 networks 43–4, 96, 97, 185
Xanadu hypertext 106
Xbox 360, and online polling 175
Xerox PARC 37, 53, 118
    Alto computer 37, 53
    PUP (PARC Universal Packet) (Alto
        Aloha) 37–8
    Xerox Star 53
xfree86 project 114
XMODEM system 68

Yahoo! 52, 98, 117
    Google, offer to buy 119
Yang, Jerry 117
Yen, Shih-Pau 109, 110
YouTube 140, 144, 150
    see also social networking

Zittrain, Jonathan 186

< 246 >